HOME HANDBOOKS

HOUSE
PLANTS

HOUSE PLANTS

Contributing editor
John Brookes

The Reader's Digest Association, Inc.
Pleasantville, New York

This is an RD Home Handbook
specially created for The Reader's Digest Association, Inc.,
by Dorling Kindersley Limited.

First American edition, 1990

Published in the United States
by The Reader's Digest Association, Inc.,
Pleasantville, N.Y.
Published in Great Britain
by Dorling Kindersley Limited, London
Printed in Singapore

Designed and edited by Swallow Books,
260 Pentonville Road, London N1 9JY

Library of Congress Cataloging in Publication Data

House plants / contributing editor, John Brookes. — 1st American ed.
  p. cm. — (RD home handbooks)
  ISBN 0-89577-349-X
  1. House plants.   2. Indoor gardening.   I. Brookes, John, 1933–
  II. Series.
SB419.H785   1990
635.9′65—dc20
                                                                    89-70332
                                                                        CIP

CONTENTS

Introduction 6

INTRODUCTION

While green thoughts, gardening books and nursery catalogues may sustain some plant lovers through the winter when their gardens are relatively dormant, others may seek a more practical outlet for their horticultural interests. For many, particularly those who live in apartments or condominiums, it may be just the sight of greenery and flower color in their home or a yearning for a contact with nature which lasts throughout the year. It is to all these that this book is directed.

Indoor plants provide contact with nature for they are living, growing things, and interesting because of it; at the same time they will enhance almost any interior by adding natural forms, colors and fragrances. However, used at random they look messy and may be at odds with the decoration of a room. Professional designers are well aware of the decorative qualities of plants and how they can be used to complement a decorating scheme. But this skill in matching plants to interior decoration, and in placing them effectively in a room, can be easily learned through practice and through an appreciation of the different decorative qualities of plants and flowers.

This book sets out to show you how to get to know your plants and flowers and appreciate their shapes, colors, sizes, textures and seasons within an interior setting.

Begin your decorating by thinking about the sort of space you want to fill with plants. Do you want one large dramatic plant to act as a single focal point, or a smaller group of plants of contrasting shapes, colors or textures? Perhaps you only have space to use plants in a hanging basket, or massed in a terrarium or bottle

Creating a plant display (right)
This colorful arrangement includes ferns, ivies and flowering plants.

garden. Step-by-step projects in the chapters on *Choosing and using containers* and *Indoor gardens* show you how to put these ideas and many more into practice. In *Choosing house plants*, decorating tips are given on how to use each of the featured plants to best effect, while *Styling with house plants* shows how plants and flowers can be used in a variety of novel and exciting ways in different parts of the home.

Styling with plants

Never has there been such a range of styles for living as there is today. Yet all – even the most modern – are subtly influenced by the past. Recognizing the component parts of a style of decor helps to define the qualities you need in a plant to enhance that style. To illustrate this, and show how to approach your decorative schemes, a selection of contemporary styles of decoration have been chosen and analyzed to show how plants contribute to the overall styling.

The history of indoor plants

Plants have been used indoors for many centuries. The Dutch interest in painting interiors and flower-pieces went hand-in-hand with an increasing interest, throughout the western world, in the cultivated plant. Again, the Dutch tulip craze of the 1630s must have influenced other countries, but travelers, since the returning Crusaders, would also have brought plants home and fostered them indoors prior to the advent of glass. We know, too, that herbs were used extensively indoors: mostly for medicinal and culinary purposes. In the seventeenth century, orangeries, structures made of brick or stone with large south-facing windows, were built to shelter orange trees in winter. But it was not until the introduction of glass structures, which could be heated, that plants could be grown inside to any degree.

Tropical fruit was initially cultivated in primitively heated houses; pineapples, guavas and limes were grown – and also the first camellias. Later, there followed the date palm and banana. Succulents, such as the aloe and agave, were also raised for medicinal purposes and to decorate terraces in summer. During the nineteenth century, the conservatory became a standard addition to larger houses; house plant cultivation moved into the realms of fashion, with fern houses, palm houses, and houses for exotic plants being all the rage. Simple potted plants too began to escape from the conservatory to become the necessary accompaniment to the heavy, draped look of the late nineteenth-century interior – although the smoke from open fireplaces did the plants little good. Floristry became a fashionable lady's accomplishment.

One reaction to this style was to seek inspiration from what must have been a continuing, unsophisticated, cottage tradition of keeping temperate plants indoors to root or over-winter, and of hanging herbs from the rafters to dry. An alternative Modernist movement at the beginning of this century used specific plants in its interiors – the lily being a great favorite. But the real origins of the use of house plants lie in Scandinavia where, traditionally, plants were brought indoors to relieve the bleakness of a long winter; and it was not until after the Second World War that they really became part of the modish interior. It was then that house plants as we know them started to make their appearance, with species from Asia and Central and South America becoming available. Since then, new varieties have been bred which can be kept very successfully indoors.

Choosing plants

The plants which are or are not suitable for you will depend on the particular type of decoration you have, for currently there are a number of interior styles. Your selection will depend on personal taste and on what it is practical to maintain – given the specific limitations of day- and night-time temperatures, light availability, the presence of drafts, children and pets, and, of course, available space.

CHAPTER ONE

CHOOSING HOUSE PLANTS

This chapter performs two functions. It demonstrates the astounding diversity of plant form, leaf and flower size, shape, color and texture to enable you to consider what decorative effects to aim for in your choice of house plants. It also provides a catalogue of nearly 120 of the most commonly used plants suitable for the home, and, in a special section on flowering house plants, allows you to tell at a glance which plants will bloom during particular months of the year. With this information, you can select plants which not only create displays of the form and color you wish, but also are compatible with each other and with their habitat.

Various plants and flowers

Plants come in an overwhelming variety of shapes, sizes and colors and, depending on their origins, need a variety of different conditions. In order to choose the right ones for your home, you need to be aware of both their decorative qualities and growing needs.

Plant form

Of all plant characteristics it is shape that probably creates the strongest initial impression. Shape has primarily to do with the general outline of the plant, but it also embraces other characteristics that contribute to the plant's overall form: the density of the growth, the size and number of individual stems and branches, the way the leaves or leaflets are arranged and the "weight" of the foliage. Of course, shape is always changing as a plant grows, but certain generalizations can be made and throughout this book eight different shape descriptions have been used: upright, arching, weeping, rosette-shaped, bushy, climbing, trailing and creeping.

Cocos nucifera
Coconut palm (see p. 45)
This plant has an *arching* shape, as do most of the palms and ferns; its sword-shaped fronds have a hard outline.

Fatsia japonica
Japanese fatsia
(see p. 54)
The overall shape of
this plant is *bushy*
but the large
fingered leaves have
a strong individual
outline.

Ficus pumila Creeping fig (see p. 56)
With its spreading shape, this *creeping*
plant resembles a green carpet when
allowed to ramble; it can also trail or climb.

Philodendron scandens
Heartleaf philodendron (see p. 74) Plants usually combine different elements of shape; this *trailing* example has beautifully shaped leaves as well as stems that trail in an attractive way.

Hedera canariensis
Algerian ivy (see p. 59) The shape of its support will dictate the overall shape of a *climbing* plant, but individual foliage will give an outline that may be delicate or bold.

Yucca elephantipes
Stick yucca (see p. 93) Plants with *upright* growth and spiky leaves have a simple bold shape.

Beaucarnea recurvata
Ponytail (see p. 33) The soft shape of this *weeping* plant is created by the mass of drooping, grasslike leaves.

Nidularium innocentii
Bird's nest bromeliad (see p. 68) Most *rosette-shaped* plants have a strong outline that demands attention.

Leaf size

In many fields successful design often relies on the simple repetition of elements of similar sizes. This principle holds good for the arrangement of plants but impressive effects can also be achieved by emphasizing differences in scale.

Howea belmoreana Kentia palm
(see p. 61)
Display large plants on their own, or in groups with spiky-leaved plants.

Ceropegia woodii
Rosary vine (see p. 132)
A plant which looks best on its
own; allow the stems to trail from
a hanging basket or shelf.

**Microcoelum
weddellianum**
Dwarf coconut
palm (see p. 65)
Juxtapose these small
slender fronds with
other larger
palms.

**Philodendron
hastatum**
Elephant's ear
philodendron
A large-leaved climber
best used as a feature
plant or as a foil for
low-growing plants.

Philodendron scandens
Heartleaf philodendron (see
p. 74) Use in a hanging
basket or arrange around a
large-leaved philodendron.

Leaf shape

Leaf shape is a very strong visual characteristic of a plant and a striking display can be achieved by concentrating solely on either contrasting or harmonizing leaf shapes. There is a great variety of leaf shapes to choose from – lance-shaped leaves, oval leaves, heart-shaped leaves, wavy-edged leaves and even leaves shaped like a violin.

Scindapsus pictus 'Argyraeus'
Pothos vine (see p. 82)
Heart-shaped leaves with acutely pointed tips.

Monstera deliciosa
Swiss cheese plant (see p. 66)
The large oval leaves become perforated as the plant gets older.

Cissus rhombifolia
Grape ivy (see p. 44)
The leaves have pointed tips and scalloped edges.

Passiflora caerulea
Passion flower (see p. 70)
Fan-shaped leaves with many deeply cut lobes.

Philodendron bipinnatifidum Finger plant (see p.73)
The young, irregularly shaped leaves become violin-shaped when mature.

Asparagus setaceus
Asparagus fern (see p. 31)
Wiry stems carry feathery triangular sprays.

Dieffenbachia maculata
Dumb cane (see p. 50)
The long oval leaves
have wavy margins and a
distinct point at their tip.

Ficus benjamina
Weeping fig (see p. 55)
Small, slender, oval
leaves with curved
edges and pointed tips.

Yucca elephantipes
Stick yucca (see p. 93)
Long, narrow, spiky
leaves with finely toothed
edges.

Grevillea robusta
Silk oak (see p. 57)
The leaves are highly
divided giving a delicate
fernlike appearance.

**Nephrolepis exaltata
'Bostoniensis'**
Boston fern (see p. 67)
The fronds are divided into
narrow leaflets giving a
graceful feathery
appearance.

Dizygotheca elegantissima
False aralia (see p. 51)
Narrow leaflets with saw-
toothed edges radiate like
spokes from the top of
each stem.

Leaf color

The range of color found in leaves is startling: from the variety of different greens to leaves with all-over colors from silver-white to deep purple, as well as those which are patterned or mottled with contrasting colors. Dramatic displays can be made with foliage plants by concentrating on the interplay between two, or at most three, colors.

Zebrina pendula
Wandering Jew (see p. 93)
The leaves are finely marked with two green stripes.

Caladium hortulanum hybrids Angel wings (see p. 39)
Paper-thin leaves with very delicate markings in combinations of red, pink, white and green.

Fittonia verschaffeltii
Nerve plant (see p. 57)
Carmine-red veins traversing olive-green leaves create a dramatic color contrast.

Neoregelia carolinae 'Tricolor' Blushing bromeliad (see p. 66)
Green- and cream-striped leaves which become suffused with red at flowering time.

Coleus blumei
Painted nettle (see p. 46)
Leaf color and pattern varies, with rich mixtures of yellow, red, orange, green and brown.

Codiaeum variegatum pictum Croton (see p. 46)
Leaves in a range of warm exotic colors mottled with spots, blotches and veins.

Hedera helix hybrids
English ivy (see p. 60)
The mid-green leaves
have darker green
blotches and cream
margins.

Cordyline terminalis
Ti plant (see p. 47)
The striped leaves are
outlined in a vivid pink.

Calathea makoyana
Peacock plant (see p. 39)
Leaves which look as if
they have been hand-
painted with a spectacular
pattern of dark blotches.

**Aglaonema crispum
'Silver Queen'** Silvered
spear (see p. 26)
Beautiful dark-green
leaves heavily marked with
silvery-green blotches.

Caladium hortulanum hybrids Angel wings (see p. 39)
This young leaf, from the same
plant as the leaf to its left, shows
the color variation which can
occur on the same plant.

**Begonia
'Tiger paws'**
Eyelash begonia
(see p. 36)
Bright-red markings on
the undersides of the
emerald-green leaves
show through as brown
on the upper surface.

**Saxifraga stolonifera
'Tricolor'** Strawberry
geranium (see p. 81)
Olive-green leaves with a
pink margin and fine
pink hairs.

Hypoestes phyllostachya
Polka-dot plant (see p. 62)
Dark olive-green leaves which
are heavily spotted with pink.

Leaf texture

There are as many variations in leaf texture as in shape, size or color. Very few leaves have no textural quality and textures can vary from glossy to matt, from hairy to wrinkled, from ribbed to quilted. Subtle displays can be made by juxtaposing plants with contrasting leaf textures.

Araucaria heterophylla
Norfolk Island pine (see p. 30)
Tiers of needle-covered
branches give an overall
filigree lightness.

Aspidistra elatior
Cast-iron plant (see p. 31)
Distinctive ribbing marks
run along the length of
these leathery leaves.

Asplenium nidus
Bird's nest fern (see p. 32)
The lance-shaped
leaves are extremely
smooth and shiny
with a central rib.

Begonia rex-cultorum
Painted-leaf begonia (see p. 34)
The highly decorative
foliage is covered
in pimples giving it a
curious rough texture.

Peperomia caperata
Emerald ripple peperomia
(see p. 72)
The heart-shaped, dark-
green leaves have a
corrugated surface with a
waxy feel to them.

Adiantum raddianum
Delta maidenhair fern
(see p. 25)
Leaves have a soft filmy
texture and are arranged
on gracefully drooping
fronds.

Gynura aurantiaca
Purple velvet plant
(see p. 58)
The toothed leaves
are covered in soft
purple hair, giving
them a furry
texture.

**Platycerium
bifurcatum**
Staghorn fern (see p. 76)
The antler-shaped fronds
are covered with fine,
white, feltlike scurf.

**Maranta leuconeura
erythroneura** Prayer plant
(see p. 64)
Bright-red veins stand out from the
surface of the satiny leaves.

Columnea 'Banksii'
Columnea (see p. 47)
The dark-green paired
leaves are fleshy with a
waxy texture.

The A–Z of house plants

In this section, nearly 120 of the most popular indoor plants (excluding cacti, succulents and bulbs) are catalogued in alphabetical order by Latin names. Color photographs of each plant provide a visual guide, and advice is given on the most effective way to display them. Additionally, *The A–Z of house plants* gives special care advice by way of readily recognizable symbols. These symbols indicate the preferred light, temperature, watering and humidity levels of each plant, plus the relative ease of its cultivation. The amount of light and heat needed by each plant is described in terms of its *mini-climate*: a system which enables you to see, at a glance, which plants are compatible. Using this, it is possible to determine which upright plants, for example, would be suitable for any sunny position, or for a warm and shady one – thus allowing you to choose easily which plants would be suitable for your habitat.

Impatiens wallerana hybrids
Pink impatiens

How to use the symbols

TEMPERATURE
⊡ **Cool with winter rest** Plants should be kept at 50-60°F from spring to autumn, and 45-50°F in winter.
⊡ **Cool** The plants which thrive in a cool climate should be kept at a temperature of between 50°-60°F all year, if possible.
⊡ **Warm** The plants which thrive in a warm climate should be kept at a temperature of 60°–70°F all year, but endure higher or lower ranges for reasonable periods.

LIGHT
☼ **Sunny** A sunny position is one near a south-, east- or west-facing window which receives unobstructed direct sunlight.
◑ **Filtered sun** This is indirect sunlight, which shines through a translucent curtain or blind, or is screened by a leafy tree outside a window.
◉ **Shady** A shady position is one close to a north-facing window, or to the side of an east- or west-facing window which never receives any direct or indirect sun.

HUMIDITY
▢ **Low humidity** The air surrounding the plant should be approximately 30-40 per cent

How to use the A–Zs

In *The A–Z of house plants* each plant is given a detailed entry arranged in alphabetical order by the Latin genus and species names. Symbols give additional information in each entry. There are separate A–Z sections in *Indoor Gardens* for cacti and succulents, and for flowering bulbs. At the end of this section there is a photographic color guide to a selection of flowering house plants, running through the color spectrum from white to violet, and there is also a seasonal guide, in the form of a chart, to indicate their flowering or fruiting periods during the year.

Scientific name (genus and species) in bold type followed by hybrid/cultivar name where applicable. Common name in italic

A general description of each plant, mentioning its main decorative qualities and how to use it

Size entry gives the maximum dimensions of the plant and tells you in what form it is offered for sale

Feeding entry gives advice on the most suitable fertilizer and how often to use it

Potting entry gives comprehensive advice on when and how to pot the plant, and the type of potting mixture to use

SELAGINELLA MARTENSII
LITTLE CLUB MOSS

These unusual plants have decorative, medium-green leaves which are packed around the branches like the scales of a fish. The creeping stems of the club mosses form a dense mat of foliage with a pleasant, soft texture. Roots are put down into the potting mixture at intervals. A terrarium or bottle garden is the best environment in which to display these small plants as they will thrive in the humid atmosphere.

Mini-climate 2 Warm, filtered sun.
Size The creeping stems may grow to 6in in length. Small plants are offered for sale.
Feeding Feed with one-quarter strength standard liquid fertilizer every two weeks.
Potting Repot every spring using a mixture of two-thirds peat-based potting mix and one-third coarse sand. Once plants are in 6-8in pots simply remove plants from their pots, clean and refill them with fresh mixture and replace the plants.

Special points Touch the plants as little as possible as this can damage the foliage.

Similar-shaped species
Selaginella pallescens has white-edged leaves which grow on erect stems of up to 1ft long.

Plant care symbols give a pictorial summary of each plant's needs: temperature, light, humidity; watering and ease of care

Mini-climate categorization enables you to see at a glance which plants are compatible and can be displayed together

Special points (where applicable) for keeping a plant in a healthy state

Similar-shaped species entry (where applicable) lists similar plants of the same genus and describes how they differ from the featured plant

---

saturated with water. Few plants tolerate low humidity.
■ **Moderate humidity** The air surrounding the plant should be approximately 60 per cent saturated with water.
■ **High humidity** The air surrounding the plant should be approximately 80 per cent saturated with water.

WATERING
• **Water sparingly** This involves barely moistening the whole mixture, and allowing it to dry out almost completely each time.
•• **Water moderately** This refers to moistening the entire mixture, but allowing the top inch or so to dry out before watering again.
••• **Water plentifully** This means keeping all of the potting mixture moist at all times, not letting even the surface dry out.

CARE
⊘ **Easy** Plants which are termed "easy" to care for are those which can be grown successfully with only the minimum of attention.
✪ **Fairly easy** Plants in this category require the basic care plus some attention to their individual growing needs.
✔ **Challenging** These plants need very specific growing conditions in order to thrive.

ABUTILON HYBRIDUM 'CANARY BIRD'

FLOWERING MAPLE

These are pretty, woody plants which can be trained when young. They have maplelike leaves from whose leaf-joints come the bell-shaped flowers. The flowers of the hybrids are red, pink, yellow or white. *Abutilon hybridum* 'Canary Bird' are long-lasting, making them suitable for use as feature plants, especially in front of a window.

Mini-climate 1 Warm, sunny.

Size They can reach a height and spread of 3ft in three years. Pinch out growing tips to maintain bushy growth.

Feeding Feed with standard liquid fertilizer every two weeks in summer.

Potting Repot every spring using soil-based potting mixture. Once plants are in 10in pots topdress instead.

Special points Water less in winter and cut back any untidy stems in spring.

Similar-shaped species

Abutilon pictum 'Thompsonii' has green and yellow variegated leaves and flowers which may be composed of one color, two colors or two shades of the same color.

ACHIMENES GRANDIFLORA

CUPID'S BOWER

Also known as "magic flowers", these plants have hairy, upright, green or red stems and dull-green leaves which are also hairy. Flowers can be pink, purple or yellow in color, with white throats. The flowering period lasts from summer to autumn. These are very useful infill plants for an indoor window-box.

Mini-climate 1 Warm, sunny.
Size *Achimenes grandiflora* grow to about 1½ft in height. Small plants are offered for sale in spring.
Feeding Feed with phosphate-rich liquid fertilizer at one-eighth strength when watering during the flowering period.
Potting Repot every spring using an equal-parts mixture of peat moss, coarse sand or perlite, and vermiculite. Divide older plants every spring.
Special points Do not water in winter.

ADIANTUM RADDIANUM

DELTA MAIDENHAIR FERN

These ferns have delicate, pale-green fronds borne on black, wiry stalks. They mix well with both foliage and flowering house plants and are useful for softening the outline of arrangements. They are also attractive on their own. Small plants can be planted in terraria.

Mini-climate 3 Warm, shady.
Size *Adiantum raddianum* grow to 1ft in height with a similar spread. Plants of all sizes are offered for sale.
Feeding Feed with standard liquid fertilizer once a month during spring and summer.
Potting Repot in spring using fern potting mixture but only when a mass of roots appears on the surface of the potting mixture.
Special points Stand plants on trays filled with moist pebbles to increase humidity.

Similar-shaped species
Adiantum raddianum microphyllum has minute, dark-green, wedge-shaped leaflets. *Adiantum hispidulum* is very small and has fingerlike fronds.

AECHMEA FASCIATA

URN PLANT

When three or four years old, these plants produce a drumstick-shaped inflorescence which rises from the center of the rosette. This flower head comprises many spiny, pink bracts through which peep short-lived, pale-blue flowers. Display large plants as specimens, or grow small plants on a dried branch covered with sphagnum moss.

Mini-climate 1 Warm, sunny.
Size The leaves of these plants reach 2ft long and the flower spikes grow 6in above the leaves. Small plants grown from offsets and mature plants are offered for sale.
Feeding Feed with half-strength standard liquid fertilizer once a month in spring and summer. Apply feed to the center of the rosette as well as the roots.
Potting Repot in spring using bromeliad potting mixture but only if the roots have completely filled the existing pot. Once plants are in 6in pots topdress instead.
Special points Keep the center of the rosette filled with fresh water.

AGLAONEMA CRISPUM 'SILVER QUEEN'

SILVERED SPEAR

The beautiful foliage of these plants is green only at the margins and main veins; the rest of the leaf is silvery-white and cream. As plants age they lose some of their lower leaves and develop a short, trunklike stem. They are excellent as part of a bold, leafy arrangement, particularly if contrasted with dark-green foliage plants.

Mini-climate 2 Warm, filtered sun.
Size *Aglaonema crispum* 'Silver Queen' reach a maximum height of 3ft with a spread of about 2ft.
Feeding Feed with standard liquid fertilizer once a month from spring to autumn.
Potting Repot every spring using soil-based potting mixture. Once plants are in 6in pots topdress instead.

ALLAMANDA CATHARTICA

GOLDEN TRUMPET

These climbing plants produce bright, buttercup-yellow flowers over a period of many weeks during the summer. The oval leaves which are carried on long stems are a glossy dark-green color. If grown in a conservatory border, or in a tub, *Allamanda cathartica* can be trained to cover a wall. For the smaller room, they can be grown in pots and trained over a wire framework of any shape.

Mini-climate 2 Warm, filtered sun.

Size These plants are fast-growing and can attain a maximum height and spread of 7ft. They should be cut back by as much as two-thirds in winter. Small plants are offered for sale in summer.

Feeding Feed with standard liquid fertilizer every two weeks in summer.

Potting Repot every spring using soil-based potting mixture. If you don't want to move an older plant into a larger pot, topdress instead.

Special points Water less in winter.

ANANAS COMOSUS VARIEGATUS

VARIEGATED PINEAPPLE

These plants are prized for their stiff, spiny leaves which curve gracefully outward, giving them a symmetrical shape. When five or six years old they produce striking pink flower heads, followed by a pink fruit which is unlikely to ripen and be edible. Large plants displayed in an urn suit formal interiors.

Mini-climate 1 Warm, sunny.
Size These plants grow to a maximum height of about 3ft with a spread of up to 6ft. Fruiting plants are offered for sale.

Feeding Feed with standard liquid fertilizer every two weeks during spring and summer.
Potting Repot in spring every two years using bromeliad potting mixture. Once plants are in 6-8in pots topdress instead.
Special points In direct sunlight, a rich-pink hue enhances the variegation of the leaves.

Similar-shaped species

Ananas bracteatus striatus is the variegated form of the wild pineapple and has boldly striped leaves which become pink if grown in bright light.
Ananas nanus is much smaller with plain, dark-green leaves and produces small, inedible fruits. It can be bought in fruit in a 4in pot.

ANTHURIUM ANDRAEANUM HYBRIDS

FLAMINGO FLOWER

The exotic flower heads consist of a bright scarlet bract encircling a tail-like flower spike. They last for several weeks and can appear at any time between February and July. When in flower, several plants grouped together make an attractive display; when not in flower, the leaves harmonize with those of other tropical plants suitable for shady spots.

Mini-climate 3 Warm, shady.
Size Small plants are offered for sale, although they can grow to 2ft in height.
Feeding Feed every two weeks with standard liquid fertilizer.
Potting Repot every spring using a mixture of one-third soil-based potting mixture, one-third coarse peat moss, and one-third coarse sand. Once plants are in 7in pots topdress instead. Cover exposed roots in peat moss.
Special points Water less in winter. Stand plants on trays filled with moist pebbles to increase humidity.

APHELANDRA SQUARROSA 'LOUISAE'

SAFFRON SPIKE

These are dual-purpose flowering and foliage plants. For about six weeks the plant has unusual flower heads of overlapping yellow bracts. When flowering has finished, pinch off the dead blooms, then use as a foliage plant. The leaves are large and glossy and marked with large, white veins. Mix with plain-leaved plants for a contrasting display in a modern living-room.

Mini-climate 2 Warm, filtered sun.
Size *Aphelandra squarrosa* 'Louisae' grow to about 1ft in height with a similar spread. Plants already in flower are offered for sale.
Feeding Feed with standard liquid fertilizer every week from spring to early autumn.
Potting Repot every spring using soil-based potting mixture. Once plants are in 6in pots topdress instead.

ARAUCARIA HETEROPHYLLA

NORFOLK ISLAND PINE

Also known as "Christmas tree plants", these are at their best when four years old. Because of their starkness, they seldom look well mixed with other plants, but a most striking effect can be created by grouping several of these conifers together to give a Japanese look.

Mini-climate 5 Cool, filtered sun.
Size *Araucaria heterophylla* are slow-growing: a ten year old plant rarely exceeds 6ft in height and 4ft width.
Feeding Feed with standard liquid fertilizer every two weeks in spring and summer.
Potting Repot every two or three years in spring using soil-based potting mixture. Once plants are in 9-10in pots topdress instead.
Special points Water more sparingly during the winter rest period.

ASPARAGUS DENSIFLORUS 'SPRENGERI'

EMERALD FERN

These plants have arching stems which begin to trail with age. Each stem is covered in tiny branchlets, giving the plants a delicate, fernlike appearance; in fact they are not true ferns but related to the lilies. Use them to soften the outline of arrangements, or group with true ferns in a hanging basket. They thrive in most conditions and have a fresh, informal look which makes them suitable for most settings.

Mini-climate 2 Warm, filtered sun.
Size The stems can grow up to 3ft in length. Small plants are offered for sale.
Feeding Feed with standard liquid fertilizer every two weeks in spring and summer, and once a month in autumn and winter.
Potting Repot in spring using soil-based potting mixture but only if the roots have completely filled the existing pot. If you don't want to move an older plant into a larger pot, topdress instead.
Special points To keep plants in a decorative state for as long as possible, faded stems should be cut out as they appear.

ASPARAGUS SETACEUS

ASPARAGUS FERN

Asparagus setaceus have light, feathery foliage made up of tiny branchlets on wiry stems. Taller growing kinds may be trained up thin canes to form a delicate column shape. Trained around east- or west-facing windows they can give a charming "cottage" effect. They can also be included in fern groups in a hanging basket.

Mini-climate 2 Warm, filtered sun.
Size These plants can produce stems up to 4ft long. Small plants are offered for sale.
Feeding Feed with standard liquid fertilizer every two weeks in spring and summer, and once a month in autumn and winter.
Potting Repot every spring using soil-based potting mixture. If you don't want to move an older plant into a larger pot, topdress instead.

Similar-shaped species

Asparagus asparagoides is a vigorous climbing vine with leafletlike branchlets up to 2in long. *Asparagus falcatus* is similar but has sickle-shaped spines on its stems.

ASPIDISTRA ELATIOR

CAST-IRON PLANT

As their common name suggests, these plants will tolerate a certain amount of neglect. They were much used in Victorian days as specimen plants, but despite these associations, *Aspidistra elatior* can be used to great effect, either massed together or grouped with other, smaller plants. They are ideal plants for filling difficult, darker spaces.

Mini-climate 5 Cool, filtered sun.
Size These plants have a maximum height and spread of 3ft. Small plants are offered for sale.
Feeding Feed with standard liquid fertilizer every two weeks in spring and summer.
Potting Repot every three years using soil-based potting mixture but only if the roots have completely filled the existing pot. If you don't want to move an older plant into a larger pot, topdress instead.

ASPLENIUM NIDUS

BIRD'S NEST FERN

These plants have shiny, apple-green fronds arranged in an upward-spreading rosette at whose base is a circle of young leaf fronds. These slowly unroll from the fibrous core of the plant. Large specimens are too bold in shape to display with other ferns and look best either arranged on their own, or included in a mixed group of large-leaved foliage plants.

Mini-climate 3 Warm, shady.
Size The fronds can reach 1½ft long. Young plants are offered for sale.
Feeding Feed with standard liquid fertilizer once a month.
Potting Repot in spring using fern potting mixture but only when a mass of roots appears on the surface of the potting mixture. If you don't want to move an older plant into a larger pot, root prune instead.
Special points Stand plants on trays filled with moist pebbles to increase humidity.

AUCUBA JAPONICA 'VARIEGATA'

SPOTTED LAUREL

Also known as "Japanese laurels", these plants were much used by the Victorians in their shrubberies and greenhouses. The modern hybrids are more cheerful, having leaves strongly variegated with yellow. They can be used in window-boxes and in cool rooms as they tolerate a certain amount of neglect, poor light and drafts.

Mini-climate 5 Cool, filtered sun.
Size These plants can reach 3-4ft high. Plants of about 8in high are offered for sale.
Feeding Feed with standard liquid fertilizer once a month in summer.
Potting Repot every spring using soil-based potting mixture. Once plants are in 8in pots topdress instead.
Special points Clean leaves regularly. Plants can be put outside in summer.

BEAUCARNEA RECURVATA

PONYTAIL

These are most bizarre-looking plants, having a ponytail-like tuft of narrow, green leaves sprouting from the top of a fat or long, woody stem. The swollen base adds to the unusual appearance of the plants, which are ideal for displaying in a modern interior and will thrive in any centrally heated room.

Mini-climate 2 Warm, filtered sun.
Size These plants reach a maximum height of 5ft with a spread of 2ft. Small and medium sized plants are offered for sale.
Feeding Feed with standard liquid fertilizer every month during summer.
Potting Repot every three or four years in spring using soil-based potting mixture. They thrive in small pots.
Special points Can easily be killed by overwatering.

BEGONIA 'ELATIOR' HYBRIDS

ELATIOR BEGONIA

These plants flower for most of the year. The large, roselike flowers range in color from deep red, through pink to yellow and white, They are best treated as annuals and discarded when flowering has finished. The foliage is usually pale green but plants with deep-red foliage are sometimes available. As their flowers are quite large they can be displayed as specimen plants or grouped together in a shallow pan. *Begonia* 'Elatior' hybrids do best in light, well-ventilated rooms.

Mini-climate 2 Warm, filtered sun.
Size These plants are usually erect with a maximum height and spread of 14-16in. Small bushy plants are offered for sale from mid-spring to early autumn.
Feeding Feed with standard liquid fertilizer every two weeks in spring and summer.
Potting Repot two or three times during summer and autumn using equal parts of soil-based potting mixture and leaf mold or coarse peat moss. If you don't want to move an older plant into a larger pot, topdress instead.
Special points Protect from powdery mildew by supplying adequate ventilation.

BEGONIA FOLIOSA MINIATA

FUCHSIA BEGONIA

These delicate-looking plants have small, oval leaves with a glossy texture. The leaves are borne on long, thin stems which begin to arch over as they get longer. Small, waxy, succulent-looking, shell-pink flowers appear in clusters between autumn and spring. They need some kind of support if they are to be seen to best effect. Display with green foliage groups in an informal setting. They can look good if allowed to trail from a hanging basket.

Mini-climate 1 Warm, sunny.
Size *Begonia foliosa* can grow to about 3ft in height, with a spread of about 20in. Pinch out growing tips to maintain bushy growth. Small plants are offered for sale.
Feeding Feed with standard liquid fertilizer once every two weeks during flowering.
Potting Repot every spring using an equal-parts mixture of soil-based and peat-based potting mixture. If you don't want to move an older plant into a larger pot, topdress instead.
Special points Water less in winter.

BEGONIA REX-CULTORUM

PAINTED-LEAF BEGONIA

Also known as "rex begonias", these are among the most handsome of the species, grown for their beautifully colored leaves rather than their flowers, which tend to be insignificant. The heart-shaped leaves, which can be up to 1ft in length, bear striking patterns made up of variations of red, black, silver and green. Leaf texture also varies: some hybrids have smooth leaves; this one has a rippled or pimpled surface.

Mini-climate 3 Warm, shady.
Size These plants can grow up to 1ft in height with a 3ft spread. Young specimens 2-3in high are offered for sale.
Feeding Feed with standard liquid fertilizer every two weeks in spring and summer.
Potting Divide overcrowded clumps and repot in spring every three years using peat-based potting mixture in a shallow container.
Special points Water less in winter. Destroy any powdery mildew you may find.

Similar-shaped species
Begonia masoniana has a deep-red, cross-shaped pattern on its pale-green leaves.

BEGONIA SEMPERFLORENS-CULTORUM

WAX BEGONIA

A profusion of white, pink or red flowers begin blooming in spring and continue well into the winter. Single- and double-flowered varieties are available. They are best treated as annuals and discarded when flowering has finished. Group them together in shallow containers or mix with colorful foliage plants in light, well-ventilated rooms.

Mini-climate 1 Warm, sunny.

Size These plants never reach more than 1ft in height when fully grown. They are offered for sale in spring as seedlings and for the rest of the year as mature plants.

Feeding Feed with standard liquid fertilizer every two weeks in spring and summer.

Potting Repot as needed, perhaps two or three times during summer and autumn, using a mixture of half soil-based potting mixture and half leaf mold or coarse peat moss. If you don't want to move an older plant into a larger pot, topdress instead.

Special points Protect from powdery mildew by supplying adequate ventilation.

BEGONIA 'TIGER PAWS'

EYELASH BEGONIA

The common name of these plants derives
from the short, coarse hairs which grow
around the edge of each lopsided, heart-shaped
leaf. The attractive foliage is bright lime-green
in color, marked with a bronze-red pattern
which gives the leaves a patched or blotchy
appearance. The stalks are also speckled with
red and arise from a rhizome which creeps
across the surface of the potting mixture. Mass
these plants together in a basket or mix them
with other foliage plants.

Mini-climate 2 Warm, filtered sun.
Size These plants grow to about 6in in
height with a 1ft spread. Small plants are
offered for sale all year.
Feeding Feed with standard liquid fertilizer
every two weeks during spring and summer.
Potting Repot every spring using an equal
combination of soil-based potting mixture and
leaf mold. If you don't want to move an older
plant into a larger plot, topdress instead.
Discard the plant after several repottings.
Special points Stand plants on trays filled
with moist pebbles to increase humidity.
Protect from powdery mildew by supplying
adequate ventilation.

BILLBERGIA NUTANS

QUEEN'S TEARS

These plants have tough leaves with toothed
edges. There may be many plants in the same
pot, as production of offsets is prolific. During
the main flowering season, May to June, the
foliage is interspersed with trailing, bright-pink
bracts. These bracts open to display the small
yellow, green and purple flowers. *Billbergia
nutans* are best displayed at eye-level as
feature plants.

Mini-climate 1 Warm, sunny.
Size The leaves reach about 2ft in length.
Spread depends on the number of offsets
produced. Small plants are offered for sale.
Feeding Feed with standard liquid fertilizer
every two weeks during spring and summer.
Potting Repot every spring using bromeliad
potting mixture. Once plants are in 6in pots
topdress instead.
Special points The rosette of leaves should
be cut away at the base after flowering to allow
the offsets around it to develop.

BOUGAINVILLEA BUTTIANA

PAPER FLOWER

    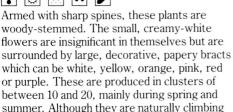

Armed with sharp spines, these plants are woody-stemmed. The small, creamy-white flowers are insignificant in themselves but are surrounded by large, decorative, papery bracts which can be white, yellow, orange, pink, red or purple. These are produced in clusters of between 10 and 20, mainly during spring and summer. Although they are naturally climbing plants, *Bougainvillea buttiana* can be trained to remain bushy indoors. They are best grown in very sunny rooms or conservatories, since they require a large amount of light to encourage them to flower.

Mini-climate 1 Warm, sunny.

Size These plants can reach a maximum height and spread of about 6ft. Pinch out growing tips to encourage bushy growth. Small plants are offered for sale.

Feeding Feed with standard liquid fertilizer every two weeks in summer.

Potting Repot every spring using soil-based potting mixture with extra peat moss mixed in. Once plants are in 8in pots topdress instead.

Special points Water less in winter. Destroy any mealy bugs you may find.

BROWALLIA SPECIOSA

AMETHYST VIOLET

These are showy plants with violet-blue flowers that appear in early summer or autumn depending on climate and when seeds were started. They are best treated as annuals and discarded when flowering has finished. The stems tend to droop so display plants in eye-level hanging baskets or massed together on a low table.

Mini-climate 1 Warm, sunny.
Size *Browallia speciosa* grow to 10-12in tall with a similar spread. Pinch out growing tips to encourage bushy growth. Mature plants are offered for sale in autumn.

Feeding Feed with standard liquid fertilizer every two weeks.

Potting Repotting is unnecessary.

Special points Destroy any greenfly you may find.

Similar-shaped species

Browallia viscosa is only half the size of *B. speciosa*, with smaller leaves and flowers. The leaves are slightly sticky.

CALADIUM HORTULANUM HYBRIDS

ANGEL WINGS

Caladium hortulanum hybrids send up long, fleshy stalks bearing the paper-thin, heart-shaped leaves. The variety of leaf colors and patterns is immense – besides green leaves with red veining, white and cream leaves veined with pink or green are also available. These plants are highly ornamental, especially if different leaf colors are grouped together.

Mini-climate 3 Warm, shady.
Size The mainly green-leaved specimens grow to a maximum height of 8-10in. Varieties with colored leaves may reach 1½-2ft high. Plants in full leaf are offered for sale.
Feeding Feed with half-strength liquid fertilizer once every two weeks during spring and summer.
Potting Repot a rested tuber in spring using peat-based potting mixture. Make provision for good drainage. Use 5in pots and cover the tuber with 1in of potting mixture.

CALATHEA MAKOYANA

PEACOCK PLANT

The leaves of these plants look as if they have been hand painted with dark-green patterns. They look best in a mixed group of foliage plants. Smaller plants can be used in bottle gardens and larger terraria.

Mini-climate 3 Warm, shady.
Size *Calathea makoyana* can grow to a height of 3ft with a spread of about 2ft. Plants of all sizes are offered for sale.
Feeding Feed with standard liquid fertilizer every two weeks during spring and summer and once a month during autumn and winter.
Potting Repot every spring using a mixture of two-thirds soil-based potting mixture and one-third leaf mold or peat. Once plants are in 6in pots topdress instead.
Special points Stand plants on trays filled with moist pebbles to increase humidity.

CAMPANULA ISOPHYLLA

ITALIAN BELLFLOWER

Campanula isophylla produce clusters of delicate-looking white or pale-blue flowers in early August and continue flowering until November. The flowers are normally so numerous that they completely hide the pale-green foliage. They are best treated as annuals and discarded when flowering has finished. These are useful plants for massing in hanging baskets or window-boxes. They look good in conservatories or informal rooms.

Mini-climate 4 Cool, sunny.

Size The slender stems reach a maximum length of 1ft. Pinch out growing tips to encourage bushy growth. Small plants are offered for sale in summer.

Feeding Feed with standard liquid fertilizer every two weeks during the flowering season.

Potting Repot every spring using soil-based potting mixture. When plants are in 5in pots topdress instead.

Special points Mist-spray plants in hanging baskets daily during summer and autumn.

CAPSICUM ANNUUM

CHRISTMAS PEPPER

An increasingly popular plant bearing brightly colored fleshy berries which appear in autumn and remain decorative for 8-12 weeks. The most familiar berries are orange-red in color but white, yellow, green and purple-berried varieties are also available. They are best treated as annuals and discarded when the fruiting has finished. They make colorful displays and are striking massed together as a table decoration.

Mini-climate 1 Warm, sunny.
Size These plants are at their best when at 12-14in height and spread, and fruiting plants of this size are offered for sale.
Feeding Feed with standard liquid fertilizer every two weeks in the fruiting season.
Potting Repotting is unnecessary.
Special points To keep plants in a decorative state for as long as possible, stand plants on trays filled with moist pebbles to increase humidity.

CHAMAEDOREA ELEGANS 'BELLA'

PARLOR PALM

These plants have dainty, deeply divided fronds arching from the central stem. The fronds are fresh green when young and darken with age. Mature plants produce small sprays of tiny, yellow, beadlike flowers. They thrive in the warm, humid conditions of bottle gardens and terraria.

Mini-climate 2 Warm, filtered sun.
Size *Chamaedorea elegans* 'Bella' is a dwarf species, reaching a height of about 3ft after several years, with a spread of 1½ft. Young plants are offered for sale.
Feeding Feed with standard liquid fertilizer once a month from spring to autumn.
Potting Repot in spring using soil-based potting mixture but only if the roots have completely filled the existing pot. Once plants are in 6-8in pots topdress instead.
Special points Water less in winter.

Similar-shaped species
Chamaedorea erumpens forms a clump of slender stems, knotted at intervals like bamboo and with sections of bare stem. They can grow to about 6-8ft in height.

CHAMAEROPS HUMILIS

EUROPEAN FAN PALM

Also known as "dwarf fan palms", these handsome, low-growing palms have wide, fan-shaped fronds. These are made up of rigid, sword-shaped segments with split ends. There is no recognizable stem, except in very mature plants, the fronds being held upright on long leaf stalks. These are ornamental plants with an oriental look to them which can be used either as specimens or in groups depending on their size.

Mini-climate 2 Warm, filtered sun.
Size These plants are slow-growing, but will eventually reach 5ft in height with a similar spread when mature. Plants of all sizes are offered for sale.
Feeding Feed with standard liquid fertilizer once a month in spring, summer and autumn.
Potting Repot every two years in spring using soil-based potting mixture. Once plants are in 12in pots topdress instead.
Special points Stand plants outside in a sheltered place during summer.

CHLOROPHYTUM COMOSUM 'VITTATUM'

SPIDER PLANT

These hybrids have a distinctive white or cream stripe down the center of each leaf. The narrow leaves arch over but the true trailing effect is produced by long stems bearing numerous plantlets. Well-grown specimens are striking when displayed from a height on pedestals or in hanging baskets.

Mini-climate 5 Cool, filtered sun.
Size The leaves can grow up to 2ft long. The spread depends on the number of plants growing in the same pot. Plants of all sizes are offered for sale.
Feeding Feed with standard liquid fertilizer every two weeks.
Potting Repot in spring using soil-based potting mixture but only if the roots have completely filled the existing pot. If you don't want to move an older plant into a larger pot, topdress instead.
Special points Allow a 1in space at the top of the pot for the development of the fat roots.

CHRYSANTHEMUM MORIFOLIUM HYBRIDS

FLORIST'S CHRYSANTHEMUM

Also known as "pot chrysanthemums", these plants are offered for sale with flowers of every color but blue. The flowers and foliage have a distinctive scent. They will remain in flower for about six weeks, and are best treated as annuals and discarded when flowering has finished. Several plants grouped together in a shallow basket or pan on a low table look particularly attractive.

Mini-climate 5 Cool, filtered sun.
Size *Chrysanthemum morifolium* hybrids have been specially cultivated to reach no more than 1ft in height. They are offered for sale in flower throughout the year.
Feeding Feeding is not required for these temporary plants.
Potting Repotting is unnecessary.
Special points When buying make sure the flower buds show color as tightly closed green buds often fail to open.

CISSUS ANTARCTICA

KANGAROO VINE

Relatives of the grapevine, these are scrambling foliage plants whose glossy, dark-green leaves have marked veining and a scalloped edge. They can be used in many striking and different ways: either trained up poles, used as specimen plants or displayed in hanging baskets.

Mini-climate 2 Warm, filtered sun.
Size These plants grow to 6ft tall with a spread of 2ft in about two years. Plants of all sizes are offered for sale.
Feeding Feed with standard liquid fertilizer every two weeks in spring and summer.
Potting Repot every spring using soil-based potting mixture. Once plants are in 6-8in pots topdress instead.
Special points Stand plants on trays filled with moist pebbles to increase humidity. Mist-spray plants in hanging baskets.

CISSUS RHOMBIFOLIA

GRAPE IVY

These plants have deeply toothed leaves. New leaf growth appears to be silver due to a fine covering of hairs on both surfaces. Older leaves have undersides covered in fine, brown hairs. Trained up a simple framework of bamboo canes, *Cissus rhombifolia* can quickly become quite large feature plants. They also make an excellent display in hanging baskets.

Mini-climate 2 Warm, filtered sun.
Size These plants grow to 6ft in height in around two years and can reach 10ft in ideal conditions. Pinch out growing tips regularly to encourage bushy growth. Plants of all sizes are offered for sale.
Feeding Feed with standard liquid fertilizer every two weeks in spring and summer.
Potting Repot every spring using soil-based potting mixture. Once plants are in 6-7in pots topdress instead.

CITROFORTUNELLA MITIS

CALAMONDIN ORANGE

These ornamental orange trees bear fragrant flowers, unripe green fruits and ripe orange fruits all at the same time. The oranges produced are small and bitter but are excellent for making marmalade. The plants will fruit when still quite young and are best as specimen plants or arranged in formal groups.

Mini-climate 4 Cool, sunny.
Size *Citrofortunella mitis* take several years to reach a maximum height of 3-6ft with a similar spread. Small specimens bearing fruit are offered for sale.
Feeding Feed every two weeks with a tomato-type fertilizer all year except in winter.
Potting Repot in spring using soil-based potting mixture but only if the roots have completely filled the existing pot. If you don't want to move an older plant into a larger pot, topdress instead.
Special points Susceptible to scale insects. Prune to keep plants shapely and compact.

COCOS NUCIFERA

COCONUT PALM

These most striking looking plants grow directly from the nut which sits on top of the potting mixture. From the nut sprout the upright stalks which bear the once-divided, arching fronds. These fronds are heavily ribbed. *Cocos nucifera* makes a striking specimen plant for a stark modern interior.

Mini-climate 2 Warm, filtered sun.
Size These plants can reach more than 5ft in height. Large plants are offered for sale.
Feeding Feed with half-strength liquid fertilizer once every two weeks during spring and summer.
Potting Repotting is unnecessary.
Special points These palms only last about two years in the home as they resent root disturbance.

CODIAEUM VARIEGATUM PICTUM

CROTON

These are striking, highly colored, tropical shrubs with many variations in leaf shape, size and color. Young leaves have a green color, reds, oranges and purples develop with age. They naturally drop their lower leaves with age but will retain them longer in a humid atmosphere. Mass together plants with different colored leaves for a vivid display.

Mini-climate 1 Warm, sunny.
Size They rarely grow larger than 3ft tall, with a similar spread. Small and medium-sized plants are offered for sale.
Feeding Feed with standard liquid fertilizer every two weeks from spring to autumn.
Potting Repot every spring using soil-based potting mixture. When plants are in 8-10in pots topdress instead.
Special points Stand plants on trays filled with moist pebbles to increase humidity.

COLEUS BLUMEI

PAINTED NETTLE

These plants have soft-textured leaves in a range of vivid colors, from red and bronze to cream and purple, some incorporating three or more colors. Although the serrated leaves closely resemble those of the stinging nettle, the two plants are not related. *Coleus blumei* are best treated as annuals and discarded after one year. Their brightly patterned foliage is suited to period rooms containing richly colored fabrics.

Mini-climate 1 Warm, sunny.
Size These plants will grow to a height of 18in in one year with a similar spread. Pinch out growing tips to encourage bushy growth.
Feeding Feed with standard liquid fertilizer every two weeks in spring and summer, and once a month during autumn and winter.
Potting Repot once every two months using soil-based potting mixture. If you don't want to move an older plant into a larger pot, topdress instead.
Special points Leaf color is stronger if plants are placed in a sunny position.

COLUMNEA 'BANKSII'

COLUMNEA

These plants have striking scarlet flowers borne among the small, waxy leaves on long trailing stems. The flowers may be produced at any time of year and a large plant may have up to 100 flowers at any one time. Use large plants as specimens in plain containers or hanging baskets in a warm room.

Mini-climate 2 Warm, filtered sun.
Size The trailing stems of *Columnea* 'Banksii' reach a maximum length of 4ft. Young plants are offered for sale in spring.
Feeding Feed with one-quarter strength high-phosphate liquid fertilizer each time the plant is watered.
Potting Repot every spring using a mixture of equal parts peat moss, perlite and vermiculite. If you don't want to move an older plant into a larger pot, prune the roots instead.
Special points Maintain high humidity throughout the year.

CORDYLINE TERMINALIS

TI PLANT

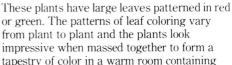

These plants have large leaves patterned in red or green. The patterns of leaf coloring vary from plant to plant and the plants look impressive when massed together to form a tapestry of color in a warm room containing richly colored fabrics.

Mini-climate 2 Warm, filtered sun.
Size *Cordyline terminalis* can grow to a height of 4ft with a spread of 1½ft. Small plants are offered for sale.
Feeding Feed with standard liquid fertilizer every two weeks from April to September.
Potting Repot every two years in spring using soil-based potting mixture. If you don't want to move an older plant into a larger pot, topdress instead.
Special points Water less in winter. Clean leaves with a damp sponge.

CRYPTANTIIUS BIVITTATUS

EARTH STAR PLANT

These small plants have some of the most beautifully colored foliage found in the bromeliads. The sharply pointed leaves have two distinctive cream stripes running along their length, which turn pink or even a strong red if placed in the direct sun. Clusters of small white flowers are hidden by the leaves. These stemless plants can be massed together in shallow bowls or terraria.

Mini-climate 1 Warm, sunny.
Size These are slow growing and will reach 6-8in across by the time they flower.
Feeding Feed occasionally by splashing with half-strength standard liquid fertilizer.
Potting Repotting is hardly ever necessary.
Special points Some time after flowering has finished cut away the parent plant to allow the offsets around its base to develop.

CYCLAMEN PERSICUM HYBRIDS

FLORIST'S CYCLAMEN

These flower in late autumn, winter and early spring. Many varieties are available, with the color of the swept-back flowers ranging from white, through red, to purple. Some varieties have frilled or perfumed flowers. Although usually treated as an annual, if the tubers are dried off in the late spring and rested during the summer months, these plants can last for many years, although they do not mix well with other plants. They are ideal for colorful displays in entrance halls or period rooms where conditions are not excessively hot.

Mini-climate 5 Cool, filtered sun.
Size They rarely grow larger than 8-10in tall. Budded plants are offered for sale from September until Christmastime.
Feeding Feed with standard liquid fertilizer every two weeks when in flower.
Potting Repotting of first year plants is unnecessary. Repot a rested tuber in soil-based potting mixture in September. Use the same pot each year.
Special points Never pour water directly on to the tuber, instead stand the pot in water for ten minutes.

CYPERUS ALTERNIFOLIUS 'GRACILIS'

UMBRELLA PLANT

The radiating grasslike bracts of these plants resemble the spokes of an open umbrella. The tall stems are very brittle and should be handled with care. *Cyperus alternifolius* 'Gracilis' have a Japanese look and suit stark modern interiors.

Mini-climate 2 Warm, filtered sun.
Size They will reach a height of 4ft given suitably wet conditions.
Feeding Feed with standard liquid fertilizer once every month.
Potting Repot in spring using soil-based potting mixture with added charcoal, but only if the roots have completely filled the existing pot. Ensure plants are repotted at the same soil level. If you don't want to move an older plant into a larger pot, topdress instead.
Special points Stand permanently in a water-filled saucer to keep the roots saturated.

DIEFFENBACHIA MACULATA

DUMB CANE

Dieffenbachia maculata are bold feature plants with handsome, variegated leaves. Older plants tend to lose their lower leaves giving a solitary plant a bizarre look; but several plants grouped together make a dramatic display in a modern setting.

Mini-climate 3 Warm, shady.

Size These plants will grow to a height of 5ft and a spread of 2ft. Plants of all sizes are offered for sale.

Feeding Feed with standard liquid fertilizer every two weeks from early spring to mid-autumn.

Potting Repot every spring using soil-based potting mixture in clay pots. Once plants are in 8in pots topdress instead.

Special points The sap is poisonous and can cause severe inflammation of the mouth.

Similar-shaped species

Dieffenbachia amoena has 1½ft long, pointed leaves which are dark green with herringbone markings in cream.

Dieffenbachia exotica has 10in long leaves marked with white and pale green.

DIZYGOTHECA ELEGANTISSIMA

FALSE ARALIA

Also known as "finger aralias", these plants are elegant, open shrubs made up of many narrow leaflets. Leaf color changes with age from bronze to a very deep green and the leaf texture becomes coarser. The dark tracery of the palmate leaves makes a delicate background to set off bolder foliage, or several plants can be grouped together to create a lacy mass of leaves.

Mini-climate 2 Warm, filtered sun.
Size These plants reach 7ft in height with a spread of 2ft. Pinch out growing tips to encourage bushy growth. Plants of all sizes are offered for sale.
Feeding Feed with standard liquid fertilizer every two weeks in spring and summer.
Potting Repot every two years in spring using soil-based potting mixture. If you don't want to move an older plant into a larger pot, topdress instead.
Special points Stand plants on trays filled with moist pebbles to increase humidity.

DRACAENA MARGINATA 'TRICOLOR'

RAINBOW PLANT

The common name "rainbow plant" is derived from the leaf markings, which form stripes of green, cream and pink. In mature plants, the topknot of leaves emerges from the bare, woody stem, giving plants a palmlike look. Three or four specimens planted in the same pot make a good display in a modern setting.

Mini-climate 2 Warm, filtered sun.
Size *Dracaena marginata* 'Tricolor' will grow to 5ft with a spread of 1½ft. Plants of 1ft in height are offered for sale, but there is more demand for older plants with bare stems.
Feeding Feed with standard liquid fertilizer every two weeks in spring and summer, and once a month in autumn and winter.
Potting Repot every spring using soil-based potting mixture. If you don't want to move an older plant into a larger pot, topdress instead.
Special points Water less in winter.

DRACAENA SANDERANA

BELGIAN EVERGREEN

Also known as "ribbon plants", these are the most dainty of this family. They are slender, upright plants with narrow, cream-striped leaves. Because they rarely branch, three or four specimens should be planted together in a pot to create a spiky mass of leaves.

Mini-climate 2 Warm, filtered sun.
Size *Dracaena sanderana* are slow-growing but will eventually reach a maximum height of 3ft. Small plants, usually three to a pot, are offered for sale.
Feeding Feed with standard liquid fertilizer once every two weeks from mid-spring to early autumn.
Potting Repot every two or three years in spring using soil-based potting mixture. Once plants are in 4½-5in pots topdress instead.
Special points Water less in winter.

EPIPREMNUM AUREUM

DEVIL'S IVY

These plants, also known as "Solomon Islands' ivies", have yellowish-green, angular stems with aerial roots and large, bright-green leaves boldly and irregularly marked with yellow. They are impressive in hanging baskets, on high shelves, or when trained up moss-covered poles. Large specimens are best displayed on their own in a warm room.

Mini-climate 2 Warm, filtered sun.
Size The stems grow to a maximum of 6½ft long with a 3ft spread. Pinch out growing tips to encourage bushy growth. Young, small-leaved plants are offered for sale.
Feeding Feed with standard liquid fertilizer every two weeks in spring and summer.
Potting Repot every spring using soil-based potting mixture. If you don't want to move an older plant into a larger pot, topdress instead.
Special points Water less in winter.

EUPHORBIA PULCHERRIMA

POINSETTIA

With their flamboyant red, pink or creamy-white bracts, *Euphorbia pulcherrima* are at their best in winter. The bracts remain decorative for two months. After this they should be cut hard back and kept for their foliage alone, as it is not easy to get these plants to bloom for a second year. These are essentially specimen plants; the common red form is particularly striking, but can look good when mixed with dark-green foliage plants.

Mini-climate 1 Warm, sunny.
Size These plants vary from 1ft up to 5ft in height when mature. They are offered for sale in autumn and winter.
Feeding Feed with standard liquid fertilizer once every month.
Potting Repotting of first year plants is unnecessary. If keeping the plant for a second year, repot in the same pot with fresh soil-based potting mixture.
Special points These plants have a sap which can cause irritation of the skin.

EXACUM AFFINE

GERMAN VIOLET

Also known as "Persian violets", these are small, bushy plants covered in bright-blue flowers with yellow eyes and shiny, olive-green leaves. They bloom in summer and the flowers can last for up to two months. They are best treated as annuals and discarded when flowering has finished. To display, mass them in a large bowl, as they make an eye-catching show in any setting – traditional or modern.

Mini-climate 2 Warm, filtered sun.
Size *Exacum affine* will quickly grow stems up to 1ft long. Young, budding plants are offered for sale in early spring.
Feeding Feed with standard liquid fertilizer every two weeks while the plant is in flower.
Potting Repot using soil-based potting mixture but only if the plant was bought in a very small pot. Further repotting is unnecessary.
Special points Stand plants on trays filled with moist pebbles to maintain high humidity.

FATSHEDERA LIZEI

TREE IVY

Also known as "aralia ivies", these plants have palmate, glossy-green leaves and can be displayed as upright feature plants, either alone or to give height to a group of smaller plants. They will also climb and can be trained, if tied to supports, to cover staircases and balconies and to frame windows.

Mini-climate 5 Cool, filtered sun.
Size *Fatshedera lizei* can grow upright to a height of 3ft with a similar spread. If allowed to wander over a support their growth will be unlimited.
Feeding Feed with standard liquid fertilizer every two weeks.
Potting Repot every spring using two-thirds soil-based potting mixture and one-third peat-moss. If you don't want to move an older plant into a larger pot, topdress instead.

FATSIA JAPONICA

JAPANESE FATSIA

An evergreen shrub which has been used for over a century as an indoor and outdoor plant. It has attractive, shiny, fingered leaves whose color and texture contrast with the stem which becomes gnarled and woody with age. The plant can be moved outside in summer, where the leaves become a deeper shade of green. *Fatsia japonica* can look extremely decorative in an architectural setting.

Mini-climate 5 Cool, filtered sun.
Size These are fast-growing shrubs, reaching 5ft in height and spread in two years. Small plants are offered for sale.
Feeding Feed with standard liquid fertilizer every two weeks during spring and summer.
Potting Repot every spring using soil-based potting mixture. Clay pots are best because these plants tend to be top-heavy. If you don't want to move an older plant into a larger pot, topdress instead.

FICUS BENJAMINA

WEEPING FIG

These plants are the most elegant of the ornamental figs with their graceful, gray-barked arching stems bearing the dangling, pointed leaves. The arrangement of the leaves gives the plant an open appearance; good for both modern and period interiors.

Mini-climate 3 Warm, shady.
Size *Ficus benjamina* have a maximum height of 5ft with a spread of about 4ft if given enough room. Medium-sized and large plants are offered for sale.
Feeding Feed with standard liquid fertilizer every two weeks in spring and summer.
Potting Repot in spring using a soil-based potting mixture but only if the roots have completely filled the existing pot. If you don't want to move an older plant into a larger pot, topdress instead.
Special points Water less in winter.

FICUS ELASTICA

RUBBER PLANT

The shiny, dark-green leaves are oval in shape with a pronounced point at their tip. The growth point is covered in a pink sheath for protection. *Ficus elastica* have a strong shape and look best displayed as specimen plants in a modern setting.

Mini-climate 3 Warm, shady.
Size These plants can grow up to 6ft in height. Plants of all sizes are offered for sale.
Feeding Feed with standard liquid fertilizer every two weeks in spring and summer.
Potting Repot in spring using soil-based potting mixture but only if the roots have completely filled the existing pot. If you don't want to move an older plant into a larger pot, topdress instead.
Special points Clean older leaves regularly. Do not clean young leaves.

Similar-shaped species

Ficus lyrata has huge puckered leaves which are shaped like a violin.

FICUS PUMILA

CREEPING FIG

These plants have small, heart-shaped, slightly wrinkled leaves borne on long, wiry stems which spread out across the surface of the potting mixture. They look good in shallow hanging baskets, alternatively, they can be used as ground cover in indoor window-boxes. Small plants make good fillers in bottle gardens and terraria.

Mini-climate 5 Cool, filtered sun.

Size The stems of the *Ficus pumila* can reach 2ft in length. Spread depends on the mode of growth. Small plants are offered for sale.

Feeding Feed with standard liquid fertilizer every two weeks.

Potting Repot in spring using peat-based potting mixture but only if the roots have completely filled the existing pot.

Special points Stand plants on trays filled with moist pebbles to increase humidity. Never allow the potting mixture to dry out as the leaves will shrivel and never recover.

FITTONIA VERSCHAFFELTII

NERVE PLANT

These plants have oval, olive-green leaves which are covered by a network of fine, carmine-colored veins creating a mosaic effect. Yellow flower spikes may occasionally be produced. These plants are suitable for massing together on a low table; they also look good in the forefront of a foliage group and are ideal for bottle gardens or terraria.

Mini-climate 3 Warm, shady.
Size These plants reach a height of 6in with a spread of about 1ft. Pinch out growing tips to encourage bushy growth. Small plants are offered for sale all year.
Feeding Feed with half-strength standard liquid fertilizer every two weeks in spring and summer.
Potting Repot every spring using peat-based potting mixture in half-pots or other shallow containers. Once plants are in 4½in pots simply remove plants from their pots, clean and refill them with fresh mixture and replace the plants.
Special points Stand plants on trays filled with moist pebbles to increase humidity.

GREVILLEA ROBUSTA

SILK OAK

These are treelike evergreen shrubs with finely divided, fernlike leaves. The leaves are bronze when they first appear, turning green later. They look good grouped with other plants and, when they are large enough, displayed as specimen plants.

Mini-climate 4 Cool, sunny.
Size *Grevillea robusta* are fast-growing and will reach 5ft high in two or three years. Encourage bushy growth by stopping the main shoot when young. Young plants are offered for sale.
Feeding Feed with standard liquid fertilizer every two weeks during spring and summer.
Potting Repot every spring using lime-free soil-based potting mixture. If you do not want to move an older plant into a larger pot, topdress instead.
Special points Water less in winter.

GUZMANIA LINGULATA

SCARLET STAR

These winter-flowering bromeliads have centers made up of bright-orange or scarlet bracts filled with small, yellow flowers. The arching leaves are soft, glossy and bright green in color. These are strongly colored plants which suit bold, modern interiors. Mass several plants together in a shallow glass bowl or display in pairs for a symmetrical arrangement.

Mini-climate 2 Warm, filtered sun.
Size These plants reach about 10in in height and have a spread of up to 1ft.
Feeding Feed with half-strength standard liquid fertilizer once a month. Ensure the feed gets on to the leaves and roots and into the central cup.
Potting Repot in spring using bromeliad potting mixture but only if the roots have filled the existing pot.
Special points Empty the central cup and fill with fresh water every month.

GYNURA AURANTIACA

PURPLE VELVET PLANT

The tooth-edged leaves of these plants are covered in fine, purple hair and are at their most colorful when the leaves first open. The stems are upright at first but sprawl as they get longer. The downy leaves are seen to full advantage when the plants are massed in hanging baskets and viewed against a sunny window. A large plant looks good displayed in a room containing richly colored fabrics.

Mini-climate 1 Warm, sunny.
Size The trailing stems of the *Gynura aurantiaca* can reach 3ft in length. Small compact plants are offered for sale.
Feeding Feed with standard liquid fertilizer once every month.
Potting Repot in spring using soil-based potting mixture. Discard the plant after the second repotting.
Special points Water less in winter. The unpleasantly scented orange flowers should be removed before they open.

HEDERA CANARIENSIS

ALGERIAN IVY

Also known as "Canary Island ivies", these plants have slightly lobed dark-green leaves with patches of gray-green variegation. They are vigorous climbers and can easily be trained up any kind of support. They make good specimen plants when very large and are most suitable for use in cool places.

Mini-climate 5 Cool, filtered sun.
Size These are fast-growing with an unpredictable maximum height and spread; certainly 6ft. Leaves can be as much as 6in long and 6in wide. Plants of all sizes are offered for sale.
Feeding Feed with standard liquid fertilizer every two weeks when actively growing.
Potting Repot in spring using soil-based potting mixture but only if the roots have completely filled the existing pot. Once plants are in 4½-6in pots topdress instead.
Special points Water less in winter.

HEDERA HELIX HYBRIDS

ENGLISH IVY

There are many *Hedera helix* hybrids, all forming low-growing bushy trailers, but with many variations in leaf shape and color. They may be used in a variety of ways: to infill the fronts of groups, as trailers in hanging baskets, or displayed along shelves. They can also be trained to climb.

Mini-climate 5 Cool, filtered sun.
Size These plants can grow very straggly so pinch out growing tips to encourage bushy growth. Plants of all sizes are offered for sale.
Feeding Feed with standard liquid fertilizer every two weeks in spring and summer, and once a month in autumn and winter.
Potting Repot in spring using soil-based potting mixture but only if the roots have completely filled the existing pot. If you don't want to move an older plant into a larger pot, topdress instead.
Special points Water more sparingly during the winter rest period.

HIBISCUS ROSA-SINENSIS

CHINESE HIBISCUS

Large, funnel-shaped flowers and glossy, dark-green leaves make these spectacular plants. Flowers can be red, pink, white, yellow or orange and appear singly, usually in spring and summer. Use in a bright, sunny setting for an oriental look, either individually or by grouping several plants of different colors together.

Mini-climate 1 Warm, sunny.
Size *Hibiscus rosa-sinensis* are fast-growing, quickly reaching about 5ft in height. Plants with opening buds are usually offered for sale in spring.
Feeding Feed with high-potash liquid fertilizer every two weeks in spring and summer, and once a month in autumn and winter. If flowers are not produced freely, increase the frequency of feeding (not the strength of the fertilizer).
Potting Repot every spring using soil-based potting mixture. If you don't want to move an older plant into a larger pot, topdress instead.
Special points Water less in winter.

HOWEA BELMOREANA

KENTIA PALM

These slender palms were great favorites in the 19th century, adding soft grace to large rooms. The arching fronds are borne on upright stems giving the plant an elegant look. Always specimen plants, they can be difficult to place due to their large size but seem to thrive in a range of conditions found in the home.

Mini-climate 2 Warm, filtered sun.
Size *Howea belmoreana* can grow to 10ft with a spread of 8ft. Medium and large plants are offered for sale.
Feeding Feed with standard liquid fertilizer once a month from spring to autumn.
Potting Repot every second year in spring using soil-based potting mixture. Once plants are in 12in pots topdress instead.
Special points Clean leaves regularly with a damp sponge.

Similar-shaped species
Howea forsterana is very similar and can only be told apart by the greater, flat-topped spread and wider gaps between the frond leaflets of this species.

HOYA BELLA

MINIATURE WAX PLANT

These are spreading plants with drooping stems and dull green, fleshy leaves. The pure white, strongly scented flowers are grouped in star-shaped clusters of eight to ten, each flower having a curious purple center. Flowers appear through the summer. *Hoya bella* are best displayed in hanging baskets as the centers of the drooping flowers can only be seen from below. They look good in a sunny conservatory or modern interior.

Mini-climate 1 Warm, sunny.
Size These plants grow to 1ft in height, the branches then begin to trail and produce a maximum spread of 1½ft.
Feeding Feed with high-potash liquid fertilizer once every two weeks from spring to early autumn.
Potting Repot every spring using soil-based potting mixture making provision for good drainage. Once plants are in 5-6in pots topdress instead.
Special points Destroy any mealy bugs.

HYPOESTES PHYLLOSTACHYA

POLKA-DOT PLANT

These are pretty plants with unusual foliage. The leaves, which range from olive-green to very dark green, are spotted with pale-pink dots. They are best treated as annuals and discarded after one year. New forms, as they are quite small, look more dramatic if several plants are grouped together, either in separate pots or planted in a shallow pan.

Mini-climate 2 Warm, filtered sun.
Size These plants can grow quite tall but will become straggly, so it is advisable to limit growth to 1ft tall by pinching out the growing tips. Small, bushy plants of 3-5in tall are offered for sale.
Feeding Feed with standard liquid fertilizer every two weeks from early summer to mid-autumn.
Potting Repot in spring but only if the roots have completely filled the existing pot. Once plants are in 5in pots topdress instead.
Special points Spray leaves with tepid water to discourage red spider mites.

IMPATIENS WALLERANA HYBRIDS

IMPATIENS

The flower color of these ubiquitous plants ranges from white, through pink, to red; some flowers are striped with another color. The foliage and thick, succulent stems also vary in color from pale green to bronze. *Impatiens wallerana* hybrids will begin flowering when only six weeks old and continue throughout the summer. They are best treated as annuals and discarded when flowering has finished. These plants look particularly attractive if grouped in a hanging basket or window-box.

Mini-climate 1 Warm, sunny.
Size These plants are fast-growing, the modern hybrids reaching a maximum height of 14in. Pinch out growing tips to encourage bushy growth. Seedlings and small and medium-sized plants are offered for sale.
Feeding Feed with standard liquid fertilizer every two weeks in spring and summer.
Potting Repot every spring using soil-based potting mixture but only if the roots have completely filled the existing pot. Once the plants are in 5in pots topdress instead.

JASMINUM POLYANTHUM

WHITE-SCENTED JASMINE

Clusters of white, scented flowers are produced by these attractive plants in winter and spring. Although delicate-looking, these plants are very vigorous climbers, easily trained around wire hoops or any other fine support. If planted in a conservatory border, they can be trained to cover a wall.

Mini-climate 4 Cool, sunny.
Size *Jasminum polyanthum* can reach 20ft if grown in a border, 3ft if grown in a pot. Spread depends upon the support used. Plants in flower are offered for sale in winter.
Feeding Feed with standard liquid fertilizer once a month in summer and autumn.
Potting Repot every spring using soil-based potting mixture. Once plants are in 8in pots topdress instead.
Special points Place plants outdoors during summer months.

LEEA COCCINEA

WEST INDIAN HOLLY

These plants have deep-green, holly-shaped leaves which are often tinged with a coppery-red. The plant has a very open appearance as the leaves are twice divided. *Leea coccinea* can be used as specimen plants or as a foil for low-growing foliage plants.

Mini-climate 2 Warm, filtered sun.
Size These plants reach a maximum height of about 5ft with a similar spread. Plants of about 1ft tall with a similar spread are offered for sale.
Feeding Feed with standard liquid fertilizer every two weeks from spring to autumn.
Potting Repot every spring using soil-based potting mixture. If you don't want to move an older plant into a larger pot, topdress instead.
Special points Water less in winter.

MARANTA LEUCONEURA ERYTHRONEURA

PRAYER PLANT

Prayer plants are so called because of the way pairs of leaves close together at night like hands in prayer. They are also known as red herringbone plants because of the leaves' deep red, raised veins. The red midrib is surrounded by a pale-green stripe on the olive-green leaf. These are among the showiest of plants and should be displayed in a prominent position. They can also be trained to grow up short, moss-covered poles.

Mini-climate 3 Warm, shady.

Size These plants will grow to a maximum of 6-12in tall with 16in spread. Small plants are offered for sale.

Feeding Feed with standard liquid fertilizer once every two weeks during spring, summer and autumn.

Potting Repot every spring using soil-based potting mixture in half-pots or other shallow containers. If you don't want to move an older plant into a larger pot, topdress instead.

MICROCOELUM WEDDELLIANUM

DWARF COCONUT PALM

These compact palms have shiny fronds which are deeply divided into many threadlike leaflets arranged in a herringbone fashion. Although the fronds look feathery they are quite tough to the touch. These palms have no true trunk; the fronds arise from a short, thickened base. They are not as arching as the larger types and therefore suitable for table tops or shelves.

Mini-climate 2 Warm, filtered sun.
Size *Microcoelum weddellianum* reach a maximum height and spread of 3ft. Small plants are offered for sale all year.
Feeding Feed with standard liquid fertilizer once a month in summer.
Potting Repot every two years in spring using soil-based potting mixture. If you don't want to move an older plant into a larger pot, topdress instead.

MIKANIA TERNATA

PLUSH VINE

These small plants have soft, slaty-green foliage covered in fine, purple hairs. The underside of the leaves and the stems are purple. They can be used in much the same way as ivies – either as trailers or climbers – although they do not grow as tall. Their unusual coloring provides a contrast to light-green plants in a mixed foliage arrangement.

Mini-climate 2 Warm, filtered sun.
Size *Mikania ternata* have a maximum height and spread of about 10ft. Small plants are offered for sale.
Feeding Feed with standard liquid fertilizer every two weeks from spring to autumn.
Potting Repot in spring using soil-based potting mixture. Discard the plant after the second repotting.
Special points Do not wet the hairy foliage.

MONSTERA DELICIOSA

SWISS CHEESE PLANT

These decorative plants have undivided, heart-shaped leaves when young; the characteristic split edges and holes appear with age. Train *Monstera deliciosa* up a moss-covered pole so that the pencil-thick aerial roots can be guided into the moss; never cut these roots off as they take in nutrients. The scale of a mature plant means that it can make a good foil for large pieces of furniture.

Mini-climate 3 Warm, shady.
Size These plants can reach a height in excess of 8ft. Plants of all sizes are offered for sale.
Feeding Feed with standard liquid fertilizer every two weeks in spring and summer.
Potting Repot every spring using a combination of two-thirds soil-based potting mixture and one-third leaf mold. Once plants are in 8in pots topdress instead.
Special points Clean older leaves regularly.

NEOREGELIA CAROLINAE 'TRICOLOR'

BLUSHING BROMELIAD

These flat-topped bromeliads have striking foliage; young leaves are a soft green striped with ivory white. As the plants mature the leaves become suffused with pink, and just before flowering the center becomes bright red. Display within a group of bold foliage plants for best effect.

Mini-climate 2 Warm, filtered sun.
Size Mature specimens grow to about 8in in height with a spread of about 1½ft.
Feeding Feed with half-strength standard liquid fertilizer once every month. Apply on to the leaves, into the cup and on to the potting mixture.
Potting Repot in spring using bromeliad potting mixture but only if the roots have completely filled the existing pot. Once the plants are in 5in pots topdress instead.

NEPHROLEPIS EXALTATA 'BOSTONIENSIS'

BOSTON FERN

These lush but graceful ferns have swordlike fronds which are available in several forms: some with crested fronds, others with very finely divided leaf sections. *Nephrolepis exaltata* 'Bostoniensis' make elegant specimen plants, used either on a pedestal or in a hanging basket, and suit almost any type of setting.

Mini-climate 3 Warm, shady.
Size Fronds are often about 3ft long and can grow up to 6ft. Plants of all sizes are offered for sale.

Feeding Feed with standard liquid fertilizer every two weeks when actively growing, otherwise feed once a month.
Potting Repot in spring using fern potting mixture but only if the roots have completely filled the pot. If you don't want to move an older plant into a larger pot, topdress instead.
Special points Stand plants on trays filled with moist pebbles to increase humidity.

Similar-shaped species
Nephrolepis cordifolia is smaller, its fronds will grow up to 2ft long.

NERTERA GRANADENSIS

BEAD PLANT

These attractive plants have tiny, green leaves, but are prized for the profusion of pea-sized, bright-orange berries that develop from the insignificant, greenish-yellow flowers. The berries appear in late summer and last several months. They are best treated as annuals and discarded when the berries begin to die off. They make colorful table displays and are also suitable for growing in dish gardens, bottle gardens and terraria as long as they are kept small.

Mini-climate 4 Cool, sunny.
Size These plants form a low mound up to 3in high, with a maximum spread of around 6in. Small plants are offered for sale.
Feeding Feed with standard liquid fertilizer every two months during the growing season of the berries.
Potting Repot every spring using two-thirds soil-based potting mixture and one-third peat moss. If you don't want to move an older plant into a larger pot, topdress instead.
Special points Water less in winter. These plants can also be placed outside, in a sheltered spot, in summer.

NIDULARIUM INNOCENTII

BIRD'S NEST BROMELIAD

These plants form low, spreading rosettes of straplike, dark-green leaves. The center of the rosette becomes very dark red, sometimes almost black, at flowering time. The small white flowers form a clump in the center of the water-filled vase and last only a short time, although the colored center remains attractive for some months. *Nidularium innocentii* can be grouped with other bold-leaved plants.

Mini-climate 2 Warm, filtered sun.
Size These plants grow to a height of 8in with a spread of 16in. Three or four year old plants about to flower are offered for sale.
Feeding Feed with half-strength standard liquid fertilizer monthly. Apply on to the leaves, into the cup and potting mixture.
Potting Repot in spring using bromeliad potting mixture but only if the roots have completely filled the existing pot. Once plants are in 4in pots topdress instead.
Special points Some time after flowering has finished cut away the parent plant to allow the offsets around its base to develop.

PANDANUS VEITCHII

VEITCH SCREW PINE

These plants get their common name from the way the leaf bases spiral round the stem but, despite their name, they are unrelated to the pine family. The long, arching leaves are a rich dark green edged in cream and have a fine-toothed edge which can rasp the skin. Use these handsome specimens in a modern setting for a dramatic effect.

Mini-climate 1 Warm, sunny.

Size *Pandanus veitchii* can reach a height and spread of about 3ft. Plants of all sizes are offered for sale.

Feeding Feed with standard liquid fertilizer every two weeks during spring and summer and once a month during autumn and winter.

Potting Repot every spring using soil-based potting mixture. If you don't want to move an older plant into a larger pot, topdress instead.

Special points Thick, stiltlike aerial roots form after two years and lift the plant base away from the potting mixture. These roots should be encouraged to grow into the potting mixture for improved anchorage.

PASSIFLORA CAERULEA

PASSION FLOWER

These exotic-looking plants have beautiful flowers. Each consists of five pinkish-white petals and five pinkish-white sepals encircling a ring of purple-blue filaments. These filaments encircle the golden anthers. The flowers may appear at any time during the summer and autumn. The foliage is dark green and stems should be trained over a wire support to make an attractive shape. *Passiflora caerulea* make striking specimen plants for conservatories or large, bright windowsills.

Mini-climate 1 Warm, sunny.
Size Plants of all sizes are offered for sale, up to a maximum height and spread of about 30ft.
Feeding Feed with standard liquid fertilizer once every two weeks during spring, summer and autumn.
Potting Repot every spring using soil-based potting mixture. Once plants are in 8in pots topdress instead.
Special points To keep plants in a decorative state for as long as possible, prune heavily in spring.

PELARGONIUM CRISPUM 'VARIEGATUM'

LEMON GERANIUM

These plants are grown for their aromatic leaves rather than the flowers they produce. The foliage is pale green with a cream-colored wavy edge, and plants can be trained to many shapes by appropriate pinching out of the growing tips. Place in a position where the leaves will be brushed against for maximum aromatic effect. *Pelargonium crispum* 'Variegatum' have a pretty, "cottage" look and suit period rooms which are not too formal.

Mini-climate 4 Cool, sunny.
Size These plants can grow to 2-3ft tall or be kept small and bushy. Small rooted plants are offered for sale.
Feeding Feed with half-strength standard liquid fertilizer twice in summer.
Potting Repot in spring using soil-based potting mixture on top of a small layer of rough drainage material, but only if the roots have completely filled the existing pot.
Special points Do not overwater in winter as plants become susceptible to black stem rot.

PELARGONIUM DOMESTICUM HYBRIDS

REGAL GERANIUM

These have large flower heads that range in color from white to red; many are bicolored or tricolored. The flowering season is short, lasting only from spring to midsummer, but the showiness of the flowers compensates for this. Very much at home in indoor window-boxes, they look equally good as specimen plants.

Mini-climate 4 Cool, sunny.
Size *Pelargonium domesticum* hybrids can be grown as single-stemmed plants of up to 2ft tall, or as small bushy shrubs. Plants of all sizes are offered for sale.
Feeding Feed occasionally with standard liquid fertilizer during spring and summer.
Potting Repot every spring using a soil-based potting mixture. Once plants are in 6in pots topdress instead.
Special points Cut off faded flower heads to encourage new growth.

Similar-shaped species
Pelargonium hortorum has ball-like clusters of flowers almost all year round.

PELLAEA ROTUNDIFOLIA

BUTTON FERN

These unusual-looking ferns have low, spreading fronds making them one of the few ferns with an almost horizontal outline. The pinnae of the fronds are also most unfernlike, consisting of leathery, button-shaped leaflets arranged in a row, one on either side of a stiff midrib. These leaflets weigh the fronds down to give an arching appearance. *Pellaea rotundifolia* make excellent infill plants to hide foreground pots in groups of plants. Display with plants of varying leaf texture in a modern setting for best effect. They can also be used in bottle gardens and terraria.

Mini-climate 3 Warm, shady.
Size The individual fronds grow to a maximum of 1ft long, giving the plant a wide but very flat shape.
Feeding Feed with standard liquid fertilizer every two weeks.
Potting Repot in spring using fern potting mixture in a shallow pot, but only if the roots have completely filled the existing pot. If you don't want to move an older plant into a larger pot, prune the roots to curb growth.
Special points These plants can be placed outside in a sheltered shady spot in summer.

PENTAS LANCEOLATA

EGYPTIAN STAR CLUSTER

These attractive plants are winter-flowering shrubs, although they may flower at any time of year. They have lance-shaped, hairy leaves and clusters of tiny, star-shaped flowers which can be mauve, white or pink in color. The almost flat-topped flower heads can be 4in across. They look best when several plants are massed together in an informal room.

Mini-climate 1 Warm, sunny.
Size *Pentas lanceolata* reach between 1ft and 1½ft in height. Pinch out growing tips to encourage bushy growth. Small plants are offered for sale.
Feeding Feed with standard liquid fertilizer every two weeks during the flowering period.
Potting Repot every spring using soil-based potting mixture. If you don't want to move an older plant into a larger pot, topdress instead.
Special points Water less in winter.

PEPEROMIA CAPERATA

EMERALD RIPPLE PEPEROMIA

These small plants have very distinctive, deeply ridged, heart-shaped leaves. The low-growing form of the leaves is offset by the vertical, white flower spikes which emerge from the rosette of leaves. These plants look good when included in foliage groups with plants of contrasting sizes and textures.

Mini-climate 2 Warm, filtered sun.
Size *Peperomia caperata* are compact plants, rarely growing taller than 6in with a similar spread. Young plants and a miniature form for use in bottle gardens are offered for sale.
Feeding Feed with half-strength standard liquid fertilizer once a month from mid-spring to autumn.
Potting Repot in spring using a peat-based potting mixture but only if the roots have completely filled the existing pot.
Special points Do not overwater these plants as they are liable to rot.

PHILODENDRON BIPINNATIFIDUM

FINGER PLANT

The leaves of these plants are heart-shaped in outline with deeply cut edges. The leaves are borne on stout stalks radiating from a central stem and unlike most of the other *Philodendron* species these plants do not climb. They make dramatic feature plants for a large room.

Mini-climate 3 Warm, shady.

Size These plants can reach a height and spread of about 3-6ft. Plants of all sizes are offered for sale.

Feeding Feed with standard liquid fertilizer every two weeks in spring and summer.

Potting Repot in spring using a combination of half soil-based potting mixture and half leaf mold, but only if the roots have completely filled the existing pot. Once plants are in 12in pots topdress instead.

Special points Destroy any scale insects you may find.

PHILODENDRON 'BURGUNDY'

BURGUNDY PHILODENDRON

These large-leaved plants have bright-red leaf stalks and undersides to their leaves. They will flourish if trained around a moss-covered pole. Large specimens look best on their own.

Mini-climate 3 Warm, shady.
Size These plants are slow-growing but will eventually reach a height of 6ft.
Feeding Feed with standard liquid fertilizer every two weeks in spring and summer.
Potting Repot in spring using half soil-based potting mixture and half leaf mold, but only if the roots have filled the existing pot. Once plants are in 6-10in pots topdress instead.

PHILODENDRON SCANDENS

HEARTLEAF PHILODENDRON

These plants have acutely pointed leaves which are fleshy and attractively bronzed when they first appear, but become dark green and leathery with age. They can be trained up a support, such as a moss-covered pole, as well as being left to trail. They are ideal for warm rooms without much sun.

Mini-climate 3 Warm, shady.
Size These plants are fast-growing; maximum size is unpredictable but a 6ft length and a 20in spread can be reached. Pinch out growing tips to encourage bushy growth. Small plants are offered for sale.
Feeding Feed with standard liquid fertilizer every two weeks in spring and summer, and once every month in autumn and winter.
Potting Repot every spring using half soil-based potting mixture and half leaf mold or peat moss. Once plants are in 10-12in pots topdress instead.
Special points Stand plants on trays filled with moist pebbles to increase humidity.

PILEA CADIEREI

ALUMINUM PLANT

The raised, silver leaf markings give the foliage of these attractive plants a quilted look. This effect is caused by pockets of air under the upper surface of the leaf. Group them with other attractively marked plants, or mass dwarf varieties together in a shallow bowl or in a bottle garden or terrarium.

Mini-climate 2 Warm, filtered sun.
Size *Pilea cadierei* will reach a height of about 1ft in one year. A dwarf variety is available, which reaches a maximum height of 6in.

Feeding Feed with standard liquid fertilizer every two weeks in spring and summer.
Potting Repot every spring using a mixture of two-thirds peat moss and one-third coarse sand or perlite. Once plants are in 3in pots topdress instead.

Similar-shaped species

Pilea spruceana has triangular, quilted, bronze-green leaves with a silver stripe.

PLATYCERIUM BIFURCATUM

STAGHORN FERN

These are most unusual ferns. All plants have two types of frond: small fronds which clasp the plant's support and large, drooping fronds which give the fern its distinctive appearance. The fronds are dark green and covered with a fine, white, felty scurf. *Platycerium bifurcatum* make striking specimen plants, particularly when displayed from a height.

Mini-climate 3 Warm, shady.
Size The fronds reach up to 3ft. Small plants are offered for sale.
Feeding Feed with standard liquid fertilizer once a month during active growth. Add feed to a bucket of water which is used to soak the pot or bark.
Potting Only small plants should be in pots– use fern potting mixture. Older plants should be grown on a piece of bark. Wrap the root ball in sphagnum moss and tie to the bark.
Special points Mist-spray regularly to maintain high humidity.

PLECTRANTHUS AUSTRALIS

SWEDISH IVY

These plants have fleshy, dark-green foliage borne on succulent, pink stems which lie flat on the potting mixture before they grow over the edge of the pot. The occasional pale-lavender flowers are insignificant and can be removed as they develop. Especially attractive in hanging baskets, this ivy also provides excellent ground cover for indoor window-boxes and other large groupings.

Mini-climate 1 Warm, sunny.
Size These plants are fast-growing; their stems quickly reach 3ft in length, with a height of 8in. Pinch out the growing tips to encourage bushy growth. Small plants are offered for sale.
Feeding Feed with standard liquid fertilizer every two weeks from spring to autumn.
Potting Repot in spring using soil-based potting mixture but only if the roots have completely filled the existing pot. If you don't want to move an older plant into a larger pot, topdress instead.
Special points Water less in winter.

PLUMBAGO AURICULATA

CAPE LEADWORT

These plants produce clusters of up to 20 pale-blue flowers from spring to autumn. A narrow, darker blue stripe runs down each of the five petals which flare from a 1½in long tube. Training these plants around a trellis produces an attractive display, or they can be trained to cover a wall.

Mini-climate 1 Warm, sunny.
Size The stems can reach over 3ft in length, but should be pruned every spring as the plants can become very straggly. Plants of all sizes are offered for sale.
Feeding Feed with tomato-type liquid fertilizer once every two weeks from spring until autumn.
Potting Repot every spring using soil-based potting mixture. Once plants are in 8in pots topdress instead.
Special points Water less in winter.

POLYPODIUM AUREUM 'MANDAIANUM'

HARE'S FOOT FERN

These plants derive their common name from the furry rhizome from which the fronds arise. The fronds are carried on long, arching stems and each bears up to ten silvery blue-green leaflets. Each leaflet has a ruffled edge. Since their color is so attractive, these ferns should be displayed as feature plants when they are large enough. Smaller plants mix well with other ferns.

Mini-climate 3 Warm, shady.
Size The fronds can grow to about 2ft in length giving the plant a large spread. Plants of all sizes are offered for sale.
Feeding Feed with half-strength standard liquid fertilizer once a week during spring, summer and autumn.
Potting Repot in spring using half soil-based potting mixture and half leaf mold in a shallow container, but only if the rhizomes have completely filled the existing pot. Once plants are in 8in pots root prune instead.
Special points Stand plants on trays filled with moist pebbles to increase humidity.

PRIMULA OBCONICA

GERMAN PRIMROSE

This is one of the prettiest flowering plants, blooming between Christmas and summer. The long-stalked clusters of flowers are white, pink, salmon or mauve with a distinctive green eye. *Primula obconica* are best treated as annuals and discarded when flowering has finished. Use singly or massed together in a shallow pan or basket in any cool area, such as a hallway or bedroom.

Mini-climate 5 Cool, filtered sun.
Size These rarely grow taller than 1ft, with a spread of 10in. Plants in flower are offered for sale.
Feeding Feed with standard liquid fertilizer every two weeks.
Potting Repotting is unnecessary.

Similar-shaped species

Primula malacoides is a very delicate plant with small white, rose-pink or lilac flowers.

PTERIS CRETICA

CRETAN BRAKE FERN

Also known as "table ferns", these plants form clumps of striped fonds which grow from short, underground rhizomes. Each frond is hand-shaped, the individual pinnae looking like fingers. They mix well with other plants, especially if used as pot hiders at the front of plant groupings. They are ideal for a plant window collection.

Mini-climate 3 Warm, shady.
Size These plants grow to 14in in height with a similar spread. Small plants of about 5in in height are offered for sale.
Feeding Feed with half-strength standard liquid fertilizer once a month.
Potting Repot in spring using fern potting mixture but only if the roots have completely filled the pot. If you don't want to move an older plant to a larger pot, topdress instead.

Similar-shaped species

Pteris tremula looks like bracken. It is fast-growing, and its fronds can reach up to 2ft long and 1ft wide.

RHAPIS EXCELSA

BAMBOO PALM

Also known as "little lady palms", these plants have stems which cluster together giving the plant a crowded look. The leaves are composed of five to nine, often blunt-tipped, segments giving an overall fan-shaped look. Each segment is deeply cut. Display with other dark-green foliage plants. Older plants lose their lower leaves making them suitable for displaying on their own.

Mini-climate 2 Warm, filtered sun.
Size *Rhapis excelsa* are slow-growing taking several years to reach a maximum height of 5-10ft tall with a similar spread. Medium and large plants are offered for sale.
Feeding Feed with standard liquid fertilizer once a month during the active growing period.
Potting Repot every second year in spring using soil-based potting mixture. Once plants are in 12in pots topdress instead.

RHODODENDRON SIMSII

AZALEA

Rhododendron simsii produce clusters of brightly colored flowers atop a mass of shiny, green leaves. Flower color ranges from white to magenta, including almost every shade of red and pink. Some flowers are bicolored. They are best treated as annuals and discarded when flowering has finished. Mass in a shallow bowl and place in a prominent position in a hallway or other cool place.

Mini-climate 5 Cool, filtered sun.
Size These plants do not grow much larger than 1ft in height with a similar spread. Budding plants are offered for sale in winter and spring.
Feeding Feed with standard liquid fertilizer once every two weeks from spring to autumn.
Potting Repot as necessary using one part soil-based potting mixture, two parts peat moss, and one part coarse sand.
Special points To keep plants in a decorative state for as long as possible, keep the potting mixture permanently moist and display in a cool place.

RHOEO SPATHACEA 'VARIEGATA'

BOAT LILY

These plants are also known as "Moses-in-the-cradle", referring to the boat-shaped cups which encase the small, white, three-petalled flowers. The long, rather stiff leaves are beautifully colored, having yellow and cream stripes on their upper surface and purple on their lower surface. They are best displayed on their own in order that the unusual flower-cups can be seen.

Mini-climate 2 Warm, filtered sun.
Size These plants reach a maximum height of 1ft with a spread of 1½ft and plants of this size are offered for sale. Maintain as an upright plant by pinching off basal shoots.
Feeding Feed with standard liquid fertilizer every two weeks in spring and summer.
Potting Repot every second year in spring using soil-based potting mixture. If you don't want to move an older plant into a larger pot, topdress instead.

SAINTPAULIA HYBRIDS

AFRICAN VIOLET

These plants have an impressive range of flower colors from white and pink to purple, magenta and violet. The flowers are held in clusters above the rosette of furry leaves. With this range of color *Saintpaulia* hybrids can be used in both modern and period interiors. One of the most effective ways to display them is massed in a shallow bowl. Miniature varieties can be displayed in a terrarium.

Mini-climate 2 Warm, filtered sun.
Size These plants will form a flat rosette of about 8in diameter. Flowering plants are available all year. Named varieties run into thousands.
Feeding Feed with specially prepared *Saintpaulia* hybrid liquid fertilizer, used at one-quarter strength, at each watering throughout the year.
Potting Repot only when the roots have completely filled the existing pot. Use a mixture of equal parts peat moss, perlite and vermiculite in half pots or shallow pans.
Special points Avoid wetting the hairy leaves when watering and feeding as they will become stained.

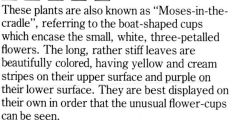

SANSEVIERIA TRIFASCIATA 'LAURENTII'

MOTHER-IN-LAW'S TONGUE

The upright leaves of this plant emerge in a cluster from an underground stem. The thick, leathery leaves are marbled with dark green and have golden bands along their margin. Display large plants as specimens or group them with other spiky-leaved plants in a modern setting.

Mini-climate 2 Warm, filtered sun.
Size The leaves can grow to a height of about 3ft. Plants of all sizes are offered for sale.
Feeding Feed with half-strength standard liquid fertilizer once a month.
Potting Repot in spring or early summer, using one-third coarse sand or perlite and two-thirds soil-based potting mixture, but only when a mass of roots appears on the surface. If you don't want to move an older plant into a larger pot, topdress instead.
Special points Water less in winter.

SAXIFRAGA STOLONIFERA

STRAWBERRY GERANIUM

These plants produce many plantlets on threadlike stems. The mother plants are small and low-growing and the plantlets hang down from the center of the plant giving a trailing effect. *Saxifraga stolonifera* are best displayed in hanging baskets so that the red undersides to their leaves may be seen. Display in cool places, such as hallways, and ensure the delicate trailing stems are not brushed against.

Mini-climate 5 Cool, filtered sun.
Size These plants are fast growing, but reach no more than 8in high. The trailing stems grow to 2ft long.
Feeding Feed with standard liquid fertilizer once a month.
Potting Repot every spring using soil-based potting mixture. Discard the plant after the second repotting.
Special points Water more sparingly during the winter rest period.

SCINDAPSUS PICTUS 'ARGYRAEUS'

POTHOS VINE

The most striking feature of these plants is their matt olive-green colored leaves covered with silver spots. The heart-shaped leaves are carried on thick stems which occasionally produce aerial roots. Mass several small plants together or put a large specimen in a hanging basket near a sunny window. These vines also make attractive feature plants when trained up moist, moss-covered poles.

Mini-climate 1 Warm, sunny.
Size These plants are slow-growing, but mature specimens can reach 5ft in height with a similar spread. Pinch out growing tips in spring to encourage bushy growth. Plants of 4-6in in height are offered for sale.
Feeding Feed with standard liquid fertilizer every two weeks from spring to autumn.
Potting Repot in spring using soil-based potting mixture but only if the roots have completely filled the existing pot. Once plants are in 6in pots topdress instead.
Special points Water less in winter.

SELAGINELLA MARTENSII

LITTLE CLUB MOSS

These unusual plants have decorative, medium-green leaves which are packed around the branches like the scales of a fish. The creeping stems of the club mosses form a dense mat of foliage with a pleasant, soft texture. Roots are put down into the potting mixture at intervals. A terrarium or bottle garden is the best environment in which to display these small plants as they will thrive in the humid atmosphere.

Mini-climate 2 Warm, filtered sun.
Size The creeping stems may grow to 6in in length. Small plants are offered for sale.
Feeding Feed with one-quarter strength standard liquid fertilizer every two weeks.
Potting Repot every spring using a mixture of two-thirds peat-based potting mix and one-third coarse sand. Once plants are in 6-8in pots simply remove plants from their pots, clean and refill them with fresh mixture and replace the plants.
Special points Touch the plants as little as possible as this can damage the foliage.

Similar-shaped species
Selaginella pallescens has white-edged leaves which grow on erect stems of up to 1ft long.

SENECIO CRUENTUS HYBRIDS

CINERARIA

These plants have large, daisy-shaped flowers which cluster together in the center of the fleshy leaves. The flowers can be of orange, red, magenta, pink, blue or purple, often with a circle of white surounding the central disc. The leaves are furry to touch and are often tinged with blue on their undersides. *Senecio cruentus* hybrids are best treated as annuals and discarded when flowering has finished. Mass several specimens of the same color together in a china dish or basket. They suit both traditional and modern rooms.

Mini-climate 4 Cool, sunny.
Size Budding plants up to 1ft tall and of similar spread are offered for sale throughout winter and spring.
Feeding Feeding is not required for these temporary pot plants.
Potting Repotting is unnecessary.
Special points To keep plants in a decorative state for as long as possible, ensure that the potting mixture does not dry out too much. Water is easily lost through the large leaves and the plant will collapse if the roots are allowed to dry out. Destroy any aphids or whitefly you may find.

SENECIO MACROGLOSSUS

CAPE IVY

These plants are very similar to the *Hedera helix* hybrids, but their leaves are smoother, softer and more fleshy. The leaves are borne on purple stems and are green marked with pale-cream streaks and patches. In some cases, where variegation is very strong, all the leaves on a shoot may be predominantly cream-colored. They should be trained around hoops of bamboo cane or wire, or planted in small hanging baskets.

Mini-climate 1 Warm, sunny.
Size These ivies grow up to 3ft in height and spread. Pinch out growing tips to maintain bushy growth. Small plants are offered for sale.
Feeding Feed with standard liquid fertilizer every two weeks during spring and summer.
Potting Repot every spring using a mixture of one part coarse sand to three parts soil-based mixture. Once plants are in 6in pots topdress instead.
Special points Water less in winter. Destroy any aphids you may find.

SINNINGIA SPECIOSA HYBRIDS

GLOXINIA

The large, downy leaves have a bold pattern of veins on them but are eclipsed by the large, showy flowers. They are borne in a cluster on top of the rosette of leaves. Trumpet-shaped with frilled edges they can be white, pink, red or purple, and are often margined in white. Although these plants can be treated as annuals they have a tuber which can be dried off in autumn and repotted in spring. They are best in period rooms, displayed either singly or massed together.

Mini-climate 2 Warm, filtered sun.
Size These plants can attain a height and spread of about 1ft. Plants in bud are offered for sale.
Feeding Feed with half-phosphate liquid fertilizer once a month during flowering.
Potting Repot the tubers in spring using equal parts of peat-based potting mixture, vermiculite and perlite. Repotting once the plant is flowering is unnecessary.

Similar-shaped species

Sinningia pusilla is very small, no more than 1in tall, but has attractive, relatively large, pale-lavender flowers.

SOLANUM CAPSICASTRUM

CHRISTMAS CHERRY

Marble-sized, orange-red berries make these small, shrubby plants an autumn favorite. The berries will last for several months if kept in a sunny but cool place; hot, dry air considerably shortens their lives. Placed on a low table or in a window-box, these plants add color and interest to a group of foliage plants.

Mini-climate 4 Cool, sunny.
Size These plants reach a maximum height of 1½ft. Specimens bearing berries are offered for sale.
Feeding Feed with standard liquid fertilizer every two weeks.
Potting Repot in spring using soil-based potting mixture. To keep for a second fruiting season cut away half the growth and move them outside in 5in pots for the summer.
Special points Mist-spray daily to increase humidity and aid pollination when in flower. The berries are not edible, so keep the plants away from small children.

SOLEIROLIA SOLEIROLII

BABY'S TEARS

These pretty plants produce masses of tiny, bright-green leaves on thin stems, and will quickly carpet all available space in the pot. A number of these mossy mounds make an attractive display if they are massed together in a wicker basket. They also look good filling in the front of foliage displays. Do not use them in bottle gardens or terraria as they quickly fill all the available space.

Mini-climate 4 Cool, sunny.
Size These plants will not exceed 2in in height, but their spread is only limited by the size of the container in which they are grown. Trim with a pair of scissors to maintain a neat shape. Small and medium-sized plants are offered for sale all year.
Feeding Feed with half-strength standard liquid fertilizer every two weeks in summer.
Potting Repot in spring using soil-based potting mixture. Discard the plant after the second repotting.
Special points Always keep potting mixture damp to prevent the leaves from turning brown.

SPARMANNIA AFRICANA

AFRICAN HEMP

Also known as "indoor limes", these plants have large, apple-green leaves, covered in fine, white hairs. A plant blooming in a cool room can produce clusters of small, white flowers nearly all year round. They look best displayed on their own as feature plants in both modern and traditional settings.

Mini-climate 4 Cool, sunny.
Size *Sparmannia africana* grow to about 5ft in height with a spread of 3ft wide in two years. Small plants are offered for sale.
Feeding Feed with standard liquid fertilizer every two weeks.
Potting Repot in spring using soil-based potting mixture but only if the roots have completely filled the existing pot. Once plants are in 12in pots topdress instead.
Special points Water less in winter.

SPATHIPHYLLUM 'CLEVELANDII'

WHITE SAILS

The striking arumlike flower heads of these plants are produced from May to August. Each flower lasts for six weeks or more, turning from white to an attractive pale green. Their elegant shape makes them ideal specimen plants for the modern interior.

Mini-climate 3 Warm, shady.
Size Mature specimens can reach a height and spread of 3ft. Plants in flower are offered for sale.
Feeding Feed with standard liquid fertilizer once every two weeks from early spring to late summer.
Potting Repot every two years in spring using peat-based potting mixture. Once plants are in a 6-8in pot root prune instead.
Special points Stand plants on trays filled with moist pebbles to increase humidity.

STEPHANOTIS FLORIBUNDA

WAX FLOWER

These plants have dark-green, glossy leaves carried on woody stems, which twine readily around any support, and delightfully scented, waxy, white flowers. The flowers grow in clusters of ten or more and each is tube-shaped, flaring out into five pointed lobes. They appear from spring until autumn. *Stephanotis floribunda* may be trained to climb a trellis or, if space is more limited, around a hoop of wire or cane inserted into the pot.

Mini-climate 1 Warm, sunny.
Size These plants are vigorous growers. Height and spread is variable, but is usually about 10ft. Pinch out growing tips to encourage bushy growth. Plants of all sizes are offered for sale.
Feeding Feed with standard liquid fertilizer every two weeks during spring and summer.
Potting Repot every second year in spring using soil-based potting mixture. Once plants are in 8in pots topdress instead.
Special points Stand plants on trays filled with moist pebbles to increase humidity. Water less in winter.

STRELITZIA REGINAE

BIRD-OF-PARADISE

These plants have spectacular orange-and-blue crested flowers which emerge in succession over a period of several weeks from a beak-shaped bud. They are unusual specimen plants for a modern interior; a large-scale setting is best as leaves and flowers become very big.

Mini-climate 1 Warm, sunny.
Size *Strelitzia reginae* will grow to 3ft in height with a spread of 2ft. Young plants are offered for sale but will not flower until they are five years old.
Feeding Feed with standard liquid fertilizer every two weeks in spring and summer and once a month in autumn and winter.
Potting Repot every spring using soil-based potting mixture. Once plants are in 12in pots topdress instead.
Special points Clean leaves regularly with a damp sponge.

STREPTOCARPUS 'JOHN INNES' HYBRIDS

CAPE PRIMROSE

These small plants have primrose-like leaves and large, tubular flowers on long stalks. Flowers may be white, pink, red, mauve or blue. Attractive twisted seed pods appear but these are best cut off to encourage more flowers. These plants are best treated as annuals and discarded when flowering has finished. Like *Saintpaulia* hybrids and *Primula obconica*, these plants should be massed together in a shallow bowl on a low table.

Mini-climate 5 Cool, filtered sun.
Size *Streptocarpus* 'John Innes' hybrids grow to about 1ft in height with a spread of 1½ft. Small plants in bud are offered for sale.
Feeding Feed with half-strength, high-phosphate liquid fertilizer every two weeks from early spring to late autumn.
Potting Repot every spring using an equal-parts mixture of sphagnum peat moss, coarse grade perlite and vermiculite. Add half a tablespoon of limestone chips to every cup of mixture. Once plants are in 6in pots root prune instead.

SYNGONIUM PODOPHYLLUM

ARROWHEAD PLANT

These climbing plants are unusual in that the shape of the leaves changes as the plant matures. Young leaves have three deeply-cut lobes but, in older specimens, the leaves have five lobes. Plants can be trained to climb up thin stakes, or up a moss-covered pole, or they can trail from a hanging basket.

Mini-climate 2 Warm, filtered sun.
Size The stems can grow up to 6ft. The spread depends on the support system used.
Feeding Feed with standard liquid fertilizer every two weeks from spring to autumn.
Potting Repot in spring using equal parts of soil-based potting mixture and leaf mold, but only if the roots have completely filled the existing pot. If you don't want to move an older plant into a larger pot, topdress instead.

THUNBERGIA ALATA

BLACK-EYED SUSAN VINE

Thunbergia alata have attractive bright-orange flowers with a characteristic deep chocolate-brown "eye". The large, round blooms are produced from spring to late autumn. These plants look particularly good when trained to climb up strings in front of a window.

Mini-climate 4 Cool, sunny.
Size These plants may reach over 6ft in height. Young plants are offered for sale.
Feeding Feed with standard liquid fertilizer every two weeks.
Potting Repot in spring using soil-based potting mixture but only if the roots have completely filled the existing pot. Once plants are in 6in pots topdress instead.
Special points To keep plants in a decorative state for as long as possible, pinch out any faded flowers.

TILLANDSIA CYANEA

BLUE-FLOWERED TORCH

These are medium-sized bromeliads with stiff, arching, grassy leaves arranged in a loose rosette. When mature, the plants produce a fleshy spear-shaped flower head, made up of pinky-green overlapping bracts, This unusual flower head is flat and wide and will remain decorative for some months. Three-petaled, bright violet-blue flowers appear in succession from between the bracts. Display on their own as feature plants.

Mini-climate 1 Warm, sunny.
Size The leaves reach about 1ft in length. Offsets give the plant a large spread. Small plants are offered for sale.
Feeding Feed with half-strength standard liquid fertilizer once a month. This can be applied to the leaves as a foliar feed.
Potting Repot every spring using bromeliad potting mixture. Once plants are in 4in pots topdress instead.
Special points Place in a sheltered part of the garden in summer to encourage flowering.

TOLMIEA MENZIESII

PIGGY-BACK PLANT

These plants, which are also known as "mother-of-thousands", derive their common names from the way that a number of mature leaves produce small plantlets on their upper surfaces. These weigh down the long leafstalks to give a trailing appearance. The fresh-green leaves and slender leafstalks are covered with soft hair. These are excellent plants to display in hanging baskets. They are easily kept in any cool place.

Mini-climate 5 Cool, filtered sun.
Size These plants are fast-growing and reach a height of about 1ft with a similar spread. Small specimens are offered for sale.
Feeding Feed with standard liquid fertilizer every two weeks during spring and summer.
Potting Repot in spring using soil-based potting mixture but only if the roots have completely filled the existing pot. Discard the plant after the second or third repotting.
Special points Water less in winter.

TRADESCANTIA ALBIFLORA 'ALBOVITTATA'

TRADESCANTIA

Tradescantia albiflora 'Albovittata' is very similar to *Zebrina pendula*. The silver and green striped leaves are almost transparent. Mass plants together in a hanging basket or allow a large specimen to trail from a shelf. They are useful for inclusion at the front of mixed arrangements in a suitably warm room and will also climb.

Mini-climate 1 Warm, sunny.
Size These plants are fast-growing, the stems reaching 1ft long. Pinch out growing tips to encourage bushy growth.
Feeding Feed with standard liquid fertilizer every two weeks from spring to autumn.
Potting Repot in spring using soil-based potting mixture but only if the roots have completely filled the existing pot. Discard the plant after the second repotting.
Special points Remove any dried or poorly colored leaves.

Similar-shaped species
Tradescantia fluminensis 'Variegata' has leaves which are a deep olive-green striped with cream and pink and covered with soft, velvety hairs.

VRIESEA SPLENDENS

FLAMING SWORD

These bromeliads have exotically marked leaves; they are shiny green banded with deep purple. The leaves form an upright vase, from the center of which a bright-red spike of bracts emerges when the plants are several years old. Small, yellow flowers poke through the red bracts. Several plants massed together make a spectacular display; alternatively, include *Vriesea splendens* with strong foliage plants or use small specimens on a dried branch covered with sphagnum moss.

Mini-climate 2 Warm, filtered sun.
Size *Vriesea splendens* can reach a height and spread of about 1½ft. The flower spike can reach 2ft in height. Plants of all sizes are offered for sale.
Feeding Feed with half-strength standard liquid fertilizer once a month. Ensure the feed gets on the leaves, roots and the central cup.
Potting Repot in spring using bromeliad potting mixture but only if the roots have completely filled the existing pot. Once plants are in 6in pots topdress instead.

Special points Keep the center of the rosette filled with fresh water except when the flower bud first appears. Change the water once a month.

Similar-shaped species
Vriesea fenestralis is a little larger with paler green leaves covered in brown markings.
Vriesea psittacina has shorter leaves which are plain green with mauve shading towards the center of the rosette.
Vriesea saundersii has a squat rosette of grey-green leaves with a dull rose-pink underside and a yellow flower spike.

YUCCA ELEPHANTIPES

STICK YUCCA

These plants have a very distinctive appearance. Many are specially grown from logs which, when planted, produce roots and leaves. The leaves are long and narrow, and can appear in clumps at any point of the upright stem. These plants have a strong shape and should be displayed on their own, or with other spiky-leaved plants in a modern setting.

Mini-climate 1 Warm, sunny.
Size Specimens up to 6½ft in height with a spread of 1½ft are offered for sale. The spread increases as more leaves are produced. Plants can also be bought which are virtually stemless; these are known as "tip yuccas".
Feeding Feed with standard liquid fertilizer once every month.
Potting Repot every spring using soil-based potting mixture. If you don't want to move an older plant into a larger pot, topdress instead.
Special points Water less in winter.

ZEBRINA PENDULA

WANDERING JEW

Zebrina pendula are highly decorative plants with attractive leaf coloring. The oval leaves have a striped, iridescent upper surface and a deep-purple underside. In spring and autumn, clusters of small, purple-pink flowers are produced. These plants make a fine display when massed together in hanging baskets, but also look attractive trailing over the edge of a bowl in a mixed planting.

Mini-climate 1 Warm, sunny.
Size The stems grow to 16in long with a spread of 1ft. Pinch out growing tips to encourage bushy growth. Small plants are offered for sale.
Feeding Feed with standard liquid fertilizer once every two weeks.
Potting Repot in spring using soil-based potting mixture but only if the roots have completely filled the existing pot. Discard the plant after the second or third repotting.
Special points Remove stems with poorly colored leaves should they appear.

Flowering house plants

Before you buy any flowering plants to decorate your home, always think about the location you have chosen for them and make sure that, however beautiful their color, they will enhance and harmonize with your existing color scheme. Concentrate on related or contrasting schemes: mass together plants in various shades of the same color for a subtle effect, or use exciting complementaries for a bold effect.

The most colorful part of a plant is not always the flower itself: in some plants, such as *Euphorbia pulcherrima* and *Anthurium andraeanum* hybrids, it is the bract, or petal-like leaf, which surrounds the flowers; in others, such as *Nertera granadensis* and *Solanum capsicastrum*, it is the berries and fruits which appear after the flowers themselves have faded.

Another consideration when choosing plants for their flowers must be the timing and duration of their individual flowering seasons. If you want to create a spectacular display of blooms and color at a particular time, make sure that your plants have the same flowering period. Alternatively, you can choose a selection of plants that between them will provide continuous color throughout the year.

The seasonal guide to flowering house plants

Key: Winter / Spring / Summer / Autumn

Plant	Jan	Feb	Mar	Apr	May	Jun	Jul	Aug	Sep	Oct	Nov	Dec	Comments
Pentas lanceolata (see p. 72)	■								■	■	■	■	Can flower at other times
Solanum capsicastrum (see p. 85)	■								■	■	■	■	Fruit
Tulipa hybrids (see p. 148)	■	■										■	Can flower at other times
Schlumbergera truncata (see p. 140)												■	Can flower at other times
Euphorbia pulcherrima (see p. 53)	■	■	■								■	■	
Hyacinthus orientalis hybrids (see p. 146)	■	■	■									■	
Narcissus hybrids (see p. 147)	■	■	■									■	
Crocus hybrids (see p. 145)	■	■	■										
Guzmania lingulata (see p. 58)	■	■	■										
Cyclamen persicum hybrids (see p. 49)	■	■	■	■							■	■	
Jasminum polyanthum (see p. 63)	■	■	■	■									
Kalanchoe blossfeldiana hybrids (see p. 137)	■	■	■	■								■	Can flower at other times
Iris reticulata (see p. 146)	■	■	■	■									
Hippeastrum hybrids (see p. 145)	■	■	■	■	■								
Primula obconica (see p. 78)	■	■	■	■	■	■							Can flower at other times
Sparmannia africana (see p. 86)	■	■	■										
Saintpaulia hybrids (see p. 80)	■	■	■	■	■	■	■	■	■	■	■		Can flower continuously
Aporocactus flagelliformis (see p. 130)			■	■	■								
Rhododendron simsii (see p. 79)			■	■	■								Can flower at other times
Muscari sp. (see p. 147)			■	■	■								
Aphelandra squarrosa 'Louisae' (see p. 29)			■	■	■	■							
Mammillaria zeilmanniana (see p. 139)			■	■	■	■							

	January	February	March	April	May	June	July	August	September	October	November	December	Comments
Pelargonium domesticum hybrids (see p. 71)			■	■	■	■							
Strelitzia reginae (see p. 88)			■	■	■	■							Only mature plants will bloom
Begonia semperflorens-cultorum (see p. 35)			■	■	■	■	■	■		■			Can flower continuously
Columnea 'Banksii' (see p. 47)			■	■	■	■	■	■		■	■		Can flower continuously
Euphorbia milii (see p. 135)			■	■	■	■	■	■		■	■		Can flower continuously
Senecio cruentus hybrids (see p. 83)			■	■	■								
Rebutia miniscula (see p. 140)			■	■	■	■							
Spathiphyllum 'Clevelandii' (see p. 87)			■	■	■	■							Can flower at other times
Stephanotis floribunda (see p. 87)			■	■	■	■							
Astrophytum myriostigma (see p. 130)			■	■	■	■							
Hibiscus rosa-sinensis (see p. 60)			■	■	■	■	■	■		■	■		Can flower at other times
Vriesea splendens (see p. 92)			■	■	■	■	■	■		■	■		Only mature plants will bloom
Bougainvillea buttiana (see p. 37)			■	■	■	■	■	■		■	■		
Impatiens wallerana hybrids (see p. 62)			■	■	■	■	■	■		■	■		Can flower continuously
Plumbago auriculata (see p. 77)			■	■	■	■	■	■		■	■		
Citrofortunella mitis (see p. 45)				■	■	■	■						Can flower at other times
Nidularium innocentii (see p. 68)			■	■	■	■	■	■		■	■		Only mature plants will bloom
Streptocarpus 'John Innes' hybrids (see p. 89)			■	■	■	■	■	■					
Thunbergia alata (see p. 90)			■	■	■	■	■	■					
Sinningia speciosa hybrids (see p. 85)						■	■	■		■	■		
Tillandsia cyanea (see p. 90)						■	■	■		■	■		Only mature plants will bloom
Abutilon hybridum 'Canary Bird' (see p. 24)						■	■	■		■	■		
Aechmea fasciata (see p. 26)						■	■	■		■	■		Can flower at other times
Achimenes grandiflora (see p. 25)						■	■	■		■	■		
Anthurium andraeanum hybrids (see p. 29)						■	■	■		■	■		Can flower at other times
Begonia 'Elatior' hybrids (see p. 33)						■	■	■		■	■		
Billbergia nutans (see p. 36)						■	■	■		■	■		Can flower at other times
Exacum affine (see p. 53)						■	■	■		■	■		
Hoya bella (see p. 61)						■	■	■		■	■		
Passiflora caerulea (see p. 70)						■	■	■		■	■		
Nertera granadensis (see p. 68)							■	■		■	■		Fruit
Allamanda cathartica (see p. 27)							■	■		■	■		
Neoregelia carolinae 'Tricolor' (see p. 66)							■	■		■	■		Only mature plants will bloom
Capsicum annuum (see p. 41)								■	■	■	■	■	Fruit
Browallia speciosa (see p. 38)								■	■	■	■		
Campanula isophylla (see p. 40)								■	■	■	■		
Chrysanthemum morifolium hybrids (see p. 43)									■	■	■		Can flower continuously

Whites, creams and yellows

1 SPATHIPHYLLUM 'CLEVELANDII'
White sails *(see p. 87)*
*White arumlike flower heads which turn pale green with age.
The color of this plant suits any kind of interior decoration.*

2 CAMPANULA ISOPHYLLA
Italian bellflower *(see p. 40)*
*Star-shaped white flowers, also available in several shades of
blue. Use plants of one color, or mix blue and white
together, and place on a high shelf or in a hanging basket.*

3 BEGONIA SEMPERFLORENS-
CULTORUM Wax begonia *(see p. 35)*
*Small white flowers, also available with pink and red
flowers. Mass plants of the same color together or mix
them with exotic-colored leaves.*

4 PRIMULA OBCONICA German primrose *(see p. 78)*
*Pure white flowers with green centers, also available with
pink, red and\mauve flowers. Use either singly, or massed up
in a bowl using different\shades from white through to mauve.*

5 CATHARANTHUS ROSEUS
Madagascar periwinkle
*White flowers with carmine-red centers, also
available with pink or all-white flowers. Use in
groups with other plants or mass together in a
bowl or basket.*

6 BEGONIA 'ELATIOR' HYBRIDS
Yellow clatior begonia *(see p. 33)*
*Primrose-yellow double flowers, also available
in many other colors. Mass plants of one
color together for a bold effect.*

7 SAINTPAULIA HYBRIDS
African violet *(see p. 80)*
Pure white flowers and white flowers edged with purple, also available in many shades of pink, blue and purple. Mass plants of one color, or in various shades of the same color, in a shallow bowl on a low table.

8 BEGONIA TUBERHYBRIDA
White begonia
Ivory-colored flowers, also available with pink, red, yellow or orange flowers. Display individually or, alternatively, in groups of one, or several, colors.

9 CAPSICUM ANNUUM
Christmas pepper *(see p. 41)*
The bright fruits may be orange, red or yellow and will change color as they ripen. Use massed to make a colorful winter table decoration.

10 BEGONIA 'ELATIOR' HYBRIDS
White elatior begonia *(see p. 33)*
Cream-colored double flowers, also available in many other colors.

11 BEGONIA TUBERHYBRIDA
Yellow begonia
Deep-yellow flowers, also available with white, pink, red or orange flowers.

12 THUNBERGIA ALATA
Black-eyed Susan vine *(see p. 90)*
Bright orange-yellow flowers with a black central eye. Let them ramble through other plants or train them up a support to create a cascade of color.

13 CHRYSANTHEMUM MORIFOLIUM HYBRIDS
Yellow chrysanthemum *(see p. 43)*
Pale yellow daisylike flowers, also available in many other colors.

14 CHRYSANTHEMUM MORIFOLIUM HYBRIDS
White chrysanthemum *(see p. 43)*
Dense creamy-white flowers, available in many other colors. Mass in a large basket and display so they can be seen from above.

15 ABUTILON HYBRIDUM
Yellow flowering maple *(see p. 24)*
Bell-shaped, creamy-yellow flowers, available in many other colors. Group several different colors together or display as feature plants when full grown.

16 CHRYSANTHEMUM MORIFOLIUM HYBRIDS
Golden chrysanthemum *(see p. 43)*
Dense golden flowers, available in many other colors.

Oranges and reds

1 BEGONIA 'ELATIOR' HYBRIDS
White elatior begonia *(see p. 33)*
Cream-colored double flowers, also available in many other colors.

2 NERTERA GRANADENSIS
Bead plant *(see p. 68)*
Beadlike, deep-orange berries cover the plant. Make a formal display on a table or low shelf.

3 KALANCHOE BLOSSFELDIANA HYBRIDS
Yellow kalanchoe *(see p. 137)*
Long-lasting deep-yellow flowers, also available with orange, pink and red flowers. Mass plants together on a sunny windowsill for winter color.

4 KALANCHOE BLOSSFELDIANA HYBRIDS
Orange kalanchoe *(see p. 137)*
Long-lasting orange flowers, also available in yellow, pink and red.

5 KALANCHOE BLOSSFELDIANA HYBRIDS
Pink kalanchoe *(see p. 137)*
Long-lasting pink flowers, also available in yellow, red and orange.

6 CHRYSANTHEMUM MORIFOLIUM HYBRIDS
Golden chrysanthemum *(see p. 43)*
Dense golden flowers, available in many other colors.

7 KALANCHOE BLOSSFELDIANA HYBRIDS
Red kalanchoe *(see p. 137)*
Long-lasting scarlet flowers, this plant is also available with yellow, orange and pink flowers.

8 HIBISCUS ROSA-SINENSIS HYBRIDS
Chinese hibiscus *(see p. 60)*
Large deep-red flowers, with a protruding stamen, also available with white, yellow, pink or orange flowers. Use either singly or in a group with different-colored forms.

9 GUZMANIA LINGULATA
Scarlet star *(see p. 58)*
Scarlet bracts surround small white flowers. Mass plants together in a container or use them in a symmetrical arrangement. They may also be cut and wired for use in large floral arrangements.

10 SINNINGIA SPECIOSA HYBRIDS
Gloxinia *(see p. 85)*
Red trumpet-shaped flowers, also available with white or violet flowers. Mass plants together on a low table.

11 BEGONIA 'ELATIOR' HYBRIDS
Pink elatior begonia *(see p. 33)*
Deep-pink double flowers, also available in many other colors.

12 ABUTILON HYBRIDUM
Red flowering maple *(see p. 24)*
Scarlet bell-shaped flowers, available in many other colors. Group several different colors together or display as a feature plant when full grown.

13 PELARGONIUM HORTORUM HYBRIDS
Bedding geranium *(see p. 71)*
Tight clusters of scarlet flowers, also available with white, mauve or pink flowers. Display in a row along a windowsill or group with foliage geraniums.

Pinks, mauves and purples

**1 IMPATIENS
WALLERANA HYBRIDS**
Pink impatiens *(see p. 62)*
*Deep pink single flowers, also
available with white, red,
orange or bicolored flowers.
Mass plants of the same
color together in a hanging
basket or window-box.*

**2 ANTHURIUM ANDRAEANUM
HYBRIDS**
Flamingo flower *(see p. 29)*
*A salmon-colored, shield-shaped bract
surrounds the central flower spike, also
available with white or red flower heads.
Mass plants together for an exotic display*

**3 BEGONIA SEMPERFLORENS-
CULTORUM**
Red wax begonia *(see p. 35)*
*Scarlet flowers with yellow centers, also available
with pink or white flowers. Mass plants of the same
color together or mix with exotic-colored leaves.*

4 IMPATIENS 'NEW GUINEA' HYBRIDS
Pink New Guinea impatiens *(see p. 62)*
*Pinky-orange flowers and strongly
variegated leaves, also with white, pink,
orange and bicolored flowers.*

5 JUSTICIA BRANDEGEANA
Shrimp plant
*White flowers emerge from pink, shrimp-
shaped bracts. Mass plants together in a
shallow basket for a subtle color effect.*

6 PLUMBAGO AURICULATA
Cape leadwort *(see p. 77)*
*Clusters of small, blue flowers, also
available with white flowers. Use trained
around a window or up a support.*

**7 BEGONIA SEMPERFLORENS-
CULTORUM**
Pink wax begonia *(see p. 35)*
*Strong-pink flowers with yellow eyes,
also available in red and white.*

8 CAMPANULA ISOPHYLLA
Italian bellflower *(see p. 40)*
*Star-shaped, bluish-mauve flowers, also
available in other shades of blue and
white. Use plants of one color, or mix
blue and white together, and place on a
high shelf or in a hanging basket.*

9 SAINTPAULIA HYBRIDS
Purple African violet *(see p. 80)*
*Intense violet-colored flowers with yellow
centers, also available with pink, blue or
white flowers. Mass plants of one color, or
several shades of the same color, in a
shallow bowl on a low table.*

**10 SINNINGIA
SPECIOSA HYBRIDS**
Gloxinia *(see p. 85)*
*Purple blooms banded
with white, also available
with white or red flowers.
Mass plants of the same
color on a low table.*

11 SAINTPAULIA HYBRIDS
Pink African violet *(see p. 80)*
*Deep-pink flowers with yellow centers,
also with blue, purple or white flowers.*

12 PASSIFLORA CAERULEA
Passion flower *(see p. 70)*
*Curious white-petaled flowers with purple-
fringed filaments, also available with pink and
purple petals. Train around a sunny window or
up a support.*

**13 AECHMEA
FASCIATA**
Urn plant *(see p. 26)*
*Short-lived, pale-blue flowers
emerge from pink bracts.*

14 EXACUM AFFINE
German violet *(see p. 53)*
*Tiny lilac-colored flowers with gold
centers, also available with white flowers.*

**15 IMPATIENS
WALLERANA HYBRIDS**
Pink impatiens *(see p. 62)*
*Sugar-pink single flowers,
available with white, red, orange
or bicolored flowers.*

Chapter Two

Choosing and Using Containers

Selecting a container for your house plants is the next step after choosing which ones are right for your environment. You can create arrangements consisting of a single plant in a simple pot, a formal grouping of associated plants, a plain rush basket overflowing with color, or a mixed display that incorporates any or all of these elements. In each case, the first thing to do is to look at the plants and flowers themselves in terms of the qualities described in the previous chapter. Only then turn to the choice of container and make your selection not just on the basis of choosing the correct size for your plant's health, but also in terms of how the container can add to your display and enhance the mood you want to create.

Matching containers to plants
These woven baskets and large terracotta and earthenware pots are suitably rustic and sturdy-looking for the profusion of large foliage plants. Where floor space is limited, as in this narrow conservatory, hanging baskets allow you to introduce a greater variety of plant shape and color, and use areas which would otherwise be neglected.

Matching plants to containers

The criteria to be borne in mind when selecting a container for your plant are many and complex, and for every rule formulated it is possible to show an example that breaks it successfully. In every case the decision will be tempered by personal taste and preference but it is worth setting down some basic guidelines.

The most important consideration is the proportion of the container to the plant. In general, the smaller the plant the more it should equal the height of its container. To find out what combinations will work together it is best to try various permutations of container with your plant; make sure that both will suit the place in which you want to put them. This is fundamental to the success of the arrangement for not only the container, but also the plant inside it, must be suitable for the setting both practically and aesthetically.

It is essential to choose a style of container and a type of plant that will reflect and enhance the ambience of the room for which they are intended. The style of the container depends on the material of which it is made and on its shape, color and texture. The style of a plant can be analyzed in a similar way: for instance, the spiky-leaved *Yucca elephantipes* (tip yucca) has a hard-edged modern look to it, while a *Begonia* sp. (begonia) with lush flowers and a soft outline will suit a more traditional setting. So do not be tempted to buy a *Yucca elephantipes* in an aluminum pot if you have a period house decorated with chintzes.

Many containers are expensive to buy, particularly if you are thinking of using several of them. It is worth having a look at everyday household objects – wastepaper baskets, preserving pans, galvanized buckets, coal scuttles, kettles, watering cans, china and enamel bowls – which can take on a new look and a new lease on life if used imaginatively. There are no rules for improvisation; it is just a question of what looks right for the plants and for the style of setting they are to inhabit. Experiment with putting potted bulbs in wicker shopping baskets, *Hedera* sp. (ivies) and other trailing plants in shiny ice coolers, small cacti in colourful pencil holders and any other combinations that suggest themselves. The delicate bars of a bird-cage could provide an elegant framework for a climbing or trailing plant to ramble over. Even an old chimney pot can make an attractive container (either stand the plant on top of it, in its own planter, or rest the planter on a pile of bricks inside the pot). If you use a container without drainage holes, line it with a layer of gravel, vermiculite or pot fragments before planting in it.

Scindapsus pictus 'Argyraeus'
Pothos vine

Guzmania lingulata
Scarlet star

Conical glass bowl
The crisp linear form of this bowl complements the red flowers and strong outline of these plants.

Spherical ceramic pot
The simplicity of the pot, both in shape and color, shows off the silver variegation in the leaves of the vine.

Hedera helix hybrids
English ivy

**Nephrolepsis exaltata
'Bostoniensis'**
Boston fern

Tall terracotta pot
*A Hedera helix hybrid displayed in this way needs a
tall pot to show off its trailing stems. A tall upright
plant would look out of proportion in such a container.*

Classical lead urn
*The height of this imitation lead urn sets off the fern's
arching fronds. The combination has a formal look
reinforced by the urn's classical design.*

Beaucarnea recurvata
Ponytail

Pellaea rotundifolia
Button fern

Low terracotta dish
*The bizarre shape of this plant
calls for a plain container such
as this terracotta dish. As the
roots like to be pot bound, the
container is very small for a
plant of this size.*

Round ceramic pot
*The simple shape of this container sets off the delicate
outline of the arching fronds. The dark matt-green leaf
color goes well with the blue of the pot.*

Fatsia japonica
Japanese fatsia

Caladium hortulanum hybrids
Angel wings

Glazed ceramic planter
The bare stems of the Caladium hortulanum *are set off by the shape of the green planter. This unassertive color allows the patterns in the leaves to stand out.*

Handled rush basket
This vigorous Fatsia japonica *with its broad-fingered leaves and bushy shape demands a simple but sturdy-looking container.*

Plumbago auriculata
Cape leadwort

Yucca elephantipes
Tip yucca

Hooped rush basket
The hooped handle of this basket forms a support for this small, climbing plant. The rough texture of the basket goes well with the rather untidy stems.

Square fiberglass planter
The austere form of the upright spiky-leaved Yucca elephantipes *is shown off by the extreme simplicity of its white fiberglass container.*

Soleirolia soleirolii
Baby's tears

Flat terracotta dish
The flat open shape of this dish suits the creeping habit of the Soleirolia soleirolii. *The rustic terracotta goes well with the fresh green of the plant's tiny leaves.*

Opuntia microdasys
Rabbit's ears cactus

Dizygotheca elegantissima
False aralia

Rustic wooden barrel
The arresting shape of this upright cactus requires a container with a simple form. The rough wooden barrel goes well with its vigorous spiny texture.

Large terracotta planter
The success of this combination relies on the contrast between the solidity of the terracotta pot and the filigree effect of this upright plant's bronze-colored foliage.

Groups of containers

Codiaeum variegatum pictum
Croton

One of the ways of adding interest to the layout of a room is by grouping pots and other containers with plants, as incidental focal points. You can use containers of the same color to hold a group of plants together and to stabilize the mood of an area within a room. Few groupings of this sort are important enough to become the focal point in a very large room, but can work well in a smaller area.

When choosing your containers, think carefully about how they will match your plants, and about how plants and containers will work together as a group, both in terms of themselves and in terms of their setting.

Begonia rex-cultorum
Painted-leaf begonia

Counterpoint with color (right)
These containers were chosen to set up a pleasing interplay of color between themselves and the plants. The black and red of the containers pick up and complement the leaf colors of both plants.

Playing with scale (left)
This group works through the repetition of container shape and texture set off by a dramatic contrast in scale of the containers. The use of the same plant in each pot contributes to the satisfying unity of the group.

Soleirolia soleirolii
Baby's tears

Tall and small (right)
Here, the contrast in shape and scale between the two containers is enhanced by the use of the same plant in each. The monochromatic color scheme of the pots helps to hold the group together and picks up the silvery-gray leaf variegation in this vine.

Scindapsus pictus 'Argyraeus'
Pothos vine

Repetition (below)
A small plant in a small pot may need reinforcement: this can be achieved by using a larger specimen of the same plant in a larger pot. These pots pick up the very dark-green color of the plants' leaves and contrast well with their pink variegation.

Hypoestes phyllostachya
Polka-dot plant

Terracotta pots (left)
A simple classical grouping of containers that share the same style and color helps control the random, profligate growth of the plants, and contributes to the effect of a balanced arrangement.

Grouping plants in a single container

For a large arrangement, quite dramatic effects can be achieved by grouping several plants together in a single container. Plants grow better when they are grouped together; a micro-climate is established with the moisture given off by one plant becoming available to its neighbor. The individual plants tend to grow into each other and show each other off.

The plants may form a mixed group of several different types with similar growing needs. Alternatively, grouping plants of the same kind together is often particularly effective as the uniformity of the colors and leaf shapes will increase their impact. Or you could choose plants of the same species but of different varieties to create a subtle interplay of colors, leaf patterns and textures.

Planting with begonias (right)
A striking and colorful foliage group can be made by planting together a number of Begonia rex-cultorum *(painted-leaf begonias). These plants have extremely decorative leaves with striking patterns in red, silver, green and black. Plant them in peat-based potting mixture and put them in a warm part of the house in indirect light.*

Equipment and materials
1 *Porcelain planter* 2 *Trowel* 3 *Peat-based potting mixture* 4 **Aechmea fasciata** *Urn plant (see p. 26)* 5 *Clay pellets* 6 *Charcoal*

They can either be knocked out of their pots and planted in a common potting mixture, as shown here, or, if they are for a temporary display, they can be left in their individual pots and stood in moist peat. If you are potting the plants, select a fairly deep container, so that the potting mixture does not dry out too quickly, and always include a layer of porous material at the base of the container if it is without drainage holes. This method has the advantage that it usually gives the plants a bigger root run, but it does make it more difficult to remove an ailing plant, or to group plants with different watering needs. Sometimes a combination of the two methods is best, allowing you to give a single plant special treatment.

PLANTS
Mini-climate 1
Warm, sunny

1

2

3

4

6

5

Planting a large container

In general, the strongest and most effective arrangements of this type are the simplest ones. Often, mixed plantings do not work because they show too much variation in shape and texture; the overall effect is untidy and difficult to place in a room. Here, several exotic-looking *Aechmea fasciata* have been grouped together. Their vigorous shape called for a simple container and a white porcelain planter was chosen whose color picked up the white sheen on the leaves of the plants.

Planting with saffron spikes
The strong shape of these plants and exciting leaf and flower color are intensified when massed together.

BUILDING UP THE ARRANGEMENT

1 *Line the bottom of the planter with ¾ in of porous clay pellets or vermiculite and scatter pieces of charcoal over them. Fill the planter half-full with potting mixture and place one of the plants on the mixture to check that the top of its pot is level with the top of the planter.*

2 *To remove the plant from its pot, first water it well and then, holding the plant between your first and second finger, hit the pot hard against the edge of a table, or strike the base hard with your fist.*

3 *Build up the potting mixture at the back of the planter, and as you position each plant in the potting mixture tilt it out slightly so that the rosette of leaves and flower heads can be appreciated.*

4 *Finally, add another plant to fill the container and, to keep the plants in good condition, put them in a warm, sunny place. Keep their natural "vase" – formed by the rosette of leaves – filled with water.*

Planting a basket

The choice of a basket as a container will dictate the types of plants which are suitable to be displayed in it. A rush basket calls for unsophisticated plants such as *Senecio cruentus* (cinerarias) and *Exacum affine* (German violets), as well as the examples illustrated here. Potted bulbs can be used in spring and should be massed together in the basket just before they begin to flower.

The plants which you select are for a temporary arrangement as you display them for their flowering period, or when their foliage is at its best. Given that their moment of glory is short there is no need to unpot the plants into a potting medium; and, since they are in separate pots, you can group together plants with different watering needs so long as they like similar amounts of light and heat.

A display with begonias
A collection of plants such as these Begonia 'Tiger Paws' *(eyelash begonias) would be suitable for a warm place in the house. Their striking green-and-bronze foliage creates a strong enough pattern for them to stand on their own.*

Equipment and materials
1 *Rush basket* 2 *Plastic lining* 3 *Clay pellets* 4 *Peat*
5 **Hedera helix hybrids** English ivy (see p. 60)
6 **Primula obconica** German primrose *(see p. 78)*
7 *Scissors*

PLANTS
Mini-climate 5
Cool, filtered sun

BUILDING UP THE ARRANGEMENT

1 *Place a piece of plastic inside the basket to form a watertight skin. Cut it to shape allowing a small overhang which will eventually be tucked in. Cover the bottom of the basket with a layer of porous clay pellets or vermiculite about 1in deep.*

2 *Fill the basket with 2in of damp peat. Stand the pots inside and start to build up the composition. Put the three taller, salmon-pink flowering plants at the back, packing peat around the pots as you go, then let the variegated ivy trail down one side of the basket to soften the overall shape.*

3 *Finally, put the remaining primroses at the front of the basket. Make sure that all the pots are standing upright because you will still need to water them – the primroses in particular like plenty of water. To keep the display looking fresh, take off individual flowers as they fade and remove any yellowing leaves. These primroses should last from 6-8 weeks provided they are kept in a cool place.*

Planting hanging baskets

Most of us are familiar with hanging baskets displayed on terraces, balconies or porches, but seldom see them used indoors to advantage. When selecting a basket for an indoor display think carefully about its setting: a wire basket is only suitable for a room with a water-resistant floor, such as a conservatory. A practical, but less attractive, alternative is a solid plastic basket with a raised platform inside, a filling tube and water-level indicator, or another type which incorporates a drip-tray. But there is nothing to stop you using a terracotta container or rush basket, if you make your own rope hangings, or using a wall basket in an appropriate material.

It is important to secure the basket properly because it will be very heavy when wet. The chain or rope support should hang from a hook firmly anchored in a ceiling joist, not set into plaster. It is a good idea to use a hook with a universal joint so that the basket can be rotated to give the plants an even supply of light.

When deciding upon a planting scheme for a basket, remember that you are trying to blend the arrangement with your decor. Limit yourself to one type of plant unless your setting is very plain. For an outdoor planting you can be less restrained with your colors, but it is sensible to choose species which are used to heat and the drying effect of wind.

Planting a wire basket

The attraction of a wire basket is that, once the plants are established, it becomes a spherical mass of flowers or foliage. Here, the effect of a large ball of flowers has been created by planting white and blue *Campanula isophylla*. These should flower continuously from August to November provided they are watered well in warm weather – a good reason for putting this in a conservatory.

PLANTS
Mini-climate 4
Cool, sunny

Equipment and materials
1 *Bucket* **2** *Scissors* **3** *Peat-based potting mixture*
4 **Campanula isophylla** *Italian bellflower (see p. 40)* **5** *Trowel* **6** *Sphagnum moss* **7** *Wire basket*
8 *Plastic lining*

1

2

3

8

7

5

6

BUILDING UP THE ARRANGEMENT

1 *Line the basket with a 2in layer of damp sphagnum moss. Then, cut a circle of plastic sheeting to fit inside, leaving an overlap of 4in. Make a circle of holes in the plastic 2in up from the bottom.*

2 *You will need to divide some of the larger plants into two to fit them through the holes. First, water the plants before taking them out of their pots; then, holding the plant in both hands, plunge your thumbs into the middle of the potting mixture and pull apart.*

3 *Insert the divided plants from the outside, pushing the roots through the sphagnum moss and the holes in the plastic. Push one row of plants around the bottom of the basket, cover with a layer of potting mixture, firming it down around them, and then place more plants higher up the sides of the basket to fill the gaps. Plant several large white specimens in the top.*

4 *Fill the gaps in the top with blue-flowered plants and, when the basket is filled, tuck in the overhanging plastic. Water the basket well before replacing the chains and hanging it in a sunny place.*

4

Planting a wicker basket

Hanging baskets can add freshness and color to a room, particularly where space at floor level is limited. Think about the place where your basket is to hang and select your plants and container with an eye to the decorative effect you want, bearing in mind that the plants should like their habitat and be broadly compatible in their requirements. A wicker basket was felt to best suit this display where ferns have been grouped together, accentuating contrasts of plant form and leaf shape.

Equipment and materials
1 *Wicker basket* 2 *Foam matting* 3 *Foil* 4 *Clay pellets* 5 **Asparagus setaceus** *Asparagus fern (see p.31)* 6 *Trowel* 7 *Peat-based potting mixture* 8 *Charcoal* 9 **Asparagus densiflorus 'Sprengeri'** *Emerald fern (see p.30)* 10 **Guzmania lingulata** *Scarlet star (see p.58)* 11 **Nephrolepsis exaltata 'Bostoniensis'** *Boston fern (see p.67)* 12 **Pteris cretica** *Cretan brake (see p.78)* 13 **Adiantum raddianum** *Delta maidenhair fern (see p.25)* 14 *Sphagnum moss* 15 **Asplenium nidus** *Bird's nest fern (see p.32)*

BUILDING UP THE ARRANGEMENT

1 *Line the basket with foil to prevent rotting, then place foam matting on top and trim to fit. Put some pieces of gravel at the back of the basket to form a higher area for planting. Line the basket with porous clay pellets or vermiculite. Then fill it with peat based potting mixture, and a handful of charcoal to prevent the mixture from turning sour.*

2 *Position the first plant where the compost has been built up. Use a bushy asparagus fern with delicate feathery fronds for height. Plan the rest of the arrangement by positioning your plants, still in their pots, until you are satisfied. Here two trailing emerald ferns were put either side of the first fern.*

3 *To give more substance to the back of the design put two Boston ferns either side of the asparagus ferns. When planting, tilt the ferns out to the side so that their fronds overhang the sides of the basket.*

4 *To fill the foreground add a delta maidenhair fern and a cretan brake. The delicate fronds of the delta maidenhair fern and the unusual branching fronds of the cretan brake provide further variation in both leaf shape and leaf color.*

5 *Placing a bird's nest fern on the left is a pleasing contrast to the surrounding feathery fronds. Finally, add the two scarlet stars to create a splash of color, cover any visible potting mixture with damp moss and water well. Place the rope hangings around the basket and hang it from the ceiling. Use a hook with a universal joint so that the basket can be rotated to ensure plants get an even supply of light.*

PLANTS

Mini-climate 2	Mini-climate 3
Warm, filtered sun	*Warm, shady*

Planting window-boxes

Window-boxes are usually thought of as outdoor containers but there is no reason why they cannot be used indoors, provided you have a window which opens outward or upward with a suitable sill.

There are many types of boxes: plastic is a light, cheap material suitable for use indoors or out and, if planted with trailers, will hardly be visible through the greenery; fiberglass comes in authentic-looking imitations of lead and stone, and is extremely light but correspondingly expensive; stone is always attractive but is too heavy for most sills and better used on the ground; terracotta suits period houses and formal interior settings; wood is a very useful material for an outdoor box as it can be made to measure and, if fitted with a waterproof zinc liner which can be lifted out, is easy to replant. As a general rule, the material of your window-box should be in keeping with the style of your house – if it is to go outside – or the style of your room – if it is to go inside. In either case, it is best to choose a box which is as low-key as possible to show off the plants. If you use a purpose-made wooden box it can be painted to match the color of your walls. Your choice of plants will depend on the season in which you are planting, and on the orientation of your window.

Your window-box should have holes at the bottom to prevent the lower layers collecting sour water and causing roots to rot. Wooden, stone and terracotta boxes have holes drilled and plastic ones have indentations which you can tap out with a screwdriver. Always fit a drip-tray underneath the box to prevent any surplus water over-flowing. Whether your box is to go indoors or out, select one that is as deep as is practical; this will prevent the potting mixture from drying out too quickly, although you will find that any box will need very frequent watering in warm weather. If your box is placed high-up where it could fall and cause damage below, secure it in place with a brace on either side attached to the window surround, or within an angled bracket fixed to the wall or window. Never use window-boxes on weak or rotten sills.

PLANTS
Mini-climate 1
Warm, sunny

Equipment and materials
1 *Shards* **2** *Soil-based potting mixture*
3 Tradescantia fluminensis 'Variegata'
Tradescantia (see p. 91) **4 Achimenes grandiflora**
Cupid's bower (see p. 25) **5** *Pruners* **6** *Trowel*
7 *Window-box and drip-tray*

Planting an indoor window-box

Begin by thinking about what types of plants will like the quality of light offered by your window and choose ones with similar growing needs. For this summer group a plain white plastic window-box was used and pink and purple *Achimenes grandiflora* and a *Tradescantia fluminensis* 'Variegata' with pink stripes were chosen. Alternative plantings for a spring box would be bulbs or herbs, and for a winter box *Narcissus medioluteus* hybrids.

The finished arrangement
Both plants like a sunny position and will be happy on a south-facing windowsill.

BUILDING UP THE ARRANGEMENT

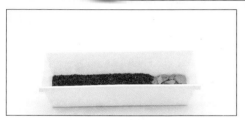

1 *Line the box with a layer of shards making sure that the pieces face downward so that water will drain off them (if you do not have any broken terracotta pots, most garden centers will supply shards free of charge). Add a 2in layer of potting mixture, putting more at the back to give height to the back of the arrangement.*

2 *Set the plants out in the box and experiment with the design until you are satisfied that it looks balanced. Begin by planting six purple Cupid's bowers along the length of the box, leaving room between them for the pink-flowered kinds and the trailing foliage of the tradescantia.*

3 *Place a tradescantia in the center of the box, letting some stems trail down in front and threading the others through the Cupid's bowers. Finally, fill the remaining spaces with more of the flowered plants and another tradescantia.*

Planting an outdoor window-box

Winter is the season when you long to see greenery and colorful flowers. One way of improving the view from your windows, particularly if you live in a city, is to plant a window-box using plants with colorful berries and evergreens with attractive foliage. The window-box that has been planted below will need protection from the frost, since the *Solanum capsicastrum* hybrids and *Chrysanthemum morifolium* hybrids are not hardy; put it at a window where it can easily be brought inside in cold weather or, alternatively, use it as an indoor window-box for a cool place in the home.

Other ideas for windows

There are other ways to decorate windows besides using window-boxes. For instance, you can set potted plants on glass or plastic shelves lined with metal to protect them from any water leaking out. Covering the shelves with rows of plants will obscure the view through the window, but can be useful for this very reason and will make an attractive display in themselves. All plants benefit from being grouped together and, if they are also given good light, they will grow fast.

Your choice of plant will, of course, depend upon the orientation of your window. Place sun-loving desert cacti and succulents and tropical species at a south-facing window; flowering plants at west- and east-facing windows; and plants which like indirect light at north-facing windows. By placing all the plants in the same type of container, you can introduce a sense of order into a crowded and varied arrangement.

Alternatively, it is possible to build a special window (essentially a glass box around the outside of the window) for plants, similar to a miniature conservatory. Plants will need some form of shade from the summer sun, and you must ensure that there is good ventilation and remember to increase the humidity when it is hot. To do this, stand the plants on trays filled with moist pebbles.

Equipment and materials
1 **Chrysanthemum morifolium hybrids** *Florist's chrysanthemum (see p. 43)* 2 **Solanum capsicastrum** *Christmas cherry (see p. 85)* 3 **Terracotta window-box** 4 **Hedera helix hybrids** *English ivy (see p. 60)* 5 *Peat-based potting mixture* 6 *Trowel* 7 *Clay pellets*

PLANTS
Mini-climate 4
Cool, sunny
Mini-climate 5
Cool, filtered sun

BUILDING UP THE ARRANGEMENT

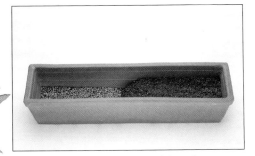

1 *Line the window-box with 1in of clay pellets or vermiculite (you can also use shards or gravel) to provide drainage. Place a layer of potting mixture over the pellets to a depth of about 2in.*

2 *With the plants still in their pots, experiment with putting the Christmas cherry in the middle, the florist's chrysanthemum at the edge and the ivies where their trailing fronds will look best.*

3 *Take the plants out of their pots and shake off excess potting mixture. Put two Christmas cherries in the center of the box and plant the florist's chrysanthemum hybrids on either side. Let the four small ivies trail down at the sides and in the front of the box. Firm potting mixture around the plants and water well before putting in position.*

Using bottles and terraria

Bottle gardens and terraria provide optimum growing conditions for plants which like a humid atmosphere, since the moisture given off by the leaves of the plants inside condenses and runs back into the soil. Any sort of bottle is suitable, provided plants can be passed through the neck. If you plan to use a bottle made of colored glass, you should move it into brighter light than would be normal for the plants inside to compensate for this. Terraria can be bought embellished with stained glass, however a simple, clear glass or plastic one with an attractive shape will show off plants to their best advantage.

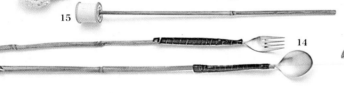

Planting bottle gardens

As it is difficult to prune and remove plants from a bottle garden, it makes sense to plant particularly slow-growing specimens if you want your garden to look attractive for a year or more. Tempting as it may be to plant *Saintpaulia* hybrids (African violets), it is not a good idea since, once the flowers fade, they can look very dull. It is best to create a colorful effect by using plants with variegated leaves and to build an interesting group with contrasts of shape and texture.

PLANTS
Mini-climate 3
Warm, shady

Equipment and materials
1 *Glass bottle* 2 *Funnel* 3 *Circle of paper*
4 **Adiantum raddianum microphyllum**
Delta maidenhair fern (see p. 25) 5 *Sphagnum moss* 6 *Clay pellets* 7 *Peat-based potting mixture* 8 *Miniature trowel* 9 *Charcoal* 10 **Fittonia verschaffeltii** *Nerve plant (see p. 57)* 11 **Fittonia verschaffeltii argyroneura 'Nana'** *Little nerve plant (see p. 57)* 12 **Adiantum hispidulum** *Australian maidenhair fern (see p. 25)* 13 *Spoon* 14 *Fork* 15 *Spool* 16 *Sponge*

BUILDING UP THE ARRANGEMENT

1 *Cut a circle of paper the same size as the planting area of the bottle and experiment with the design until you are happy with it – placing the taller plants at the back and the low-growing ones in the foreground.*

2 *Pour a 1in layer of clay pellets into the bottle through a funnel made of stiff paper. Add a handful of charcoal, and fill the bottle with 2-3in of damp peat-based potting mixture. Build up the potting mixture at the back and use the spoon to smooth out the surface.*

3 *Make a hole for the first plant. Take a delta maidenhair fern and stick the fork into the root ball. Lower into the hole. Cover the roots and firm down the mixture around it. Put another delta maidenhair fern at the back and then add an Australian maidenhair to vary the outline. Leave about 2in between them to allow room for growth.*

4 *Place the little nerve plants in the foreground. Then, to give the arrangement a focal point, plant a nerve plant in the center. Finally, decorate any bare area with sphagnum moss, and pour in a cup of water by directing it against the glass. You can cork the bottle but it will make the glass mist up more quickly.*

Planting terraria

Terraria are glass cases which offer the same humid environment as bottle gardens and allow pruning and removal of the plants inside. For this reason you can use suitable fast-growing kinds such as the species of *Selaginella* and the *Hypoestes phyllostachya* planted in the terrarium opposite. Similarly, small flowering plants such as *Sinningia pusilla* (miniature gloxinias) can be planted, and replaced when they have faded. Here, a leaded-glass terrarium resembling a tiny conservatory was used, which suggested the choice of palms to form the background of the group.

Terraria need to be cleaned regularly to remove build ups of condensation or algae from the inside surface of the glass. This can be easily done using a small sponge attached to a bamboo stake.

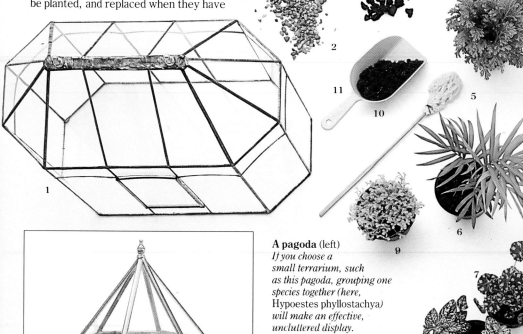

A pagoda (left)
*If you choose a
small terrarium, such
as this pagoda, grouping one
species together (here,
Hypoestes phyllostachya)
will make an effective,
uncluttered display.*

PLANTS
Mini-climate 2
Warm, filtered sun

Equipment and materials
1 *Terrarium* 2 *Gravel* 3 *Charcoal* 4 **Selaginella
kraussiana** *Spreading club moss (see p. 83)*
5 *Sponge* 6 **Chamaedorea elegans 'Bella'**
Parlor palm (see p. 41) 7 **Begonia 'Tiger Paws'**
Eyelash begonia (see p. 36) 8 **Hypoestes
phyllostachya** *Polka-dot plant (see p. 62)*
9 **Selaginella martensii** *Little club moss (see p. 83)*
10 *Peat-based potting mixture* 11 *Miniature trowel*

BUILDING UP THE ARRANGEMENT

1 *Line the terrarium with ½in of gravel, spread lumps of charcoal over it and then fill with 2in of damp potting mixture. Place some of the plants you have chosen inside the terrarium and plan your group. Make a depression in the potting mixture ready for the first plant.*

2 *Plant the tallest parlor palm, spreading the roots out horizontally and gently packing potting mixture around them. Plant another palm at the back of the terrarium on the left side. Then, below, place a begonia next to a little club moss.*

3 *Put another little club moss in the front of the terrarium and a spreading club moss behind the larger palm to give the arrangement more bulk. Then, fill the remaining spaces around the palm with polka-dot plants and decorate any bare area of potting mixture with gravel. Mist-spray plants and potting mixture and close any aperture in order to make the atmosphere more humid.*

CHAPTER THREE

INDOOR GARDENS

The variety of plants and containers
suitable for the home is by no means
limited to house plants and traditional
plantings in pots and baskets. This section
shows how you can use more unusual
plants and growing methods to achieve
impressive effects. Cacti and succulents,
for instance, can be grouped together
to make miniature landscapes that imitate
their natural desert habitat. Garden bulbs
planted indoors will make a mass of bright
color in the colder months of the year.
Water gardens, made by growing plants in
containers of water and aggregate instead
of soil, are easy to care for and visually
striking. There is also advice on how to
train and maintain bonsai, and suggestions
on growing plants in artificial light where
natural light is unavailable or inadequate.
These ideas are particularly useful for
anyone who has restrictions on space or
habitat or on the amount of time to be
spent on maintenance.

Growing plants in artificial light
*This small light fixture is equipped with a special bulb
which should provide the light needed to keep this*
Nephrolepsis exaltata *'Bostoniensis' (Boston fern)
healthy in a position which would otherwise be too dark
for it. The light also serves a decorative purpose,
casting an interesting shadow on to the wall behind.*

Cacti and succulent gardens

Cacti and succulents add a different range of shapes and textures to a collection of house plants and can be used to make interesting desert landscapes. Most of the cacti have abandoned leaves and developed their unusual body shapes to prevent excessive loss of water. Some are ribbed or segmented and they may be covered with decorative spines, bristles or hairs. One species, *Cephalocereus senilis*, is so closely covered with white hair that it resembles a ball of wool. Desert cacti (usually covered in spines), such as *Mammillaria* and *Rebutia*, have the added attraction of striking flowers. The jungle cacti (often without spines), such as *Schlumbergera* sp., have stems which are notched at intervals and produce brightly colored flowers in early spring or mid-winter.

Succulents are those plants which have fleshy stems or leaves that store water. They may be upright and treelike in shape, or have thin trailing stems, or be spherical or columnar in outline. Some are just a few inches high; others can grow to 6ft tall and make large, striking plants. Leaf shape varies from the thick, succulent leaves of *Crassula arborescens* and *Cotyledon undulata* to the thin, narrow leaves of *Euphorbia milii*. Leaf color also varies from the green of *Aloe aristata* and *Kalanchoe blossfeldiana* hybrids to the silvery-mauve of *Ceropegia woodii* or the green and white of *Agave victoriae-reginae*.

A desert garden
A suitably rugged and arid-looking miniature landscape for these desert plants has been created by scattering pebbles and stone chippings in between the cacti.

The A-Z of cacti and succulents

The A-Z of cacti and succulents uses the symbols below to indicate preferred light, temperature, watering and humidity levels for each plant, and the relative ease of its cultivation. The symbols are explained in detail in *The A-Z of house plants* (pp. 22-3).

AGAVE VICTORIAE-REGINAE

QUEEN AGAVE

These succulents have three-dimensional scalelike leaves. Each fleshy leaf is dark green with a white margin and bears a sharp black spine at its tip. They are the most attractive of the *Agave* genus and should be displayed so that they can be seen from above.

Mini-climate 4 Cool, sunny.
Size These plants are slow-growing, reaching a maximum height of 8in, but they can attain a spread of about 1½ft. Small plants are offered for sale.
Feeding Feed with standard liquid fertilizer once a month during spring and summer.
Potting Repot every second year in spring using two-thirds soil-based potting mixture and one-third coarse sand. If you don't want to move an older plant into a larger pot topdress instead.
Special points Water less in winter.

ALOE ARISTATA

LACE ALOE

These stemless succulents are made up of many fleshy leaves arranged in tight rosettes. The triangular leaves are dark green and covered with raised white spots. The small orange-red flowers are borne on a long stalk which appears from the center of the rosette in summer and last only a few days. Offsets are readily produced from the base of mature plants. Group plants together and place them so that they are seen from above.

Mini-climate 1 Warm, sunny.
Size *Aloe aristata* reaches a maximum height of 6in. If offsets are left to develop in the same pot as the parent, spread is only limited by the size of the pot.
Feeding Feed with standard liquid fertilizer once a month from spring to autumn.
Potting Repot every spring using soil-based potting mixture. If you don't want to move an older plant into a larger pot topdress instead.
Special points Water less in winter. Avoid trapping water in the rosette of leaves.

APOROCACTUS FLAGELLIFORMIS

RAT'S TAIL CACTUS

These cacti have long streamers of narrow, fleshy stems covered with many rows of fine, prickly spines. Striking crimson-pink flowers appear in spring; each bloom lasts several days and the flowering season extends for up to two months. Display them in hanging baskets or on shelves, and position them where they will not be brushed against, as the spines are very difficult to remove from the skin. They can also be displayed in a cactus garden.

Mini-climate 4 Cool, sunny.
Size *Aporocactus flagelliformis* is fast-growing and its stems can reach 3ft (occasionally much more) in three or four years. Plants of all sizes are offered for sale.
Feeding Feed with tomato-type fertilizer from late December to the end of flowering
Potting Repot every spring after flowering using soil-based potting mixture. Once plants are in a 6-10in pot topdress instead.
Special points Water less during the rest period following flowering.

ASTROPHYTUM MYRIOSTIGMA

BISHOP'S CAP

These spherical cacti are divided into wide segments, each covered with a silvery meal instead of thorns. They look rather like de-spined sea urchins. The bright-yellow flowers resemble daisies and appear from the top of the plant in summer. *Astrophytum myriostigma* looks good in cactus gardens or massed in a shallow bowl with a gravelly surround.

Mini-climate 4 Cool, sunny.
Size These cacti are slow-growing, reaching about 10in in height with a spread of 5in. Plants of all sizes are offered for sale.
Feeding Feed with tomato-type fertilizer once a month from spring to autumn.
Potting Repot in spring using two-thirds soil-based potting mixture and one-third coarse sand, but only if the plant has completely filled the existing pot.
Special points Water less during the winter rest period.

CEPHALOCEREUS SENILIS

OLD MAN CACTUS

The common name of these cacti is derived from the long, fine, white hair that shrouds the fleshy columnar body and hides the sharp spines. Flowers are only produced on older plants. *Cephalocereus senilis* looks best massed with other cacti in a cactus garden.

Mini-climate 4 Cool, sunny.
Size These cacti are slow-growing and unlikely to grow taller than 10-12in. Plants of all sizes are offered for sale.
Feeding Feed with tomato-type fertilizer once a month from spring to mid-autumn.
Potting Repot in spring using three parts soil-based potting mixture and one part coarse sand, but only if the plant has completely filled the existing pot. If you don't want to move an older plant into a larger pot topdress instead.
Special points Do not water during the winter rest period. The long hairs may be washed in a weak solution of detergent to keep them clean.

CEREUS PERUVIANUS 'MONSTROSUS'

PERUVIAN APPLE CACTUS

These cacti have bright-green columnar bodies which are twisted and contorted into most unusual shapes. They are in fact mutations of the true species. The yellow spines are short and inconspicuous. Large but short-lived white, scented flowers are produced in summer on older specimens. Their sculptural quality can be quite spectacular when several plants are grouped in a modern interior.

Mini-climate 4 Cool, sunny.
Size *Cereus peruvianus* 'Monstrosus' is slow-growing and each mutation varies in maximum height and spread. Small plants are offered for sale.
Feeding Feeding with tomato-type fertilizer once a month from spring to early autumn.
Potting Repot every spring using two-thirds soil-based potting mixture and one-third coarse sand. If you don't want to move an older plant into a larger pot topdress instead.

CEROPEGIA WOODII

ROSARY VINE

These small, tuber-forming succulents have trailing threadlike stems bearing heart-shaped leaves. These fleshy leaves, which appear in pairs at intervals along the stems, are marbled with silvery-gray and have purple undersides. Small, tube-shaped flowers appear amongst the leaves in summer. Several plants displayed together in a small hanging basket in a warm room make an unusual display. Position them where they will not be brushed against. Alternatively, the stems may be coiled in the pot so the flowers stand upright.

Mini-climate 1 Warm, sunny.

Size *Ceropegia woodii* stems do not usually grow longer than 3ft. Cut back any bare stems to encourage leafy growth. Small plants are offered for sale.

Feeding Feed mature plants with standard liquid fertilizer once a month during spring and summer.

Potting Repot young plants every spring using an equal-parts combination of soil-based potting mixture and coarse sand. Older plants thrive in 3-4in half pots. Hanging baskets should have a 1in layer of drainage material at the bottom.

Special points Water less in winter.

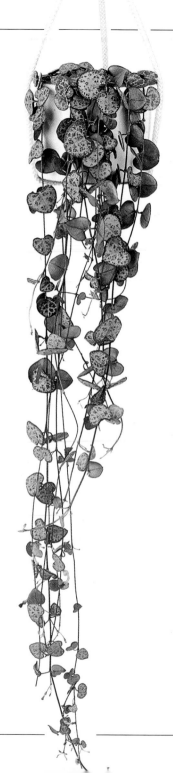

COTYLEDON UNDULATA

SILVER CROWN

These most unusual plants have fleshy fan-shaped leaves with undulating edges and a dense covering of fine, silver-white scurf. Although orange-yellow flowers may appear on older plants in summer, it is for their leaves that they are grown. Mass several plants together in a bowl on a low table.

Mini-climate 4 Cool, sunny.
Size *Cotyledon undulata* is slow-growing reaching a height of about 20in in three years. Plants of all sizes are offered for sale.
Feeding Feed with standard liquid fertilizer once a month from spring to early autumn.
Potting Repot every spring using two-thirds soil-based potting mixture and one-third coarse sand, making provision for good drainage. Once plants are in 6in pots topdress instead.
Special points Avoid handling the plants as the meal will rub off. Water less in winter.

Similar-shaped species

Cotyledon orbiculata grows taller and has gray-green leaves edged with red, with just a little meal. Orange flowers appear in summer.

CRASSULA ARBORESCENS

CHINESE JADE

These succulents have fleshy, almost round leaves which are gray in color and rimmed with red. These are borne on thick, branching, woody stems which are symmetrical in shape when the plant is mature. Small specimens can be used as "trees" in dish gardens or miniature oriental gardens.

Mini-climate 4 Cool, sunny.
Size Very young *Crassula arborescens* are offered for sale; they will eventually reach 3ft in height, when the stems will resemble gnarled tree trunks.
Feeding Feed with standard liquid fertilizer once a month from spring to early autumn.
Potting Repot every spring using a mixture of three parts soil-based potting mixture and one part coarse sand. Once plants are in 8in pots topdress instead.
Special points Water less in winter.

ECHEVERIA AGAVOIDES

MOLDED WAX PLANT

These succulents have triangular fleshy leaves which are light green with brown tips. Yellow flowers tipped with red are produced in spring. *Echeveria agavoides* should be viewed from above for best effect – place them on a low table, or use in a succulent garden.

Mini-climate 4 Cool, sunny.
Size Grow to about 3½in in height with a spread of about 6in. Plants of all sizes are offered for sale.
Feeding Feed with half-strength standard liquid fertilizer once a month from spring to autumn.
Potting Repot plants every second spring using a combination of four parts soil-based potting mixture and one part coarse sand. If you don't want to move an older plant into a larger pot topdress instead.
Special points Water less in winter.

ECHEVERIA DERENBERGII

PAINTED LADY

These pretty succulents have tightly packed bluish-gray leaves with a coating of silvery scurf and red margins. Yellow and orange bell-shaped flowers borne on spikes are produced in winter and early spring. They make good, small specimen plants for the kitchen windowsill all year round.

Mini-climate 4 Cool, sunny.
Size *Echeveria derenbergii* forms cushions 4-6in across. Young single plants are offered for sale.
Feeding Feed with half-strength standard liquid fertilizer once a month from spring until autumn.
Potting Repot every second spring using four parts soil-based potting mixture and one part coarse sand. If you don't want to move an older plant into a larger pot topdress instead.
Special points Water less in winter.

ECHINOCACTUS GRUSONII

GOLDEN BARREL CACTUS

These cacti are armed with stout, golden-yellow spines arranged in rows on the ribbed stems. Older plants develop the typical pattern of raised vertical ribs. *Echinocactus grusonii* can be grouped with other cacti or displayed with foliage plants.

Mini-climate 4 Cool, sunny.
Size These plants grow quickly to 3-4in across, but then it takes many years for the plant to double its size, though they can eventually reach a diameter of 8in. Small plants are offered for sale.
Feeding Feed with tomato-type fertilizer once a month from spring to autumn.
Potting Repot in spring using two-thirds soil-based potting mixture and one-third coarse sand, but only if the plant has completely filled the existing pot. When repotting is not necessary topdress instead.
Special points Do not water during the winter rest period or plants will rot.

EUPHORBIA MILII

CROWN-OF-THORNS

These succulent shrubs have horizontal branches bearing many sharp spines and relatively few leaves. The clusters of yellow or red "flowers" are in fact bracts which last for months, appearing in greatest profusion from February to September. They are excellent plants for modern interiors.

Mini-climate 1 Warm, sunny.
Size *Euphorbia milii* can grow to about 3ft in height with a similar spread. Plants of all sizes are offered for sale.
Feeding Feed with standard liquid fertilizer once a month from spring to autumn.
Potting Repot young plants every second year in spring using half soil-based potting mixture and half coarse sand, making provision for good drainage. If you don't want to move an older plant into a larger pot topdress instead.
Special points These plants "bleed" a white latex if damaged: this latex should not be allowed to touch the eyes or the mouth.

FEROCACTUS LATISPINUS

FISH-HOOK CACTUS

These cacti are noted for their fierce-looking spines which are grouped in clusters. Spines within individual clusters vary in size, shape and color, with one being broader and more prominently hooked than the others. Really mature plants can produce violet-colored flowers in summer. Large plants make good specimens – otherwise mix them with cacti of contrasting shapes in a cactus garden.

Mini-climate 4 Cool, sunny.

Size *Ferocactus latispinus* can reach a maximum of 1ft in height and 8in across. Plants of all sizes are offered for sale.

Feeding Feed with tomato-type fertilizer once a month from spring to autumn.

Potting Repot in spring using a combination of two-thirds soil-based potting mixture and one-third coarse sand, but only if the plant has completely filled the existing pot.

Special points Do not water during the winter rest period or plants will rot.

KALANCHOE BLOSSFELDIANA HYBRIDS

KALANCHOE

These attractive succulents flower in late winter and early spring, and remain in flower for about three months. The small flowers are grouped in closely packed flower heads borne on long stems. Each head has between 20 and 50 flowers. Color ranges from pink, through red, to orange and yellow. The fleshy leaves are dark green and often edged in red. *Kalanchoe blossfeldiana* hybrids are best treated as annuals. Use massed together on a low table for a splash of winter color.

Mini-climate 1 Warm, sunny.
Size These plants reach a maximum height of about 14in tall. A dwarf form is available and reaches 8in in height. Plants in flower are offered for sale during winter.
Feeding Feed with standard liquid fertilizer once a month whilst in flower.
Potting Repotting is unnecessary.
Special points To keep plants decorative, remove flowers as they fade.

MAMMILLARIA HAHNIANA

OLD LADY CACTUS

These globular cacti get their common name from the white, silky hairs which cover and hide the grayish-green body and the sharp spines. When the cacti are about four years old, crimson flowers appear in early May. Group several specimens together for a dramatic display or use in a cactus garden.

Mini-climate 4 Cool, sunny.
Size *Mammillaria hahniana* grows to 4in tall with a spread of 3in. Small plants are offered for sale.
Feeding Feed with tomato-type fertilizer once a month from spring to autumn.
Potting Repot in spring using two-thirds soil-based potting mixture and one-third coarse sand, but only if the plant has completely filled the existing pot.
Special points Water less during the winter rest period.

MAMMILLARIA RHODANTHA

GOLDEN PINCUSHION

These spherical cacti have bright-green bodies covered in small knobs which bear long, yellow-orange spines. These are arranged in circular groups over the whole body. Pink daisylike flowers appear in a ring around the top of the body in summer. Display the plants in a cactus garden or group with other cacti.

Mini-climate 4 Cool, sunny.

Size *Mammillaria rhodantha* grows to about 4in in height and 3in in spread. Small plants are offered for sale.

Feeding Feed with tomato-type liquid fertilizer once a month from spring to autumn.

Potting Repot in spring using two-thirds soil-based potting mixture and one-third coarse sand, but only if the plant is pot-bound.

Special points Water less during the winter rest period.

MAMMILLARIA ZEILMANNIANA

ROSE PINCUSHION

The spherical body of the *Mammillaria zeilmanniana* is densely covered in regularly arranged yellow and brown spines. The numerous flowers are produced in summer and form a ring at the top of the body. They are reddish-purple in color. Allow this cactus to form large clumps.

Mini-climate 4 Cool, sunny.
Size Individual plants grow to 2in in height but will form clumps of 10in across in around five years. Small plants are offered for sale.
Feeding Feed with tomato-type fertilizer once a month from spring to autumn.
Potting Repot in spring using two-thirds soil-based potting mixture and one-third coarse sand, but only if the plant has completely filled the existing pot.
Special points Water less during the winter rest period.

OPUNTIA MICRODASYS

RABBIT'S EARS CACTUS

These arresting cacti are made up of flattened oval segments which fit on top of one another. These segments are densely covered in tufts of tiny, yellowish spines. Yellow flowers are produced very occasionally. *Opuntia microdasys* has a spectacular outline and a large one can be used as a specimen plant. Group smaller plants in a cactus garden.

Mini-climate 4 Cool, sunny.
Size These cacti can reach a maximum height of about 3ft and spread of about 2ft. Plants of all sizes are offered for sale.
Feeding Feed with tomato-type fertilizer once a month from spring to autumn.
Potting Repot in spring using two-thirds soil-based potting mixture and one-third coarse sand, but only if the plants have completely filled the existing pot.
Special points The tiny spines can be very painful if they touch the skin. Water less during the winter rest period.

REBUTIA MINUSCULA

RED CROWN

These small, white-spined cacti are almost completely round and quickly become surrounded by many offsets. They flower when very young and are crowned with red, funnel-shaped flowers from spring through the summer. The flowers open in the morning and close in the afternoon. Mass flowering specimens together for a spectacular display in a modern setting.

Mini-climate 4 Cool, sunny.
Size *Rebutia minuscula* is fast-growing and can make clumps 6in across in a year or two.
Feeding Feed with tomato-type fertilizer once a month from spring to mid-autumn.
Potting Repot in spring using three parts soil-based potting mixture and one part coarse sand, but only if the roots have completely filled the existing pot.
Special points Do not water during the winter rest period or plants will rot.

SCHLUMBERGERA TRUNCATA

CLAW CACTUS

These jungle cacti have flattened, segmented stems which are notched at intervals. Bright-magenta, pink or white flowers are produced in late autumn. The stems are erect at first but begin to trail as more segments are produced. They make good specimen plants for hanging baskets or shelves.

Mini-climate 2 Warm, filtered sun.
Size The stems of *Schlumbergera truncata* can grow to about 2ft in height and spread. Plants of all sizes are offered for sale.
Feeding Feed with tomato-type fertilizer once a month from early November to the end of flowering.
Potting Repot every second year in spring using two-thirds peat-based potting mixture and one-third coarse sand. Once plants are in 8-10in pots repot every year.
Special points Water less during the rest period following flowering.

Similar-shaped species
Schlumbergera 'Bridgesii' is similar but blooms later and has less sharply defined notches.

SEDUM MORGANIANUM

DONKEY'S TAIL

These most unusual-looking plants have trailing stems which are densely packed with small, fat, succulent leaves. The individual leaves are a pale green, covered with a fine white bloom. Pink flowers may appear in spring, but these plants do not flower readily in the home. Ideal plants for hanging baskets, *Sedum morganianum* should be displayed in a place where they will not be brushed against, as the leaves drop off very easily.

Mini-climate 1 Warm, sunny.

Size The stems of these succulents can grow to a maximum of 3ft in length. Plants of all sizes are offered for sale.

Feeding Feeding is unnecessary.

Potting Repot every spring using a combination of one-third coarse sand and two-thirds soil-based potting mixture. They grow best in half-pots or hanging baskets where they have room to spread. Once the plants have grown too big for an 8in pot, discard the plant and grow a new one by taking and planting a cutting.

Special points Water less in winter.

Making a desert landscape

Cacti and succulents with similar growing needs can be planted together to make a miniature desert landscape. As they do not have deep root systems, they can be planted in shallow containers. If your container does not have drainage holes, line it with porous material to prevent the roots from rotting, and water the plants less than is recommended in *The A-Z of cacti and succulents*.

PLANTS
Mini-climate 4
Cool, sunny

Equipment and materials
1 *Gravel* 2 *Trowel* 3 *Coarse sand* 4 **Agave victoriae-reginae** *Queen agave (see p. 129)* 5 **Astrophytum myriostigma** *Bishop's cap (see p. 130)* 6 *Terracotta dish* 7 **Mammillaria sp.** *Mammillaria (see pp. 137-9)* 8 *Brown paper* 9 **Mammillaria bocasana** *Powder-puff cactus (see pp. 137-9)* 10 *Soil-based potting mixture*

Decorating a cactus arrangement
Large areas of potting mixture around plants look dull. Using stone chippings and shells to build up a series of decorative concentric rings in contrasting colors is simple and effective.

BUILDING UP THE ARRANGEMENT

1 *Line the container with 1in of gravel. Spread over the gravel a mixture of one part coarse sand and two parts soil-based potting mixture in a 1in layer.*

2 *With the plants still in their pots, experiment with the design. Consider any decorative pebbles which can be used on the surface of the potting mixture.*

3 *Fold up a piece of brown paper, wrap it around the spines of the cactus and lift the plant out with one hand, pulling the pot away with the other.*

4 *Lift the queen agave out of its pot and place it at the back of the dish. Plant the two bishop's caps and mammillarias, trickling the potting mixture gently around their roots.*

Decorative finishes

Most nurseries and garden centers stock a wide variety of stone chippings, pebbles and gravel that can be used to decorate the surface of the potting mixture. Marble chips can be obtained from stone masons, and aquarium dealers often have a good selection of colored pebbles. Coverings of pebbles and gravel tend to look best with cacti and succulents, since they are in keeping with the plants' arid or semi-arid natural habitat, but try out other finishes as well, such as different shaped and colored shells.

Adding a decorative finish
Using a small scoop or spoon, add a thin layer of decorative material to the top of the potting mixture.

Growing bulbs indoors

A mass of temporary flowering bulbs can make a beautiful grouping, particularly when there is little other color around. Most bulbs can be grown in containers without drainage holes, as well as conventional pots. Plant them in soup tureens, vegetable dishes, china pots or glass vases using potting mixture, or grow them hydroponically in pebbles and water.

Bulbs and corms are the food storage organs of plants which have a distinct dormant period when all top growth dies down and no further growth takes place. Bulbs are made up of tightly packed modified leaves surrounding an embryo shoot and usually a complete embryo flower. Corms consist of modified stem bases covered in thin, papery scales and do not contain the young plant, but a bud from which the shoots and roots appear. Most bulbs and corms are "hardy", in that they need a period of "wintering". Hardy bulbs are bought in their dormant state during autumn and early winter and, when potted and provided with the right growing conditions, they start to come into flower in a matter of a few weeks. These special cold (30°-45°F), dark conditions are known as wintering and it is during this period that roots are produced. To produce good flowers, the wintering recommendations for each bulb should be adhered to, as it is essential that adequate roots are established before flowering is induced. You can buy "prepared" bulbs which do not need to be kept in the dark (although they must be kept cool)

but these are more expensive. Buy bulbs as soon as you see them on sale – usually in early autumn – and plant them right away.

It should be noted that the care symbols for each entry in *The A-Z of bulbs* refer to conditions applicable when the plant is in full flower. Some corms, such as crocuses, need to be kept cool right up to the stage when the flower buds start to show color, and their early development cannot be enjoyed in the home. Most spring bulbs, such as tulips, narcissi and hyacinths, especially those treated by the nurseryman, can be potted and most of their development watched and enjoyed.

Hardy bulbs and corms provide temporary house plants but tender bulbs, such as the amaryllis, can be brought into flower season after season providing they are given a rest period in autumn.

Pots of daffodils (right)
Grass seeds have been sown on the surface of the potting mixture for decoration.

The A-Z of bulbs

The table below gives a brief description of each symbol used in *The A-Z of bulbs*. See pp. 22-3 for a detailed explanation.

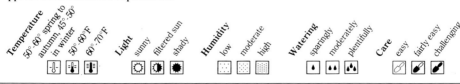

CROCUS HYBRIDS

CROCUS

The most commonly seen indoor crocuses are large-flowered Dutch hybrids which have green-and-white striped leaves and white, yellow, bronze, purple or striped blooms. These are cup-shaped and appear during winter and early spring. It is best to mass one variety of crocus in a shallow bowl.

Mini-climate 5 Cool, filtered sun.
Size Crocuses grow to about 5in in height. Dry corms are offered for sale in late summer. Pre-planted pots are offered for sale at Christmastime.
Feeding Feeding is unnecessary.
Potting Plant several corms together in early autumn, using soil-based potting mixture or bulb fiber. Plant the corms just below the surface of the potting mixture.
Special points Corms must be "wintered" for ten weeks and only brought into a warm room when the flower buds are seen.

HIPPEASTRUM HYBRIDS

AMARYLLIS

These plants have spectacular trumpet-shaped blooms borne in groups of up to four on a bare stem. Straplike leaves develop after the flowers. A large bulb may produce two flower stalks. The flowers, which are produced in spring, can be white, red, orange or yellow, and are often striped or patterned.

Mini-climate 1 Warm, sunny.
Size The flower stems of these plants grow to 20in long, with flowers up to 6in in diameter. Ordinary bulbs are offered for sale in autumn. Specially prepared bulbs which flower at Christmastime are also offered for sale.
Feeding Feed with standard liquid fertilizer every two weeks from the time the flowers fade until mid-summer. Switch to high-potash fertilizer to ripen the bulb and to ensure flowering the following year. Stop feeding from early autumn.
Potting Plant new bulbs by themselves in 4½-6in pots using soil-based potting mixture.
Special points These tender bulbs should not be "wintered". During the autumn rest period, leave the bulbs in their pots and water very sparingly.

HYACINTHUS ORIENTALIS HYBRIDS

HYACINTH

Flowers appear in spring and may be single or double, red, pink, yellow, blue or white. Their color and distinctive scent make them really welcome in the home. A group known as Roman hyacinths may produce two or even three flower stalks, but these are less tightly packed with the bell-shaped flowers. These bulbs should be massed together in a shallow bowl for the best effect.

Mini-climate 5 Cool, filtered sun.
Size The single flower stalks are 8-12in tall. Bulbs are sold according to size, from 7-9in in circumference, and the size of the flower spike depends on the size of the bulb. Specially prepared bulbs which flower slightly earlier are offered for sale.
Feeding Feeding is unnecessary.
Potting Plant the bulbs "shoulder to shoulder" in soil-based potting mixture or bulb fiber. Leave the tips of the bulbs above the potting mixture. Hyacinths can also be grown in gravel, or water alone.
Special points Prepared bulbs should be "wintered" for six weeks, ordinary bulbs for ten weeks.

IRIS RETICULATA

MINIATURE IRIS

These lovely bulbous plants produce flowers early in the season, sometimes even before the leaves have developed, although the leaves eventually become taller than the flowers. The flowers are the typical iris shape and may be light or dark blue or mauve in color, with bright-yellow markings. Each bloom rarely lasts more than two days, even if they are displayed in a cool place. However, their delicate fragrance makes it worth displaying them so that they can be appreciated close-up.

Mini-climate 5 Cool, filtered sun.
Size The flower stalks of *Iris reticulata* grow to about 6in in height, with leaves which are slightly longer. The tiny bulbs are sold dry in autumn or planted and in leaf in winter.
Feeding Feeding is unnecessary.
Potting Plant the bulbs in the autumn in a shallow container using bulb fiber. Good drainage is essential as these tiny bulbs rot very easily. Plant them 2in deep and close together – about 12 in a 12in pot.
Special points Bulbs should be "wintered" for six weeks. *Iris reticulata* can be planted outside when flowering has finished.

MUSCARI SP.

GRAPE HYACINTH

The tiny bulbs of *Muscari* sp. produce long, narrow stalks topped with an elongated cluster of tiny blue or white flowers. Each individual flower is bell-shaped, and rimmed with a frilled white edge. The clusters of flowers open from the bottom upward. The narrow leaves are strap shaped and channeled, meaning they have a definite rounded outer surface and a concave inner surface. Plant in small pots and display several of them along a windowsill.

Mini-climate 4 Cool, sunny.
Size These plants reach a height of about 6in, with leaves of nearly the same length. Bulbs already in leaf are offered for sale.
Feeding Feeding is unnecessary.
Potting Plant about twelve bulbs in a 6in pot in soil-based potting mixture or bulb fiber. Leave the tips of the bulbs showing above the potting mixture.
Special points These bulbs should be "wintered" for ten weeks.

NARCISSUS HYBRIDS

DAFFODIL AND NARCISSUS

These bulbs have bright, graceful flowers in all shades of orange, yellow, cream and white. Many different shapes are available: trumpets, clusters, double-flowered and many other forms. Both hybrids bloom naturally in late winter and early spring. Display them in bowls filled with potting mixture or bulb fiber, or grow them hydroponically in glass containers.

Mini-climate 5 Cool, filtered sun.
Size Plants grow to 6-18in in height. Bulbs are offered for sale in three sizes, "rounds" which produce one flower, "double-nosed" which produce two flowers, and "mother" bulbs which will produce three. Bulbs which produce more flowers are more expensive. Specially prepared bulbs which will flower earlier in the year are also offered for sale.
Feeding Feeding is unnecessary.
Potting Plant in early autumn in peat-based potting mixture or bulb fiber. Plant several bulbs in a pot, with the tip of the bulb showing. They can also be grown in gravel or shingle.
Special points Prepared bulbs should be "wintered" for six weeks, ordinary bulbs for ten weeks.

TULIPA HYBRIDS

TULIP

Tulips have an extraordinary variety of shapes, colors and patterns; even the leaves can be plain or variegated. The flowers are produced during late winter and early spring. It is best to plant just one variety in a pot, rather than mixing colors in the same container.

Mini climate 5 Cool, filtered sun.
Size Plants grow to about 30in tall. Dwarf varieties grow to 8-12in. Most bulbs are "rounds", producing only one flower. Specially prepared bulbs which will flower earlier are also offered for sale.

Feeding Feeding is only necessary if the bulbs are to be planted outside the following season. Feed every ten days from the time the buds appear.

Potting Plant in early autumn using either peat-based potting mixture or bulb fiber. Five or six bulbs should be planted close together, with just the tips exposed above the potting mixture.

Special points Prepared bulbs should be "wintered" for eight weeks, ordinary bulbs for ten weeks.

Planting bulb displays

Such an enormous range of hybrids is available that it is worth looking through a specialist catalog to select bulbs whose colors and shapes particularly appeal to you. For fresh color and delicate fragrance, daffodils are a good choice. Certain species, including 'Cragford' which are used here, can be grown in gravel or stones instead of potting mixture or bulb fiber. Plant them in glass containers which allow the texture of the gravel to be seen. If you plant your bulbs in October, they should be in flower by Christmas.

Indoor bulbs which flower later in the spring or in the summer include the *Hippeastrum* hybrids (amaryllis), which has huge, trumpet-shaped flowers, and several lilies including the fragrant *Lilium longiflorum* (Easter lily).

PLANTS
Mini-climate 5
Cool, filtered sun

Equipment and materials
1 Glass containers 2 Scissors 3 Black plastic bag 4 Charcoal 5 Gravel **6 Narcissus 'Cragford'** *Daffodil bulbs (see p. 147) 7 Garden twine 8 Plant ties 9 Thin stakes*

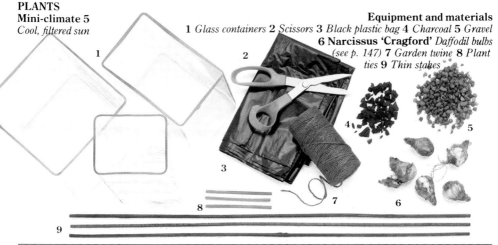

BUILDING UP THE ARRANGEMENT

1 *Mix some washed gravel with about 20 small pieces of charcoal and fill the container three-quarters full. Place each bulb in a slight depression, with their "noses" coming out. Fill the spaces between with more gravel and add water until it is close to the bottom of the bulbs.*

2 *If you use prepared bulbs, they can grow in the light, but other bulbs must be kept in the dark. Cut a black plastic bag in half, secure it around the container with garden twine or string and stand in a cool, dark place. Look at the bulbs after about four weeks to see if they need more water.*

3 *After eight to ten weeks, about ½in of growth should be visible and the bulbs can be brought out into the light. Attach any untidy leaves or bending stems to thin green stakes with plant ties. When the flowers have died, remove them and plant the bulbs outdoors.*

Making water gardens

Hydroculture is a relatively new name for an old practice of growing plants in containers filled with water and aggregate to which soluble plant foods are added. In place of soil, plants are held in position by the aggregate. The beauty of a water garden is that the plants need very little attention. Other advantages include vigorous and healthy growth, and freedom from soil-borne diseases and pests.

It is best to use plants that have already made roots in water before putting them into the new medium, since the roots made in water are quite different from those made in soil. "Prepared" plants can be bought, or you can use cuttings of soft-stemmed plants that have been rooted in water.

PLANTS
Mini-climate 1
Warm, sunny

Equipment and materials
1 *Glass containers* 2 **Scindapsus pictus 'Argyraeus'** *Pothos vine (see p. 82)* 3 **Tradescantia albiflora 'Albovittata'** *Tradescantia (see p. 91)* 4 *Miniature trowel* 5 *Aggregate* 6 *Charcoal* 7 *Pebbles*

An oriental garden
This Cyperus sp. (umbrella plant) *likes boggy conditions in the wild and is therefore a natural candidate for hydroculture.*

Materials

The basic materials for hydroculture are the aggregate, usually packed in plastic bags, and the container, which may be used on its own or have a liner.

Aggregate
The aggregate must be clean and inert and can be grit, pea-gravel, perlite or, more commonly, a purpose-made granule composed of ex-panded clay. One name given to a particular aggregate is hydroleca – "hydro" meaning water, and "leca" standing for "lightweight

BUILDING UP THE ARRANGEMENT

1 *Line the container with ¾ in of aggregate which has previously been soaked to wash away impurities. Place a layer of pebbles over it and add some charcoal in order to keep the water sweet.*

2 *Fill the container two-thirds full with aggregate. Pour in enough water to fill the container one-third full and let the aggregate absorb the water.*

3 *Place the plant inside the container and trickle aggregate around its roots. If you are moving a plant grown in potting mixure, carefully wash all traces of it away before planting.*

The finished arrangement
A Scindapsus pictus *'Argyraeus' and a* Tradescantia albiflora *'Albovittata' have been planted in aggregate decorated with pebbles to create layers of different textures in the transparent containers. Plants are fed by adding food in the form of powder or a sachet which releases nutrients into the water when they are needed.*

expanded clay aggregate". This consists of lightweight pellets of varying sizes and fairly random shape that have been fired in a rotary kiln. As a result, most of the clay has been forced to the outside wall of the pellet, leaving a honeycombed center. The great advantage of the pellets is that their outside cases conduct water from the bottom of the container, thus moistening all the pellets.

Containers
There are two main types of container that can be used – the single container and the double container. The single container may be made of any kind of watertight material (other than untreated metal that would affect the chemicals put into the water and would probably rust), ideally with a broad base to give stability. Glass is probably the best material to use. Apart from

TYPES OF CONTAINERS

Hydroculture is easy to do and virtually foolproof. Containers range from the simple bulb glass, to the more complex double container. Most plants can be grown in hydroculture and growth is usually vigorous.

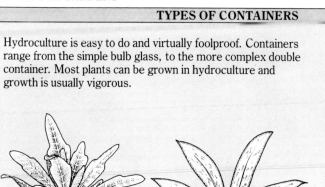

Using a bulb glass
This is a very old method of hydroculture traditionally called hydroponics. The bulb glass is specially designed to hold a column of water underneath the base of the bulb. The bulb senses the water is there and roots down into it. Use a bulb that is large enough not to fall over when the top growth appears.

Using a single container
The plant is grown in aggregate. Water is poured directly onto it and sits in a reservoir at the bottom of the container.

Using a double container
The plant is grown in aggregate, but its roots may grow out of the inner container and come into direct contact with the reservoir of water in the outer container.

looking attractive, a glass container allows you to keep a check on the water level and the amount of roots in the container.

The double container has a similar watertight outer container into which fits a smaller container. The small container hangs on the rim of the larger container and holds the aggregate and plant. The inner container is usually made of plastic and has holes or slits in its sides and base to allow air and water to circulate around the pellets and the plant's roots.

In both cases, the water should only be in the lower regions, never in the upper ones. With the single container, the bottom quarter or third of the aggregate should be submerged; with the double container, it is normally enough that the inner container, filled with the aggregate, be in direct contact with the reservoir of water. A water gauge will indicate when more water is needed.

Feeding methods

To feed plants grown in hydroculture, fertilizer is put into the water. The simplest way is to use a standard liquid fertilizer in the water used for filling the reservoir. The danger with this method is that nutrients which are not used immediately by the plants tend to crystallize out of the liquid on to the pellets and roots of the plant, and should really be washed out of the base periodically, which can be messy. It is much simpler to use a specially designed hydroculture fertilizer bonded into a pad or disc, or packed in a sachet which is placed in the water. The advantage of these pads or discs is that they do not release multi-chemical fertilizer all the time, but only when the water lacks the particular element, and so no harmful build-up of chemicals is possible.

Potting rooted cuttings in hydroculture

Cuttings from soft-stemmed plants are suitable for rooting in water. When the cuttings have made roots in water, they can be planted in hydroculture containers in much the same way as cuttings are planted in potting mixture. Hold the cuttings upright and carefully trickle the aggregate around the roots, then tap the container gently to settle the aggregate. Never bury the cuttings deeper than you would if planting them in potting mixture, and shade the planted cuttings for a few days until they have settled down in their new home. When they have made strong root growth, carefully transfer the pots to their permanent position.

Rooting cuttings in hydroculture
Cuttings of ivies, Tradescantia *sp. (tradescantias) and* Zebrina pendula *(wandering Jews) can be rooted in "nursery beds" – small pots of aggregate which stand in saucers of water to which a little ordinary fertilizer at quarter strength has been added.*

TRANSFERRING A PLANT FROM POTTING MIXTURE TO HYDROCULTURE

It is not normally recommended that you transfer a well-developed or mature plant out of potting mixture into hydroculture because of the trauma it would suffer. However, it is possible. If you do, you must wait for the old roots to be replaced by new succulent ones. Because of the shock, it will be necessary to give the plant warmth and high humidity for 10-12 weeks to aid its recovery. A heated propagator provides the best conditions, but a warm greenhouse is also suitable, provided that the air around the plant is made very humid by the use of a plastic, tentlike cover and the temperature maintained at a constant level. During this time, all of the old, soil-adapted roots will die and new, succulent ones adapted to the semi-aquatic life will be made.

1 *Using both hands, remove the mature plant from its pot, being careful not to damage the root ball. It is not advisable to use a rare or treasured specimen.*

2 *Supporting the plant with one hand, carefully tease apart the root ball, removing as much of the potting mixture as is possible without tearing the roots.*

3 *To remove the final traces of the potting mixture, wash the roots thoroughly under a gently running tap. Make sure the water is not too cold, as this will cause further trauma to the plant.*

Growing in artificial light

The use of artificial light is becoming more widespread among indoor gardeners, either as a substitute or supplement for natural light, or to allow plants to be grown in places where the light level is otherwise too low for healthy plant growth or regular flower production.

Incandescent bulbs can scorch plants if placed too close to them, and do not produce enough light for a plant's growing needs if placed the right distance away to avoid scorch. Incandescent floodlights are more effective, as they concentrate a beam of light by means of built-in reflectors, but this is still only sufficient for display purposes.

Fluorescent tubes are the most satisfactory and economical way of providing artificial light for plants in the home. They are available in several different colors; the coating on the outside of the tube determines the color of the light. If you are using a fitting with two tubes, a combination of "natural white" and "daylight" gives the closest approximation to natural light. Plants require the violet/blue and red wavelengths: "daylight" bulbs are high in blue but low in red; "warm white" and "natural white" are high in red, but low in blue. The simplest units consist of a reflector which holds one or two tubes and is supported on legs, enabling plants to be positioned underneath the lights. Multi-layered units are also available which have lights under each shelf to illuminate the plants immediately below. Alternatively, you can provide lights for plants in a bookcase or shelf-unit, or in the space between a kitchen countertop and wall-hung cabinets. It is important that any home-constructed units be fitted by a competent electrician.

Plants vary in their light needs (see pp. 181-4) in natural conditions, and equally so under artificial light tubes. If they are too close, the foliage will be scorched, if too distant they will become etiolated and flowering species will produce fewer blooms than they should. Plants grown for their flowers, such as *Saintpaulia* hybrids (African violets), need to be 7-8in from the tubes, but most foliage plants are better placed 1ft away.

To grow plants exclusively under lights, the tubes must be kept on for around 12-14 hours per day for foliage plants and 16-18 hours per day for flowering plants, unless they are short-day types – such as *Euphorbia pulcherrima* (poinsettias) – which require less light. Electric timer switches can be installed so that the lights will come on when it is most convenient. When using units to provide additional light in winter, plants should have as much normal daylight as possible, and then the tubes should be illuminated for around 5 or 6 hours in the evening.

Types of bulb (above)
*Fluorescent light tubes are the most efficient.
Incandescent bulbs are more maneuverable.*

Self-contained unit (right)
Saintpaulia *hybrids (African violets) can be encouraged to flower all through the winter in this way.*

Providing extra light

A simple unit, like this one suspended from a wooden beam, is quick and easy to install. It can light a large number of plants in places which would otherwise be too dark.

Simple but effective strip lighting

A single, 6ft long fluorescent bulb suspended from the ceiling provides uncomplicated artificial lighting for the plants below, enabling them to be grown in a place which would otherwise be too dark for healthy growth. This type of bulb generates more light per watt than any other form of lighting and wastes less of its energy as heat.

Bonsai

The word bonsai means literally "plant in a tray". It is a technique by which any tree or shrub can be turned into a dwarf specimen by restricting its growth, and by pruning its roots and branches. Developed by the Japanese and Chinese, the technique was applied mainly to hardy trees of all kinds, such as maple, silver birch, beech, larch and pine. Today, these are referred to as "outdoor" bonsai since they need to spend most of the year outdoors. They should not be brought into a heated room for more than a few days in winter, but in summer, when the temperatures inside are similar to those outside, they can be brought in more frequently. A new development is the "indoor" bonsai: these are tropical or semi-tropical species which are happy to be kept indoors all year.

All bonsai need a great deal of light and, as their roots are restricted in a very small container, they must be watered frequently, particularly in warm weather.

Bonsai can be grown from seed or cuttings, or bought as young and mature plants. If properly cared for, these trees can live for many years; their price depends on age and the complexity of the shape of the tree. They should be grown in special shallow frost-proof pots with large drainage holes which are imported from Japan.

Equipment and materials
1 Stoneware bonsai pots **2** *Green wire* **3** *Perlite and flint chippings* **4** *Bonsai wire* **5** *Garden twine* **6** *Bonsai potting mixture* **7** *Branch clipper* **8** *Root teaser* **9** *Leaf pruner* **10** *Root clipper*

An indoor bonsai (above)
This Ficus retusa *(fig) is 15 years old and its trunk has splayed roots with an interesting shape.*

Complementary shapes (left)
The smaller tree will be trained to a fan shape with a flat top to complement the taller specimen behind it.

TRAINING AND PRUNING

The Japanese have many different styles of bonsai, named according to their shape and the angle of the trunk in the pot. You can train your tree to grow in unusual shapes with wires, and by pruning the branches and leaves. To wire branches, it is best to use specially imported bonsai wire, which is very stiff, to hold branches rigid in the position you want to train them to follow. Training and pruning should be done in the very early spring, just before the new growth appears. Leaf pruning can be done all through the growing season.

1 *Loop the bonsai wire around the trunk of the tree and push it into the shape you want the branch to follow. Secure the branch to it with thinner garden wire.*

2 *Prune the stem back almost to the point at which it is wired. Cut just above the leaf axil as this is where new growth will develop.*

3 *Cut out all unwanted branches and shorten any long branches by half. Shorten all stems, and where there are multiple shoots crowded together leave just one.*

ROOT PRUNING AND REPOTTING

Established bonsai need repotting every two or three years in spring in order to replenish the potting mixture, and to restrict their roots. They should not be moved into a larger pot because this will encourage them to grow bigger. Use a special soil-based potting mixture which is well-aerated and rich enough to sustain active growth. Allow three weeks between pruning and repotting for the plant to recover its strength.

1 *Take the plant out of its pot. Remove excess potting mixture by gently teasing it from the roots with a special tool or kitchen fork.*

2 *Prune the roots with a pair of root clippers, cutting away about half the growth and removing any damaged roots.*

3 *Line the pot with perlite and flint chippings. Tie the roots up with garden twine and thread the ends through the drainage holes.*

CHAPTER FOUR

STYLING
WITH
HOUSE PLANTS

The arranging, grouping and positioning of plants is an art, not a science. It is a matter of taste, and therefore not an area in which there are hard-and-fast rules. However, there are guidelines, and it is possible to give advice on what is likely to look good and what is not. Perhaps the most important thing to remember is that every plant arrangement must be designed in context. This means taking into account not only the appearance of the plant itself, but also the container you intend to put it in (and if it is a climber, what kind of support would be most appropriate), the background against which it will be seen, the features or items of furniture by which it will be surrounded, and, of course, the compatibility of the plant with the mini-climate of the position you are proposing to place it in.

Using plants in a room
In this simple, country-style room, the traditional tiled fireplace has been filled with a variety of leafy plants to make it an attractive focus when not in use. The density of their foliage makes a strong display without swamping the small room, and the different greens pick out the colors of the tiles.

The principles of arrangement

Making an arrangement of growing plants means grouping plants together with their containers, as you might on a shelf or table-top for example, as well as placing plants in a room. Special advice for arranging plants in room settings appears in *Using house plants in the home*; the best way to begin is by looking at groupings of plants together with their planters which seem to work well.

The key to a good arrangement is that it should have visual balance. As a simple rule of thumb, a larger plant generally has more visual weight than a smaller one. However, certain plants have striking leaf color, shape or texture which attracts the eye instantly; so a small example of such a plant will usually have as much visual weight as a large example of a less dramatic plant.

SYMMETRICAL ARRANGEMENTS

Symmetry
Two identical Ficus pumila *(creeping figs) either side of an* Araucaria heterophylla *(Norfolk Island pine) create a perfectly symmetrical arrangement. If a vertical line ran through the middle of the group each side of the line would be seen to mirror exactly the other.*

ASYMMETRICAL ARRANGEMENTS

Asymmetry
The pine has more visual weight than a single Ficus pumila *and needs to be balanced by two of the latter. Space can be used to adjust balance: here, merging the two trailing plants together a little gives them more visual weight than when they are separated.*

Using contrast

If a successful arrangement is one that balances visually, what makes it not merely successful but outstanding? The answer: contrast – the setting off of opposites against one another. You can use bold contrasts of shapes and scale or more subtle contrasts of textures and colors. Compose your groups by experimenting with several different plants – choosing ones which like similar conditions – relying upon your eye to tell you what works and what does not. Restrict the contrast to just one, or at most two, elements. The effect of contrast will always be stronger if it is part of an arrangement that displays some sense of overall order and harmony.

Shape
The upright, spiky-leaved stick Yucca elephantipes *(tip yucca) contrasts with the low, rounded forms of the cacti. The strong form of the yucca gives it a visual weight that needs to be balanced by a number of small cacti. The introduction of the spiky-leaved but low-growing* Agave victoriae-reginae *(queen agave) on the left creates a pleasing visual link between the two dominant elements in the composition.*

Texture
The filigree lightness of the large Adiantum raddianum *(delta maidenhair fern) has a similar visual weight to the dense mass of the* Peperomia caperata *leaves (emerald ripple peperomia) because of the different sizes of the plants. The plants balance visually simply by being placed side-by-side.*

Scale (left)
*The three plants in this group
share the same sort of shape and
the same sort of texture – they are
all spiky-leaved. Yet they vary
enormously in scale. The small*
Agave victoriae-reginae *(queen
agave) is only a few inches
high, whereas the large* Yucca
elephantipes *(stick yucca) rises
to a height of about 5ft.
Their similarity in shape and
texture, and the fact that they are
displayed in all-white containers,
serve to emphasize the contrasts in
scale. Another way of using
contrasts of scale effectively is to
group plants in a row – along a
mantelpiece or shelf, for example
– using plants of the same kind
but of different heights.*

Color (below)
Three pink Begonia *'Elatior'
hybrids (elatior begonias) are
offset by a single white-flowered
variety. Another way of using
color is to juxtapose a plant with
variegated leaves with a flowering
plant that picks up one of the
colors in the leaves.*

Lighting plants

The chances are that your plants are seen as often in the evening, when they are lit by artificial light, as they are during the day. In addition to background lighting, you can use directional lighting to highlight plants and flowers. This type of lighting, where the beam of light is narrow enough to pick out a single object, throws plants into relief, accentuating shape, defining color and emphasizing texture. Dramatic effects can be achieved through the interplay of light and shade created by directional lights, and the most ordinary of plants can be made into something outstanding. Another consideration is the quality of light that you want. Incandescent tungsten bulbs, which are the most popular, give out a warm light which emphasizes yellows and reds; while tungsten halogen bulbs give out a more concentrated beam of colder light. To increase the warmth of a light, buy color-coated bulbs or translucent shades in warm colors. Plants should not be placed right next to the light source, as the heat transmitted by the bulb will damage the leaves.

Natural light
Light acts on the green pigment chlorophyll, which is present in all plants, to start the process called photosynthesis. The violet/blue and red wavelengths are most important for plant growth: the blue stimulates foliage and the red flowering. Incandescent bulbs are low in blue wavelengths and have only a limited effect on plant growth; but there are special lights which can be used as a substitute for daylight (see pp. 154-5).

The amount and quality of daylight that a plant needs depends upon its original habitat in the wild. Some plants need full sunlight, some prefer filtered light, which can be given by diffusing daylight with Venetian blinds, lace or muslin, and others prefer indirect light. The quality of the natural light in your room will, of course, dictate the areas in which you can display your plants.

Sun on a windowsill
A symmetrical group of a white Streptocarpus *sp. (Cape primrose) set between two carved birds.*

Training climbing plants

Climbing plants need to be provided with some kind of support in order for them to grow upright. Plants that use aerial roots to climb, such as *Philodendron* sp., *Monstera deliciosa* (Swiss cheese plants) and *Scindapsus pictus* 'Argyraeus' (pothos vines), like to grow over a constantly moist medium. A pole made out of wire netting stuffed with sphagnum moss is an excellent, sturdy support, and particularly suitable for climbing plants with thick stems and large leaves. Plants which climb by means of curly leaf tendrils, such as *Passiflora caerulea* (passion flowers) and *Hedera* sp. (ivies), can be trained on canes, wire hoops and trellis work.

Training plants in the house

Climbing plants can be trained up a blank wall, to make it an attractive feature, and trained around mirrors, doors and windows, to frame them with fresh greenery. To provide support for the plant, string runs of wire or strong nylon cord between nails or screw eyes, and then attach the plant to the support with plant ties, to help maintain the shape that you want.

Equipment and materials
1 *Bamboo sticks* 2 *Sphagnum moss* 3 *Terracotta half-pot* 4 *Drainage dish* 5 *Peat-based potting mixture* 6 *Trowel* 7 *Wire* 8 **Philodendron scandens** *Heartleaf philodendron (see p. 74)* 9 *Chicken wire* 10 *Roll of corrugated paper* 11 *Wire cutters* 12 *Tamping stick*

PLANTS
Mini-climate 3
Warm, shady

Making a moss-pole

Moss-poles can be bought ready-made, but if you make your own with wire netting you can provide far moister moss for the roots of climbing plants. You will need about three or four small climbing plants to grow up a moss-pole about 3ft high. Once it is made, it is very important that you keep the moss constantly moist. If you do not, the aerial roots will not grow into it and the plant will die.

BUILDING UP THE ARRANGEMENT

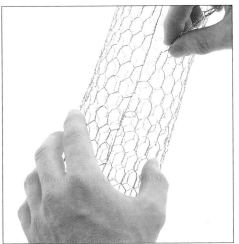

1 *To form the shape of the moss-pole, take a roll of corrugated paper and wrap chicken wire around it. Cut the wire so that it is 2in wider than the paper. Join the two cut edges together to form a column shape.*

2 *Cut two lengths of bamboo, thread them through the netting about 1½ in from the bottom. Lash them together where they cross each other, and to the wire column, then wedge them into the pot.*

3 *Fill the pot two-thirds full with potting mixture. Start to fill the empty column of chicken wire with sphagnum moss, using a wooden stick to pack it together tightly. Continue until full.*

4 *Pot the heartleaf philodendrons and attach their stems to the pole with wire, bent so that it forms a hairpin shape.*

5 *Water the sphagnum moss and the potting mixture well before putting the moss-pole in a warm, shady position. Spray the pole every day to keep the moss thoroughly moist.*

Making a wire support

Many plants suitable for indoor use are rampant climbers in the wild. They are often bought trained around a wire support which is soon outgrown. It is then a good idea to open the plant out and train it around a larger support which will show off foliage and flowers more effectively. Try to match the scale of the plant to the scale of the support: here *Passiflora caerulea* were trained around wire hoops which suited the delicate tracery of the plants' foliage.

Rattan canes

Bamboo stakes

Bamboo trellis

Rattan hoop

Plastic trellis

PLANTS
Mini-climate 1
Warm, sunny

Equipment and materials
1 **Passiflora caerulea** *Passion flower (see p. 70)* 2 *Clay pellets*
3 *Plant ties* 4 *Wire* 5 *Pliers*
6 *Glazed ceramic container*
7 *Soil-based potting mixture*

Other ornamental supports
Using bamboo, rattan or wire you can make many different shapes of support. Bamboo stakes can be made into trellis or, for a more unusual effect, into obelisks. Rattan is flexible and can be used to make any sort of rounded form.

BUILDING UP THE ARRANGEMENT

1 *Cut two lengths of wire of the same size to form two hoops. Place them in the container to check that they are in scale with it. Put the hoops to one side. Place a piece of broken shard over the drainage hole in the bottom of the pot.*

2 *Line the pot with 1in of vermiculite or clay pellets and fill three-quarters full with potting mixture. Repot a passion flower, firming potting mixture around its roots. Place one hoop in the pot and wind the plant's stems around it.*

3 *Place the other wire hoop in the container at a 90 degree angle to the other and attach them together with plant ties. Remove any dead leaves or unwanted shoots as you go. Plant the last passion flower, training one stem up the remaining bare hoop.*

The finished arrangement
Covering one hoop less thickly than the others made the arrangement a more interesting shape. It also gave it a lightness of effect which will make the transitory opening of the curious flowers more visible. You will need to tie in the shoots very regularly in order to maintain the overall shape of the display. If you cut the plants back, as far as the main stems, at the beginning of winter and put them in a cool, frost-free place they should grow back again in the spring.

Matching plants to interiors

Few of us have the opportunity of designing a room from scratch – in one go selecting all the materials, furniture, decorative objects and plants needed to create a recognizable style of interior decoration. In spite of practical limitations on the scope of your ideas, it is well worth looking at how plants can be used to evoke and enhance particular decorative styles. Plants and flowers are an integral part of many styles, often being the inspiration for decorative motifs of all kinds. On the following pages you will find an analysis of some of the most popular contemporary styles of interior decoration, combined with advice on what types of plants and flowers are most suitable to display with them.

Country style

Country style seeks to bring the garden into the house. Flower patterns are everywhere – on wallpaper, curtains, cushions and china – and can be given added freshness by the presence of fresh flowers. Country style can be formal or relaxed, suitable for the town as well as the country. Objects do not have a particular place but rely on number to create a comfortable, lived-in atmosphere. Nostalgia for rural values is an important ingredient of this style which prizes wooden furniture, homely designs, natural fabrics and warm colors.

Elements of country style
Color is more important than shape in country style. Here, foliage and flowering plants with a soft shape complement the patterns found on wallpaper, china and fabric, as do the fresh flowers which are those commonly found in an old-fashioned garden.

Oriental style

The Far East has been a source of inspiration for decoration over several hundred years. As a decorative style it can be interpreted in a number of different ways, since each area – China, Malaya and Japan – has its own recognizable national style influenced in part by the indigenous flora.

Elements of oriental style

A key element in oriental style is the concentration on a few simple shapes and large areas of neutral color, offset by focal points of bright color. Here, the contrast in texture between the coarse-weave bamboo mat and the glistening lacquer table is typically oriental. The feathery Cyperus sp. (umbrella plant) suggests bamboo, while the vivid Aeschynanthus lobbianus (basket plant) adds a more tropical Malaysian feel to the group.

Contrasting textures in the Japanese style

The spiky leaves of the bonsai are echoed by the floating chrysanthemum heads, and the harsh texture of the rock is offset against the smooth ceramic plate.

Ethnic style

The many manifestations of what can be termed "ethnic" style reflect the traditional cultures of various groups throughout the world. It is based on artefacts made by traditional methods and characterized by the use of lively patterns, which can be abstract or figurative.

Elements of ethnic style
Plants with a strong outline and solid shape are needed to stand up against the abundance of patterns in the decorative scheme of this room. Cacti are an obvious choice, particularly with objects of South American origin as shown here. Plants should be chosen in warm colors in order to harmonize with the colors of natural dyes.

Art deco

The art deco style of the 1920s and 1930s is still a source of inspiration for interior decoration. It is characterized by the use of strong geometric forms, monochromatic colors and reflective surfaces, such as chrome and lacquered wood.

Elements of art deco
Plants with a strong outline are needed to complement the hard lines and solid forms of this style. Here, the hard-edged shape of the sculpture is repeated in the form of the lily flowers. The linear form of the silvery-mauve Ceropegia woodii *(rosary vine) in the ceramic light fitting is silhouetted against the wall*

High tech

This is a style based on utilitarian shapes and industrial materials. Decoration is minimal and the overall effect is hard and clinical-looking; it is the antithesis of anything organic. Plants need to have a vigorous outline, and flowers must be strong in color so that they are not swamped by gleaming metallic surfaces and vibrant primary colors.

Elements of high tech
Suitable plants are those with a great deal of visual weight, such as large agaves, yuccas and cacti. Here, the plants have a well-defined shape and foliage whose plain green color goes well with the red container and flooring.

Using house plants in the home

Potted plants and flowers have been used to decorate rooms since as early as the seventeenth century, but it was the start of the nineteenth century that saw a vast influx of exciting new plants into Europe and America. This was when the first painted-leaved begonias, paper flowers and a large array of tropical foliage plants arrived, and those who could afford them began to display them in their homes and conservatories. However, it is only recently that an enormous range of plants have become available to everyone.

The following pages show how plants can be actively incorporated into the decorative scheme of a room, rather than featuring merely as added extras. Each room in the home has a different function and its practical use will determine the sort of environment, or *mini-climate*, it can offer to plants. Each room also has a specific mood and plants can be used to enhance this particular atmosphere.

The period of your house and the style of your room will determine the way in which you display your plants. A traditional interior calls for plants to complement an existing setting and, for instance, co-ordinate with fabrics or a collection of objects. A modern interior may call for plants to be used in an architectural way, as an integral part of the landscaping of the room.

The setting and overall styling
This is an attractive corner, but the decor shades are muted and monotone, and something bright and colorful was needed to guide the eye towards the large window. The solution was found in Cyclamen persicum *hybrids. The arrangement needed to be large, without dominating the corner. To continue a period feel, a pair of Victorian dolls and a small footstool were added. The red of the footstool and the velvet pillow picks up the exact red of the plants.*

Living rooms and bedrooms

For most people, the living room is the showpiece of the home and the room in which most entertaining takes place. A considerable amount of money may be spent on furnishings, fabric and general decoration. On the other hand, the bedroom is a highly personal part of your house and one where you can indulge your most imaginative ideas about decoration. Plants provide a restful background and fresh colors, and should enhance the room layout.

Living rooms usually contain large items of furniture, and plants should be of an appropriate size to counterbalance them: one or two large ones usually look much better than a clutter of smaller ones. Arrangements of small-scale plants can be used for incidental groupings on coffee tables, end tables and shelves. In a bedroom, if space is a problem, consider fixing up a hanging arrangement in the form of a garland, or using a pedestal to support a plant arrangement in one corner. Position your plants away from radiators or fireplaces, in an area which provides adequate light for their specific needs, and where you can water them easily.

MAKING A PLANT GROUPING FOR A CORNER OF A ROOM

Part of creating a comfortable, inviting living space is building up one or more attractive seating areas. Whether these are in the corners of the room, at one end, or in alcoves, window bays and recesses, house plants can play a large part in making the most of them. Plants can highlight a fabric, either by forming a total contrast or by echoing colors and patterns in the curtains or soft furnishings. Alternatively, the shape and form of plants can enhance and soften these settings.

Here a little period piece has been composed to accompany the easy chair and draped curtain. The site is a corner of a living room decorated in neutral shades, next to an east-facing window. Since the room is not in constant use, and therefore not always heated, the plants must be suitable for a cool room. When you are aiming to create a particular atmosphere like this, you may find that certain of your most treasured possessions suggest themselves as "props".

PLANT KEY

Spider plant

Japanese fatsia

Cyclamen

English ivy

Purple grapes

PLANTS
Mini-climate 5
Cool, filtered sun

Making up the arrangement
A plastic tray was used in which to stand the various pots, so that the plants could be watered according to their individual needs. The arrangement was planned around the two Cyclamen persicum *hybrids (cyclamen), making sure they were offset by the solid greenery of the* Fatsia japonica *(Japanese fatsia). Then a spiky green* Chlorophytum comosum *(spider plant) was added to provide outline interest, and the whole effect was lightened with trailing stems of variegated* Hedera helix *hybrids (ivies) to mask the edge of the table. Finally, just for fun, a bunch of grapes were included, and these actually had the effect of "lifting" the green/red/beige color scheme.*

Bathrooms

The relaxing surroundings of a bathroom can form a stylish setting for some of your more striking plants, and matching containers to the bathroom fixtures ensures a successful display.

Provided that they have good light, bathrooms come nearest to providing the ideal growing conditions for a number of the most popular house plants. They are generally warm places and, two or three times a day, the air becomes saturated with moisture. Quite a high level of humidity can continue for some time after someone has taken a bath, while damp towels dry out and moisture on surfaces and fabrics gradually evaporates. Even if obscured glass is fitted to windows, there is little light loss; in this case, direct sunlight becomes bright, filtered light.

DISPLAYING AIRPLANTS IN A BATHROOM WINDOW RECESS

Airplants make a fascinating display in a bathroom. Most bromeliads are native to the tropical regions of the Americas, where they cling to rocks or trees. Their roots are used merely for support – the plants survive on the moisture contained in the atmosphere, so be sure to spray them regularly with rain water or distilled water.

Making up the arrangement
Single airplants are difficult to display well; the best approach is to mass them together. A collection of shells and coral provides decorative support for the plants and gives them an under-water look suitable for the bathroom. Tuck or gently tie the plants into the shells, or use a special airplant adhesive; in time they will attach their roots to the support.

PLANTS
Mini-climate 1
Warm, sunny

Kitchens

Kitchens can be of two types: working galley kitchens and kitchens to live in. By definition, the countertop surfaces are practical and do not lend themselves to too much decoration – add to this the hazards of steam and constantly changing temperatures and you may not have ideal growing conditions. However, some plants will prefer the added humidity and warmth of the kitchen. Window-sills can often be utilized, but plants must be protected from the fall in temperatures at night if there is no double glazing. Plants can be displayed in hanging baskets, but only in places where it is easy to water them frequently.

In a compact kitchen, the chances are that you will not want any plants cluttering up your valuable countertops. Yet it seems a shame to do without greenery, and there are several ways of solving the problem practically and safely, while keeping plants off surfaces and away from kitchen appliances.

DECORATING A KITCHEN HUTCH

A collection of blue-and-white china looks very appealing set out on the shelves of a traditional country hutch. But perhaps the scene is a little stark. Kitchen hutch shelves are quite narrow and normally used for display, rather than as functional shelves for much-used items. So a kitchen hutch is an ideal "showcase" for plants, provided you observe the rules of lighting and watering, and change the plants when necessary.

Making up the arrangement
The areas of white wall behind the hutch looked rather austere and needed some "filling in". But introducing a random collection of plants would interrupt the subtle styling of the kitchen. As a solution, five plants of the same variety were selected – the Solanum capsicastrum. *Its orange berries provide a color-contrast, without being too distracting to the eye, and complement the china collection. They need a relatively humid environment and should be misted regularly. Transfer the plants to a sunnier position for a few hours every day to give them the direct light that their position on the hutch prevents them from getting.*

PLANTS
Mini-climate 4
Cool, sunny

Mini-climates

Throughout this book a system of mini-climates has been used to identify the different environments offered by the average home. Each plant featured in *The A–Z of house plants, The A–Z of cacti and succulents* and *The A–Z of bulbs* has a mini-climate reference indicating its optimum levels of heat and light. This need not be interpreted too rigidly; a great attribute of many of our most popular house plants is that they are able to tolerate a wide range of growing conditions.

Mini-climate advice may need to be adjusted in some cases. For instance, plants grown in the middle of a large city receive a lower quality of light than that found in the country, so plants that thrive in the country in filtered sun may need direct sunlight to do well in the city. Day length varies with latitude, as does the outside air temperature.

Winter sunshine will not harm any plant grown in temperate latitudes, and one that ideally needs filtered sun when the sun is high may need direct sunlight in winter, when the sun is weaker and days shorter.

Very few plants will suffer if placed in a slightly higher temperature than that recommended – as long as higher levels of humidity, and probably a little more water, are provided. Water plants less if you grow them cooler than the given mini-climate, and remember that it is much better to underwater than to overwater.

Very high summer temperatures often cannot be brought down without the aid of air conditioners, which dry the air. A high level of humidity, adequate watering and frequent mist-spraying will all help to counteract this but, in any case, do not keep plants near an air conditioner.

When choosing plants to group together in the home, it is not enough merely to consider their decorative qualities; if the display is to remain attractive, you must also ensure that the mini-climate requirements of the plants are compatible. A plant which likes direct sunlight can be happily placed next to a plant that likes filtered light, but it is not sensible, for instance, to group a tropical shade-lover with a temperate flowering plant.

MINI-CLIMATE 1

Warm, sunny

A *warm* room is one kept at a temperature of 60°-70°F – the range preferred by many popular house plants – but all plants can tolerate a slightly higher, or lower, level for a short time. A normal heating system prevents temperatures from falling below 60°F.

A *sunny* position is one that gets direct, unobstructed sunlight for part of the day. A plant standing in or very near to a south-facing window is in a sunny position; those in east- or west-facing windows tend to receive less sun each day.

MINI-CLIMATE 2

Warm, filtered sun

A *warm* room is one kept at a temperature of 60°-70°F – the range preferred by many popular house plants – but all plants can tolerate a slightly higher, or lower, level for a short time. A normal heating system prevents temperatures from falling below 60°F.

A room receiving *filtered sun* may face south, east or west (or south-east or south-west) but direct sunlight is screened by translucent blinds or curtains, a tall building or leafy tree outside a window.

MINI-CLIMATE 3

Warm, shady

A *warm* room is one kept at a temperature of 60°-70°F – the range preferred by many popular house plants – but all plants can tolerate a slightly higher, or lower, level for a short time. A normal heating system prevents temperatures from falling below 60°F.

A *shady* position, in our definition, receives no direct or filtered sunlight, but does not have "poor" light (which is too low for healthy plant growth). Plants that like some shade can be grown away from the window in a room that is well-lit, or, alternatively, in the window of a room that is not well-lit.

MINI-CLIMATE 4

Cool, sunny

A *cool* room is one kept at a temperature of 50°-60°F. This is the range preferred by many temperate zone plants, although plants from warmer climates may also be able to thrive – and temporary flowering house plants often live longer – at these temperature levels.

A *sunny* position is one that gets direct, unobstructed sunlight for part of the day. A plant standing in or near to a south-facing window is in a sunny position; those in east- or west-facing windows receive less sun.

MINI-CLIMATE 5

Cool, filtered sun

A *cool* room is one kept at a temperature of 50°-60°F. This is the range preferred by many temperate zone plants, although plants from warmer climates may also be able to thrive – and temporary flowering house plants often live longer – at these temperature levels.

A room receiving *filtered sun* may face south, east or west (or south-east or south-west) but direct sunlight is screened by translucent blinds or curtains, or a tall building or leafy tree outside a window.

Mini-climate 3
Ferns like the warm and humid conditions of a bathroom, and small shelves above a basin surround make a suitable home for various potted specimens including an Asplenium nidus *(bird's nest fern).*

· CHAPTER FIVE ·

PLANT CARE AND PROPAGATION

Outdoors, plants are able to fend very much for themselves, needing only occasional assistance on our part. In the indoor garden, however, plants depend on us to meet all their needs: we decide what level of light and humidity they are given, the quantity and regularity of watering and feeding, how big a root-run they should be allowed, and what the minimum winter temperature should be. Successful gardeners and those whose house plants thrive are said to have a green thumb. Certainly some people seem to have a built-in feel for what plants need, and how they should be cared for. There is, however, no mystery about growing plants successfully; good results can be achieved by anyone who is prepared to understand the needs of particular plants and establish a routine for taking care of them.

Caring for plants in the home
By following simple guidelines and common sense, almost all house plants will thrive in any home. The profusion of flowers and the healthy leaves of these Sinningia speciosa *hybrids (gloxinia) and* Streptocarpus *'John Innes' hybrids (Cape primrose) indicate that they are enjoying the correct care and environment.*

Requirements for healthy plants

The plants we grow in our homes come from temperate, sub-tropical and tropical areas where widely differing growing conditions exist. For example, some are exposed to direct sunlight, others are protected from the fierce rays of the tropical sun by neighboring plants or are given some shade from over-hanging trees, while still more grow on the forest floor in considerable shade. This diversity of natural habitat explains why different plants require different conditions when grown indoors.

Having said this, however, the ability to adapt to unfamiliar conditions is a major reason for the popularity of many common house plants. Most generally dislike widely fluctuating temperatures, although a drop of temperature at night is natural and preferred by most plants in the home. Cool conditions during the day (when heating may be turned off) followed by much warmer conditions during the evening (when heating may be turned on) are therefore against the natural pattern, but house plants have proved to be very adaptable to the varying conditions of the home. Of course, some are inevitably more resilient than others.

There is much pleasure and fulfilment to be derived from growing and caring for house plants. Maintaining healthy and attractive plants does not involve complicated or time-consuming procedures but just sensible and sensitive attention to the plants' basic needs. To thrive, plants need adequate light at the preferred intensity and for the right duration, a comfortable temperature, and the right level of

Basic tools and equipment for the indoor gardener

atmospheric humidity. They have to be watered when they start to dry out a little, and some need a dormant period during the winter when the water supply needs to be curtailed – allowing the plant to rest and often encouraging flower-bud production. Food must be provided, the right kind of growing medium made available and, as the roots fill the pots, plants will need potting on. These and other needs are described in the sections that follow.

Light

Light is essential to all plants. Without enough light, growth suffers, and leaves become small and pale. Healthy growth depends on the process of photosynthesis which produces carbohydrates and is triggered by the action of light on the green pigment chlorophyll. This pigment is present in red, bronze, purple and gray leaves as well as green ones; the other color is just an overlay to the green beneath. Variegated-leaved plants, however, are at a disadvantage as the yellow, cream or white sections on their leaves contain no chlorophyll. For this reason, variegated-leaved plants generally need brighter light if their strong leaf color contrast is to be maintained.

Indoor light levels

Plants in their native habitats have adapted to a wide range of different light levels. Indoors, you should try to provide the light intensity preferred by each plant as far as possible. To do this, you need to assess the amount of light present in various parts of any particular room. This can be difficult because the human eye is not a good judge of light intensity; it

BASIC TOOLS
The basic tools and equipment you need for indoor gardening: **1** *Fork* **2** *Trowel* **3** *Wooden stakes* **4** *Pruners* **5** *Wooden plant supports* **6** *Anvil pruner* **7** *Bamboo stakes* **8** *Scissors* **9** *Knife* **10** *Twine* **11** *Long wire ties* **12** *Powdered fertilizer* **13** *Terracotta pots* **14** *Hormone rooting powder* **15** *Fertilizer spikes* **16** *Drip saucers* **17** *Stub wires* **18** *Short wire ties* **19** *Paintbrush* **20** *Mist-sprayer* **21** *Liquid fertilizer* **22** *Plastic plant ties* **23** *Pesticide dusting powder* **24** *Liquid fungicide* **25** *Pesticide aerosol spray* **26** *Watering can*

SIGNS OF ILL-HEALTH

Slow or sluggish growth
If symptom occurs during summer months: –
Are you overwatering? (see p. 192)
Are you underfeeding? (see p. 195)
Does the plant need repotting? (see p. 203)
If symptom occurs during winter months: –
Is this a natural rest period?

Wilting
Is the potting mixture very dry? (see p. 191)
Are you overwatering? (see p. 192)
Is there adequate drainage? (see pp. 198-9)
Is the location too sunny? (see p. 184)
Is the temperature too high? (see p. 185)

Drooping leaves and wet soil
Are you overwatering? (see p. 192)
Is there adequate drainage? (see pp. 198-9)

Brown leaf tips/spots on leaves
Are you overwatering? (see p. 192)
Is the plant too close to the sun or another source of heat? (see pp. 185-6)
Is the humidity level too low? (see p. 187)
Is the plant standing in a draft? (see pp. 185-6)
Are you overfeeding? (see pp. 195-6)
Have you splashed water on the leaves? (see p. 189)

Falling flowers, leaves and buds
Are you overwatering? (see p. 192)
Are you underwatering? (see p. 191)
Is the temperature inconsistent? (see pp. 185-6)
Is the light inconsistent? (see pp. 183-5)
Is the humidity level too low? (see p. 187)

Variegated leaves turning green
Is the plant getting enough light? (see pp. 183-5)

Rotting at the leaf axils
Has water lodged in the axil? (see pp. 189-91)

Leaves turn yellow
If growth is straggly: –
Are you overwatering? (see p. 192)
Is the plant getting enough light? (see pp. 183-5)
Is the temperature too high? (see pp. 185-6)
Are you underfeeding? (see p. 195)
Does the plant need repotting? (see p. 203)
If leaves fall off the plant: –
Are you overwatering? (see p. 192)
Is the plant standing in a draft? (see pp. 185-6)
Is the humidity level too low? (see p. 187)
Is the temperature too low? (see pp. 185-6)

PHOTOSYNTHESIS

This is the process undertaken by the parts of plants containing the green pigment chlorophyll, in which light energy is used to produce carbohydrates from water and carbon dioxide. During daylight hours, carbon dioxide is taken from the air through the pores (stomata) of the leaves. Photosynthesis occurs through the action of light on the chlorophyll in the leaves. The light energy is used to split water molecules into oxygen and hydrogen. The hydrogen combines with the carbon dioxide taken in through the stomata to form carbo-hydrates, such as glucose, which provide the plant with food. Certain minerals are required for these chemical reactions, and these are taken up, with water, by the roots. The flow of oxygen and carbon dioxide is reversed as the plant respires or "breathes".

Light

Carbon dioxide and light enter the plant through the upper and lower leaf surfaces.

Oxygen

Water vapor

Carbon dioxide

Oxygen and water vapor are expelled into the air as by-products of photosynthesis.

Water

Minerals

Water and minerals from the potting mixture are absorbed by the roots and used to produce sugars by photosynthesis.

compensates for different light levels to give the impression of even overall lighting. The only really accurate way of measuring light intensity is to use a small hand-held photographic light-meter, or a camera with a built-in meter, which both give a good indication of light levels. You will probably be surprised at how low the levels of light are indoors: on a south-facing windowsill your plants will only get about half as much light as they would if they were growing outside, due to reflection from the glass. And as little as 3ft into the room there is only about three-quarters as much light as at the window. However, most popular house plants are extremely tolerant, their adaptability being the main reason for their popularity.

Day length

In addition to intensity, light duration or day length is an important factor in determining how much light a plant receives. Most plants

need about 12 to 16 hours of daylight to sustain active growth. Foliage house plants fall into two main groups: those that stop growing in the late autumn and need resting during the winter, and those that will continue to grow throughout the winter and remain attractive. Foliage plants from the tropics, which in the wild receive around 12 hours of sunlight each day throughout the year, will only continue to grow all the year round in temperate regions if they are given as much light as possible in winter, by using supplementary artificial light, and are kept in a warm room. Plants from more temperate regions stop growing (or slow down their growth very considerably) with the onset of winter and a shorter day.

In general, flowering plants need more light than foliage plants in order to initiate flower bud production and to allow the buds to develop properly. In many plants, flower production is triggered by day length. These plants fall into two groups: long-day plants and short-day plants. Long-day plants flower when they have received more than 12 hours of light a day over a certain period. (It does not matter whether the light is natural or artificial – *Saintpaulia* hybrids (African violets) can be induced to flower at any time of year under artificial light.) Short-day plants flower when they receive less than 12 hours light a day over a certain period. *Euphorbia pulcherrima* (poinsettias), *Chrysanthemum* hybrids (chrysanthemums), *Rhododendron simsii* (azaleas) and *Schlumbergera* sp. (claw cacti) are short-day plants which flower naturally in the autumn, but *Chrysanthemum*

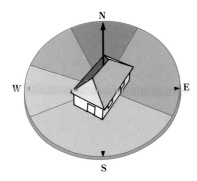

Light intensity and orientation
Levels of light intensity striking a house from all points of the compass. The lighter area corresponds to the strongest light, and the darkest area to the weakest, (assuming the sun is shining from the south). By finding out the orientation of your house, you will be able to place plants in appropriately lit positions.

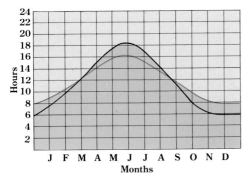

Daylight levels
In northern regions (B) plants receive more but less intense daylight in summer and less adequate light in winter than those further south (A).

hybrids can now be bought all through the year because growers can simulate the short day and initiate flower production by covering the plants in black plastic for the requisite number of hours each day. Many plants appear to have no strong preference with regard to day length, and flower through most or all of the year. These are known as day-neutral plants.

How plants seek light
All plants turn their leaves towards the source of light, except for stiff-leaved species such as *Sansevieria* sp. (mother-in-law's tongue), many palms and *Dracaena* sp. (dracaenas), and rosette-shaped bromeliads. Rooms with white or pale walls will reflect light back on to plants, whereas those decorated in darker colors absorb light and will cause plants to turn towards the window. To counteract this natural tendency, and to promote balanced, upright growth, you should turn your plants around frequently.

Suitable light levels for different plants
In *The A-Z of house plants, The A-Z of cacti and succulents* and *The A-Z of bulbs*, the light preference of each plant is indicated by one of three symbols. These stand for sunny, filtered sun and shady, described in detail below.

Sunny A sunny position is one that gets direct sunlight for all, or part of, the day. South-facing windows will receive sunlight for most of the day, east-facing windows receive sunlight for several hours in the morning, and west-facing ones for several hours in the afternoon. The strength of the sunlight will depend on latitude and on the orientation of the room. South-facing rooms receive more intense light, but in summer it reaches less far into the room than in east- or west-facing rooms. At the coast where light is brighter due to reflection from the sea, some form of shading may be necessary at a large south-facing window in summer, to prevent possible leaf scorching and too-frequent drying out of the potting mixture. This type of bright light is most suitable for plants such as desert cacti, succulents from open bush or savanna, hard-leaved bromeliads from the tree-tops and certain sun-loving flowering plants.

Filtered sun Filtered sun is direct sun that has been filtered through a translucent curtain or blind, or screened by a tree or building outside. This level of light is also found between 3 and 5ft from a window which receives sun for all, or part of, the day. Although no direct sun falls here, the general level of brightness is high. Filtered sun is about a half to three-quarters as intense as direct sunlight. If you are in any doubt about the amount of light your plant needs, place it in filtered light, as few plants like direct, hot summer sunlight. In general, too little light is less harmful than too much light. Palms, tropical rain forest plants, and shrubs, including *Dracaena* sp. (dracaena), *Cordyline terminalis* (ti plants), and *Dizygotheca elegantissima* (false aralias), and soft-leaved bromeliads, such as *Guzmania lingulata* (scarlet stars) and *Vriesea splendens* (flaming swords), prefer this kind of light, as it is similar to the dappled light of their native forest.

Levels of light intensity in a room
Different levels of light in a typical room, in the northern hemisphere, on a summer day when direct sunlight is not obscured by clouds. In lower latitudes the light would be brighter, but would extend less far into the room. Obviously, the amount of light entering a room will be affected by local factors such as the number and size of the windows, and the presence of nearby buildings and trees.

Curtains absorb light, reducing the levels on either side of the windows.

East- or west-facing windows get good light all day and direct light for a few hours. South-facing windows receive direct sun for much of the day.

Blind for shading plants on the windowsill from hot summer sun.

Dracaena sanderana
Belgian evergreen

Asplenium nidus
Bird's nest fern

Yucca elephantipes
Stick yucca

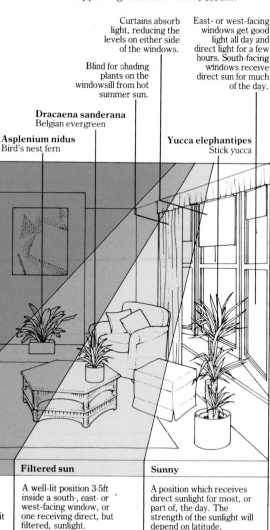

Poor light	Shady	Filtered sun	Sunny
An area more than 6ft away from the source of light. No plant will thrive here, even though the area seems to be bright.	A moderately-lit area 5-6ft away from a sunny window, usually along a side wall or near a well-lit north-facing window.	A well-lit position 3-5ft inside a south-, east- or west-facing window, or one receiving direct, but filtered, sunlight.	A position which receives direct sunlight for most, or part of, the day. The strength of the sunlight will depend on latitude.

Shady This position is one that receives no direct or indirect sunlight, yet does not have poor light. This level of light is found in, or just a little distance from, a well-lit north-facing window. It is also found in shaded areas within sunny rooms – for instance, along side walls – where the plant is well out of reach of direct sunlight, yet no more than 5-6ft from a sunny window. Shady positions receive about a quarter as much light as sunny ones. This amount of light suits plants from low-down in the jungle canopy where they are shielded from the rays of direct sun. However, day length in tropical jungles is considerably greater than that in northern hemispheres in winter, and you may need to move shade-loving plants nearer to the source of light during our winter. In a shady position, flowering plants, or foliage plants with variegated leaves, will lose most of their leaves, and those that remain will lose their variegation.

Temperature

House plants have a preferred temperature range in which they thrive, and usually another that they will tolerate. Most popular house plants are from tropical and sub-tropical areas and do best in a temperature range of 60°-70°F. (Seeds usually germinate best when temperatures reach 64°F or more; and tip-cuttings and divided sections root well at 64°-75°F.) Other types of plants – evergreens and flowering species – prefer cooler conditions in the range of 50°-60°F. These are the two temperature ranges described by the mini-climates in the A-Zs of house plants, cacti and succulents, and bulbs as "warm" and "cool". Although these are the conditions to which the plants are best suited, they will almost certainly be tolerant of slightly higher or lower temperatures for part of the time.

Monitoring temperatures (below)
It is always a good idea to monitor temperatures. The photograph shows a simple thermometer and a minimum/maximum thermometer which measures the daily fluctuation in temperature by recording the highest and lowest levels reached.

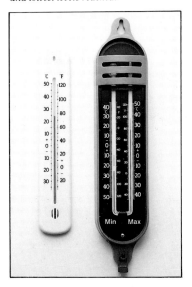

Variable temperatures (below)
This typical kitchen does not have a uniform temperature, and this factor should be borne in mind when positioning plants.

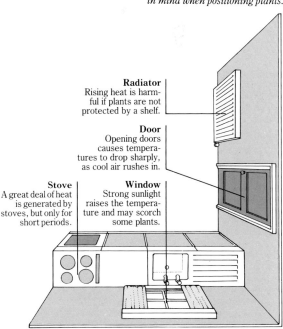

Radiator
Rising heat is harmful if plants are not protected by a shelf.

Door
Opening doors causes temperatures to drop sharply, as cool air rushes in.

Stove
A great deal of heat is generated by stoves, but only for short periods.

Window
Strong sunlight raises the temperature and may scorch some plants.

Plants that grow naturally in cool places will grow faster when given higher temperatures. Some may adapt and thrive, perhaps growing more quickly than is convenient indoors, although the blooming period of certain short-term flowering plants is greatly reduced if they are given higher temperatures than they need. It is rare that plants from a warm place do well in much cooler conditions.

In general, a fall in temperature of 5°-10°F at night is natural in the wild and advisable if plants are kept indoors. Some plants, such as cacti, can tolerate a much sharper fall, but fluctuations of more than 15°-18°F between daytime and night-time temperatures should be avoided in the home.

Winter- and spring-flowering bulbs must have their "wintering" at around 40°-50°F – a period when root growth is encouraged and active top growth discouraged. In addition, many house plants, especially evergreen species, require a winter rest period, away from the steady winter warmth of most domestic rooms. If possible, it is best to set aside a specific room which can be kept reasonably cool for several months.

Humidity

Humidity is the amount of water vapor contained in the air. It is affected by changes in temperature: warm air is capable of carrying more moisture than cold air, and it will cause water to evaporate from all available sources, including the leaves of plants. The amount of water in the air is measured on a scale of "relative" humidity – that is, the amount of water in the air compared to saturation point at a given temperature. 0 per cent equals absolutely dry air and 100 per cent equals absolutely saturated air. A relative humidity of at least 40 per cent is a requirement for most plants. To maintain this degree of humidity, a greater amount of water will need to be present in warm air than in colder air.

Cacti and succulents are used to a level of around 30-40 per cent, but the average tolerant house plant does best with a level of around 60 per cent. The thin-leaved jungle plants, such as *Adiantum raddianum* (delta maidenhair ferns) and *Coleus blumei* (painted nettles), however, are happiest with a level

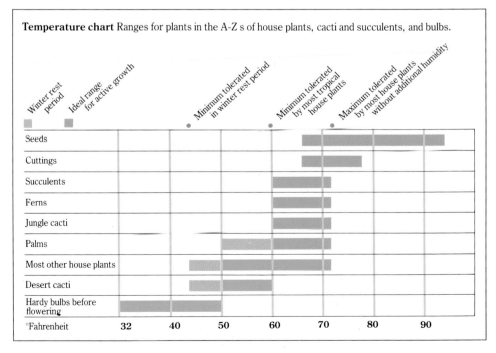

Temperature chart Ranges for plants in the A-Z s of house plants, cacti and succulents, and bulbs.

	Winter rest period	Ideal range for active growth		Minimum tolerated in winter rest period	Minimum tolerated by most tropical house plants	Maximum tolerated by most house plants without additional humidity
Seeds						
Cuttings						
Succulents						
Ferns						
Jungle cacti						
Palms						
Most other house plants						
Desert cacti						
Hardy bulbs before flowering						
°Fahrenheit	32	40	50	60	70	80	90

WAYS OF INCREASING HUMIDITY

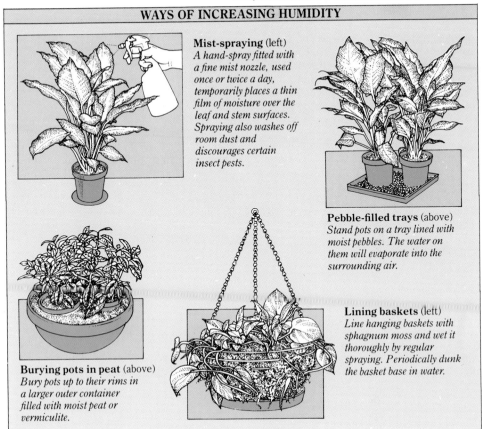

Mist-spraying (left)
A hand-spray fitted with a fine mist nozzle, used once or twice a day, temporarily places a thin film of moisture over the leaf and stem surfaces. Spraying also washes off room dust and discourages certain insect pests.

Pebble-filled trays (above)
Stand pots on a tray lined with moist pebbles. The water on them will evaporate into the surrounding air.

Lining baskets (left)
Line hanging baskets with sphagnum moss and wet it thoroughly by regular spraying. Periodically dunk the basket base in water.

Burying pots in peat (above)
Bury pots up to their rims in a larger outer container filled with moist peat or vermiculite.

nearer 80 per cent. These three figures correspond to the "low", "medium" and "high" humidity categories given in the A-Zs of house plants, cacti and succulents, and bulbs. The relative humidity level of the average living room with the heating switched on, but with no humidifying device, is only around 15 per cent so the air in bathrooms and steamy kitchens makes them better homes for most plants than living rooms.

Signs of humidity deficiency

There are a number of signs which indicate that a plant is suffering from a lack of humidity: its leaves may begin to shrivel or show signs of scorching – watch out for the drying out of leaf tips on plants with long, narrow leaves, such as *Chlorophytum comosum* (spider plants) and palms; other indications are that the buds may fall off, or flowers may wither prematurely.

Plants lose moisture from the tiny pores (stomata) of the leaves. These open during the day to take in carbon dioxide from the air but, at the same time, water from the tissues of the leaves escapes; this process is known as transpiration. Low levels of humidity mean that plants lose more moisture through transpiration. House plants grown in warm rooms, therefore, suffer all the disadvantages: the warm air encourages them to grow, but "sucks" moisture from their leaves and causes water in the potting mixture to be taken up more quickly, making more frequent watering necessary. You can alleviate this condition by increasing the humidity.

How to increase humidity

Portable humidifiers powered by electricity can be bought to increase the level of humidity throughout the room. These are effective –

keeping humidity levels between 30 and 60 per cent in heated homes – benefiting people and furniture as well as plants. Growing several plants in proximity helps to make the air around them more humid, as moisture transpired by one plant increases the humidity for its neighbor. Arrangements of plants in bowls and large containers therefore offer good growing conditions. Other methods of increasing humidity include mist-spraying and standing plants on trays of moist pebbles.

The ultimate solution for those plants which must have a very high level of humidity is to grow them in closed or almost-closed containers such as bottle gardens and terraria.

Watering

In the wild, water appears as rain, mist or fog and is taken up mainly by the root system. Plants in the home are reliant on us to meet all their watering needs. Water is essential to all plants; without it they will die. The length of time this takes may vary from one day for young seedlings to several months in the case of a succulent plant, but death will always occur eventually. Water acts as a transport medium, in the way blood does for animals, and it is also essential for the process of photosynthesis, which supplies the plant's food. Water from the potting mixture is passed by the roots to all parts of the plant, carrying with it the nutrients vital for the food-manufacturing process. It charges stems and leaves and makes them sturdy and plump (turgid); without it they cannot stay erect. Any shortage of water results in stems and leaves becoming limp and drooping, flowers fading quickly, and buds falling before they can open. A temporary drought often means that leaves shrivel and turn brown at the edges and the tips, making the plants look unattractive.

When to water

Knowing when to water can be difficult but, as a general rule, you should water potted plants when they need it. This may seem to be an over-simplification, but it is accurate. The real problem is to judge when that is. Drooping leaves and limp stems are obvious signs that

WATERING CHECKLIST

Plants needing plenty of water

- Plants which are actively growing.

- Plants with delicate-looking, thin leaves, e.g., *Caladium hortulanum* hybrids (angel wings).

- Plants in very warm rooms, especially those near windows in summer.

- Plants with many large leaves that clearly transpire a lot of water.

- Plants that have filled their pots with a mass of healthy roots.

- Plants that are grown in relatively small pots.

- Plants grown in dry air.

- Plants from bogs and marshy areas, e.g., *Cyperus* sp. (umbrella plants).

- Plants grown in free-draining potting mixes, including peat-based mixtures.

- Plants in clay pots.

- Plants with budding leaves and young flower blossoms.

Plants needing less water

- Plants which are resting and those without buds or flowers.

- Plants with thick, leathery leaves, e.g., *Ficus elastica* (rubber plants).

- Plants grown in cooler rooms, especially during winter.

- Plants which are succulent and therefore naturally adapted to store water for future use, e.g., cacti; they transpire much less than more leafy plants.

- Plants that have recently been repotted and whose roots have not yet penetrated through all of the mixture.

- Plants that are given a high level of humidity, e.g., ferns, and those grown in a shady position or in bottle gardens and terraria.

- Plants grown in water-retentive potting mixtures, including soil-based mixtures.

- Plants grown in plastic and glazed clay pots.

- Plants that have thick, fleshy roots or water-storing sections on their roots.

more water is needed, but you should not wait for such an advanced stage to be reached. There are more subtle signs: some plants' leaves take on a paler, translucent look when water is needed; on others, the flower buds dry and shrivel. Each plant has its own watering needs, dependent on its size, its natural environment and, most importantly, the time of year; actively growing plants need a lot of water, the same plants can manage with much less during the winter rest period. Never water routinely just because someone tells you to water every so many days. It is far better to test the potting mixture first, as this will indicate whether or not the plant needs watering. "Weighing" the pot in your hand regularly can also give an indication of the amount of water in the potting mixture; a mixture that is saturated with water weighs more than one that is dry. This method is reliable, but it takes a little practice to gauge whether or not the plant needs water, and is not always practical with larger plants in bigger pots. Moisture gauges are available which record on a dial the exact moisture content of the potting mixture. Readings such as "wet", "moist" or "dry" can be seen at a glance and allow you to act accordingly. Quite simple small indicator "sticks" or probes can be bought which are pushed into the mixture and change color according to the moisture content. Generally, play safe and, if in doubt whether to water, wait a day or two before making the decision. This is because, though both under- and overwatering can cause damage to plants, overwatering is probably more usually fatal (see also pp. 191-2). In the A-Zs of house plants, cacti and succulents, and bulbs, three symbols have been used to indicate the correct amount of water to give each plant shown; these recommend watering plentifully, moderately or sparingly. A detailed explanation of the three main instructions is given overleaf.

How to water

Most plants prefer to be given a really thorough drink, and like the dose to be repeated only when a given amount of the potting mixture has dried out. To water frequently in dribbles is bad practice. To give too little often means that the water never reaches the lower layers of the mixture which become compacted around the roots; and to give too much often results in a waterlogged potting mixture. Waterlogging forces air out of the potting mixture and provides ideal conditions for the action of bacteria and fungi that will rot the roots of the plant.

METHODS OF APPLYING WATER

Topwatering
Pour water on the surface of the potting mixture; this gives more control over the amount of water the plant receives and flushes away any excess mineral salts which may have accumulated.

Watering from below
Stand the pots in saucers filled with water. This method forces mineral salts to the upper layer of the potting mixture, but these can be flushed away with an occasional topwatering.

Bromeliad watering
Empty any water out of the cup-shaped central reservoir of the plant and pour in fresh water with a narrow-spouted watering can.

WATERING SPARINGLY

Give enough water at each watering to barely moisten the potting mixture throughout. Do this in several stages, adding a little water each time. Never give so much water that it appears in any quantity through the drainage hole in the bottom of the pot. When watering from below, put no more than ¼in in the saucer at a time.

1 Test the potting mixture with a stake. It is time to water when approximately two-thirds of the mixture has dried out.

2 Add just enough water to the surface of the potting mixture to allow percolation without water appearing in the saucer.

3 Test again with the stake. Add a little more water if you find any dry patches. Never leave water in the saucer.

Type of water to use

Tap water is safe to use on most plants, even though it can have a high lime content. It is always best to apply it when it is tepid, or at least at room temperature; stand a can filled with water overnight in the same room as the plant, to allow the water to reach room temperature and some of the chlorine to dissipate. Ideally, the water should be as lime-free as possible. Rain water is good if you live in the country but, if collected in cities, it is liable to be polluted by chemicals. Water can be boiled (and allowed to cool) for the real lime-haters such as *Rhododendron simsii* (azaleas); distilled water is also lime-free, but rather expensive for use on anything but the

WATERING MODERATELY

This involves moistening the mixture all the way through, but allowing the top ¼-1in to dry out between applications. When watering from below, stand pots in ¼in of water and repeat until the surface of the potting mixture becomes moist.

1 When the potting mixture feels dry to the touch, give the plant a moderate amount of water.

2 Pour on enough water to moisten, but not saturate, all of the potting mixture.

3 Stop adding water when drops start appearing from the drainage hole. Pour away any excess water from the saucer.

WATERING PLENTIFULLY

This involves keeping all of the potting mixture moist and not letting even the surface of the mixture dry out. Give enough water at each watering to let some flow through the drainage holes at the bottom of the container. If watering from below, keep re-filling the saucer until no more water is taken up. Half an hour is usually sufficient.

1 *When the potting mixture feels dry to the touch, give the plant plenty of water.*

2 *Flood the surface of the potting mixture with water until it flows through the drainage hole in the base of the pot.*

3 *Empty the saucer under the pot once the excess water has drained through the potting mixture.*

most precious of plants. Do not use water from any ordinary domestic water-softener, as this is full of chemicals and can cause damage.

Possible watering problems

If the instructions in the A-Zs of house plants, cacti and succulents, and bulbs are followed, your plants should receive the right amount of water. However, there can be problems if plants are underwatered, or overwatered – particularly during the winter rest period.

Underwatering

Underwatering can still occur if you apply water "little and often", as the plant may need a large dose of water to thoroughly soak its roots. Should the potting mixture get over-dry (this happens particularly readily with peat-based potting mixtures), it can shrink appreciably, leaving a gap between root ball and pot sides. Any water applied to the plant just runs quickly away. The only solution is to soak the pot in a bowl or bucket of water until the mixture has swollen up again and the gap closed. The symptoms of underwatering are easily recognized and can often be arrested in time to save the plant. Plants particularly susceptible to problems if underwatered are those with succulent-looking stems, such as *Coleus blumei* (painted nettles), *Impatiens* sp. (impatiens), and all *Primula* sp. (German primroses) and *Selaginella* sp. (selaginellas).

DANGER SIGNS

Too little water

- Leaves rapidly become wilted and limp.
- Leaf growth slows.
- Lower leaves become curled or yellow in color.
- Lower leaves fall prematurely.
- Leaf edges become brown and dried-out.
- Flowers fade and fall quickly.

Too much water

- Leaves develop soft, rotten patches.
- Leaf growth is poor.
- Leaves become curled or yellow in color, and their tips brown.
- Flowers become moldy.
- Young and old leaves fall at the same time.
- Roots rot away.

Overwatering

The symptoms of overwatering can take much longer to show themselves than those of underwatering. Again, watering "little and often" can lead to overwatering. Many plants need to start to dry out before they can be re-watered and, if the potting mixture is kept permanently wet, the mixture soon becomes waterlogged. A warning sign that your mixture is waterlogged is the presence of green moss on the surface, since it will only grow in a constantly wet medium. Waterlogging leads eventually to plant death. The first indication that something is wrong with the plant is when a few leaves fall or become yellow, or when the plant makes poor growth. The lack of air and excess of water in the potting mixture cause the roots to become rotten, and cut off the supply of water and food to the plant. To save an overwatered plant, carefully remove it from the pot and check the roots; if they feel soft and come away easily, they are rotten and best removed. Replace the plant in the pot with some fresh potting mixture containing at least 25 per cent sand to aid drainage. Plants susceptible to problems if over-watered include many of the cacti or succulents, whose bodies or leaves are adapted to store water.

REVIVING A PARCHED PLANT

If a plant does become parched and dried-out, it is often best to cut back the top growth and wait for next year's growth. If, however, you rescue it just in time, you could try the following emergency treatment.

Root ball problems (below)
Often, the root ball has shrunk away from the sides of the pot so that any water given runs away. Alternatively, the potting mixture often becomes compacted so that water cannot penetrate it.

Dried-out root ball

Compacted root ball

1 This plant has clearly wilted, as the drooping leaf and flower stalks are much too limp to support themselves.

3 Immerse the pot in a bucket filled with water until the air bubbles cease to rise from the potting mixture. Use a mist-sprayer on the leaves.

2 Begin reviving the plant by using a fork to break up the dried-out potting mixture. Do not injure the roots.

4 Allow any excess water to drain away, and put the plant in a cool place. Within a few hours the plant should begin to revive and stand up again.

Some plants, however, thrive on plenty of water. Their natural habitat is the swamp or bog and, consequently, their potting mixture should always be kept saturated.

Watering in winter
At some time during the twelve month season, most plants need a period of rest. Many should be fed and watered more sparingly than during the rest of the year, others need no food or water at all. The rest period is brought on by the reduction in the amount of light available to plants that occurs naturally during certain months (so it coincides with winter), and to give too much water at this time stimulates growth which is not supported by adequate light. This results in poor, and often moldy growth, browning of leaves and early leaf fall.

Watering while away
Going away on vacation can present problems if you have a collection of healthy house plants and no-one to take care of them. An absence of just a few days should not cause any harm to your plants; if they are given a thorough watering and moved into a cool room, they should quite happily survive. Increasing the

TEMPORARY SELF-WATERING METHODS

Temporary wicks (left)
Simple wicks for short-term use can be made using water-absorbent materials such as oil-lamp wicks, cotton shoe-laces or old pantyhose. Place one end in a reservoir of water and the other firmly in the potting mixture.

Covering with transparent material (below)
Plants can be put into large plastic bags or into purpose-made domes. Respiration and photosynthesis produce water vapor which condenses on to the sides. Only use this method for short periods.

Capillary mats (above)
Place the capillary mat on a drainboard or a shelf next to the bath and let at least half of it trail into the sink, or bath, which should be filled with water. As the mats are made of thick felt or felt rubber, the water will be carried up to the plants. The plants then take up what water they need by capillary action. Use capillary mats for plants in plastic pots; the thinness of a plastic pot and the many holes in its base allow the easy passage of water. Clay pots are too thick – the pot tends to absorb the water, rather than passing it to the plant.

humidity by installing a portable humidifier, or by placing your plants on a tray lined with moist pebbles can also help at this time (see pp. 187-8). For longer periods, some form of self-watering system is required so that your plants do not suffer or even die.

Certain of the methods shown below and on the preceding page are better suited to plants in plastic pots; others are suited to plants in clay pots, as they need a larger, more constant supply of water. Automatic methods of watering are not suitable for plants in containers without drainage holes because of the risk of water-logging the potting mixture. Happily, such containers are usually glazed and, therefore, water loss is much less than with porous clay pots, which tend to absorb any available water. Plants in these kinds of containers should be well watered before leaving on vacation, placed out of direct sun or strong light and stood on trays filled with moist pebbles or even a thick wad of wet newspaper – either of which will improve the humidity and allow a plant to survive drought.

MAKING A "SELF-WATERING" WICK

This type of wick, made in a similar way to a temporary wick, is actually embedded in the potting mixture and is suitable for permanent or long-term use. It enables the plants to take up their water needs automatically, by capillary action, and saves the grower time and effort, particularly if the plant is in a position that makes regular watering inconvenient or awkward, such as a high shelf.

Some growers "wick" their plants throughout the year. However, regular checks should be made to ensure that the plant is not being overwatered (during the plants' rest period, for instance) or under-watered by the wick. If this happens, remove the wick immediately.

These wicks are suitable for plants in either clay or plastic pots. The reservoir can be any container which will safely support the plant pot and should be covered by a lid (pierce a hole to thread the wick through) to prevent the water from evaporating.

1 *Carefully remove the plant from its pot, taking care not to damage the stem or root ball in any way as you do so.*

2 *Make a wick using a strip of cotton or nylon material. Push it through one of the holes in the bottom of the pot.*

3 *Carefully push one end of the wick up into the root ball using a thin cane or a pencil.*

4 *Lower the plant back into the pot. Stand the pot over a reservoir, ensuring that the "tail" extends into the water.*

Feeding

Plants are capable of manufacturing their own food but, in order to do so, they must have a supply of light, minerals and water. Minerals are present in garden soil and in most potting mixtures, and manufactured fertilizers are made up of a mixture of the minerals that plants need to carry out the essential processes in photosynthesis. The plant does all the work of converting the raw materials to form the food it needs for healthy growth (see p. 182). When plants are bought ready potted, sufficient minerals should already be in the potting mixture to last the plant several weeks. Soil-based potting mixtures contain loam, which is normally rich in nutrients. Their main advantage is that they release minerals over a period of several months, so plants grown in these mixtures will last longer without supplementary feeding than those grown in peat-based potting mixtures. However, the loam content of soil-based mixtures may vary considerably in its nutrient value.

Peat-based potting mixtures were introduced because of their convenience and efficiency. They contain a mixture of peat moss and sand to which is added perlite and vermiculite. The mixture has no food value, but some manufacturers add nutrients to the base and, by looking at the list of ingredients on the packet, you can check whether or not they are present. The nutrients that are added are of the slow-release kind and should be sufficient to feed the plants for around eight weeks. However, some nutrients are soon leached away from the mixture by regular watering, or are used up quickly by the plants, so it is advisable to start giving supplementary feeds to plants grown in peat-based potting mixture about six weeks after purchase, or eight weeks after repotting.

Signs of a hungry plant

A hungry plant has an unhealthy "washed-out" look. Hunger signs are very slow – or a lack of – growth; weak stems; small, pale or yellowing leaves; lower leaves falling before they should, and few or no flowers. Ideally, plants should not be allowed to reach these extremes before you notice that they need feeding.

How often to feed

The A-Zs of house plants, cacti and succulents, and bulbs recommend the feeding frequency for each featured plant. Fertilizer should only be applied during the active growth period, since feeding during the rest period will result in pale, spindly growth.

"Each-time feeding" is practiced by many specialist growers. It involves feeding at every watering with a considerably reduced strength of feed (half or quarter strength). This is a way of keeping a constant but weak supply of food always available – which is particularly important to plants that are grown in relatively small pots, and in peat-based potting mixture. It also prevents an unnecessary and harmful reserve of nutrients from building up.

New plants or recently repotted plants will not need feeding for some time: those in soil-based potting mixture should not need feeding for about three months; plants in soilless mixture (peat-based, etc.) will need feeding after about six weeks.

The feeding tips given in the A-Zs of house plants, cacti and succulents, and bulbs assume that you are looking for the maximum of strong and vigorous growth. In some cases, you may feel that you would like to keep a plant at about its present size, but in a healthy state. Three

FEEDING CHECKLIST

Too little fertilizer

- Slow growth, with little resistance to disease or attack by pests.

- Pale leaves, sometimes with yellow spotting.

- Flowers may be small, poorly colored or absent altogether.

- Weak stems.

- Lower leaves dropped early.

Too much fertilizer

- Wilted or malformed leaves.

- White crust on clay pots and over the surface of the potting mixture.

- Winter growth is lanky while summer growth may be stunted.

- Leaves may have brown spots on their surface and scorched edges.

feeds of standard liquid fertilizer spread over the active growth period (roughly, mid-March, mid-June and mid-September) would keep most plants healthy without encouraging rampant growth.

Feeding guidelines

• Fertilizer is not medicine for an ailing plant; feeding will often only make matters worse. If a plant looks unhealthy, examine it for possible causes, including pests and disease, before dosing it with fertilizer.

• Overfeeding can do as much damage as underfeeding. Feed only at the strength (or much less) given in the instructions on the fertilizer label.

• Feed no more frequently than recommended on the label or in the A-Z s of house plants, cacti and succulents, and bulbs.

Types of fertilizer

Fertilizers can be bought in many different forms: as liquids, soluble powders and crystals, pills or tablets and "spikes" or "pins". Liquid fertilizers, bought in concentrated form, are very convenient, as the bottles are easy to store and the contents need only to be diluted with water. Water-soluble powders and crystals are also easy to handle and only need a thorough stirring in the prescribed amount of water to be dissolved completely. "Spikes" and "pins" are cards impregnated with chemicals that release foods when watered. These are often called slow-release fertilizers, as they work over a period of three to six months,

slowly giving up their stored minerals. Their disadvantage is that they tend to produce "hot-spots" – concentrations of food around the pill or "spike" – which can burn nearby roots. In addition to fertilizers applied to the potting mixture, there are foliar feeds: fertilizers that are diluted with water and then sprayed on to the leaves of those plants which do not readily absorb minerals through their roots. Foliar feeds act very quickly, and have an immediate tonic effect on any plant which looks starved. Always follow the instructions given on the packet, as an excessive amount of fertilizer can damage roots and leaves.

What fertilizers contain

Balanced growth relies on three essential minerals. Nitrogen (supplied as nitrates) is vital for producing energy-forming chlorophyll, and healthy leaf and stem growth. Phosphorus (supplied as phosphates) allows healthy roots to develop. Potassium (supplied as potash) is essential for fruiting and flowering and the general sturdiness of the plant. The packaging of fertilizers always indicates the relative chemical contents (shown as percentages) of the three main foods and many mention other ingredients, such as iron, copper and manganese, often under the general heading of "trace elements". The three most important elements may be spelled out fully, as nitrogen, phosphorus and potassium, or be given the codes N, P and K. Sometimes, only the percentage numbers of these minerals appear, but the coding is always arranged in the same order to avoid confusion.

EFFECT OF FERTILIZERS

Fertilizer	Supplied as	Effect	Use
N Nitrogen	Nitrates N	Manufacture of chlorophyll. Active leaf and shoot growth.	All foliage house plants, especially at start of growing season.
P Phosphorus	Phosphate P_2O_5	Healthy root production. Flower bud production.	All house plants, especially those grown for their flowers.
K Potassium	Potash K_2O	Healthy formation of leaves; flower and fruit production.	All flowering house plants, bulbs and plants grown for their berries.
Trace elements	Iron, zinc, copper, manganese, magnesium	Essential processes such as photosynthesis and respiration.	All house plants.

METHODS OF FEEDING

The method of feeding depends upon the type of plant you have and the form of fertilizer you have chosen to use. If you are using liquid fertilizer, or powders and crystals which have to be mixed with water, apply when watering the plant in the normal way. Before giving any type of food, ensure the potting mixture is already moist – to add food to dry soil is to risk root damage by "burning" with high concentrations of minerals. Foliar sprays are best applied with a mist-sprayer, used outside or in the bath-tub to avoid inhalation and marking furnishings. This type of food is rapidly absorbed, and will act very quickly on a plant with unhealthy foliage. Fertilizer pills are very convenient as they can be inserted into the mixture and left to release their food gradually. Spikes, on the other hand, can be easily removed if a plant would benefit from a period without the stimulus of fertilizer. Feeding mats are also available; these are placed underneath the pot and the nutrients they contain are absorbed into the potting mixture.

Slow-release spikes
As they tend to produce "hot-spots" of concentrated fertilizer, push the spike in at the edge of the potting mixture. Water well to help dissolve the food.

Foliar sprays
Always dilute to the correct concentration before spraying over both sides of the foliage with a mist-sprayer because they are readily absorbed.

Liquid fertilizers
Add to the water you would give the plant at its normal watering time. These can be applied either from above or from below.

Slow-release fertilizer pills
These should be pushed deep into the potting mixture with the blunt end of a pencil without damaging the roots.

What to feed

Fertilizers suitable for use with house plants are usually ones with an even balance of the essential nutrients. These are known as standard or balanced fertilizers and will promote generally good growth in most plants. There are, however, specialist fertilizers for more specific purposes. High-nitrate fertilizers encourage healthy leaf growth and are suitable for foliage plants. High-potash fertilizers are often called "tomato-type" fertilizers because they are used for tomatoes when they start to flower and fruit; these are useful for encouraging flowering and fruiting house plants that have reached a similar stage. High-phosphate fertilizers build up a strong, healthy root system and encourage the formation of flower buds, although foliage growth is slower.

Pots and potting mixtures

Most house plants are sold in plastic pots, as this is the cheapest way of packaging them, but many other kinds are available including traditional, unglazed clay pots, and purpose-made ceramic and china pots. They should never be filled with soil from a garden as it is full of bugs, disease spores and weed seeds, and its chemical content and physical make up are uncertain.

Types of pot
Almost any domestic container can be used to display plants effectively (see pp. 104-8), but they may not all provide ideal conditions for healthy growth. Purpose-made containers will have one or more drainage holes to allow any excess water to drain away. In all pots, from the smallest available (with a diameter of 1½in) to the largest (with a diameter of 12in) the depth of the pot is equal to the rim diameter.

It is possible to grow plants directly in bowls and other containers without drainage holes, but they need to be lined with drainage material and greater care is required when watering to prevent roots from rotting.

Potting mixtures
House plants should be grown in ready-prepared potting mixtures or a do-it-yourself mixture based on one of the standard prepared mixes. The contents of these have been very carefully tested as to their suitability to particular plants, and the ingredients have been sterilized to kill off unwanted visitors. The range of potting mixtures may seem large but a few basic potting mixtures will provide for the different needs of all the house plants featured in this book; details are given in the A-Zs of house plants, cacti and succulents, and bulbs. There are two main mixtures, soil-based and peat-based. Soil-based mixtures have a heavy texture suitable for large plants; although sterilized, the soil contains some micro-organisms which break down organic matter into essential minerals, thus maintaining soil fertility. Peat-based mixtures are lighter and cleaner to handle but they often do not contain any built-in nutrients, so regular feeding is still necessary.

The depth of the pot *Measured from the lip of the lip to the base, this is equal to the diameter.*

The diameter of the pot *Measured at the rim, this is equal to the depth.*

Types of potting mixture
The basic mixes are loam (soil) or peat. Specialized mixtures contain added ingredients. Additives for the mixes can be bought separately for home-made potting mixtures.

Bromeliad potting mixture A very open, porous mixture which suits the shallow root system of the bromeliads, high in humus and almost lime-free. A suitable home-made mixture consists of half coarse sand or perlite and half peat moss. Specialist growers add other ingredients to the above mixture, including chunky pieces of partly composted bark chips (available in small bags) and pine needles (sometimes available locally) – all ensure that excess moisture drains away swiftly.

Bulb fiber Use only for indoor bulbs; it does not contain enough nutrients for other pot plants. It gives good drainage which is essential to prevent bulbs from rotting. A suitable home-made mixture consists of six parts peat moss, two parts crushed oyster shell and one part charcoal.

Fern potting mixture A high-humus mixture, containing perlite or sand, and charcoal to keep it well drained. A suitable home-made mixture consists of three-fifths peat-based potting mixture and two-fifths coarse sand or medium-grade perlite. Add one cup of charcoal granules to every quart of the mixture and add a balanced granular or powdered fertilizer (according to the instructions on the pack).

Peat-based potting mixture A lightweight, standardized mixture, containing very few nutrients. A suitable home-made mixture consists of one-third peat moss, one-third medium-grade vermiculite, and one-third coarse sand or medium-grade perlite. Add two tablespoonsful of dolomite limestone powder to every two cups of the mixture to counteract the acidity of the peat.

Soil-based potting mixture A very heavy mixture suitable for large, established and top-heavy plants. A suitable home-made mixture consists of one-third sterilized fibrous loam, one-third medium-grade peat moss, leaf mold or bark chips and one-third coarse sand or fine perlite. A balanced fertilizer should also be added to the mixture.

Useful additives

Aggregate Made of clay pellets, it has excellent water-retentive properties and is used for hydroculture and to provide drainage.

Bark chips Hold water and added fertilizer.

Charcoal Absorbs excess minerals and waste, keeping the mixture "sweet".

Coarse sand Opens up potting mixtures for better aeration and drainage.

Dolomite limestone powder Acts to reduce the acidity of potting mixtures.

Eggshell/oystershell Reduces the acidity and assists drainage of potting mixtures.

Humus (leaf mold) Retains nutrients and gives an open texture.

Limestone chips Reduces the acidity and assists drainage of potting mixtures.

Manure Used as a dried powder, cow manure is nutrient rich.

Peat moss Holds water and added fertilizer very well.

Perlite Gives potting mixture an open texture for aeration and drainage.

Sphagnum moss Has excellent water-retaining properties.

Sphagnum peat moss A peat moss derived from the decay of sphagnum moss.

Vermiculite Absorbs and retains nutrients and water.

Bromeliad potting mixture

Soil-based potting mixture

Bulb fiber

Peat-based potting mixture

Charcoal

Fern potting mixture

Aggregate

Perlite

Vermiculite

Sphagnum moss

Repotting and potting on

Plants in gardens have a free root run. Their roots spread as far as they need to in search of water and food. With a few exceptions (bromeliads and other epiphytic plants), most wild plants have roots that run under the surface of the soil, where some moisture and food is usually present and where the soil temperature (which is cool) stays fairly constant. By contrast, the roots of house plants are confined within a relatively small container. Young, healthy plants quickly fill their pots with roots, and then find that there is nowhere else for them to go but through the hole in the bottom of the pot, or over the surface of the potting mixture. A clear indication of this is when the mixture dries out quickly and needs very frequent watering and feeding. "Potting on", or planting in a larger pot, is then necessary.

Sometimes it is not obvious just by looking at plants that they need potting on, so you must take them out of their pots and examine the root ball and root system. Look to see whether the roots have penetrated all the available potting mixture; if they have, it is time to move the plant into a larger pot – usually the next size up; if not, return the plant

to its original container. Some plants thrive in small pots, in which case the plant should be put back in the same pot with some fresh potting mixture. This is known as "repotting", but the same term is often used to describe moving a plant to a larger pot.

When the maximum pot size has been reached, or if the plant is very large, the potting mixture can be revitalized by removing the top couple of inches and replacing it with fresh mixture containing added fertilizer. This is called "topdressing".

As repotting and potting on can be messy, it is best to deal with several plants at the same time, protecting furniture and the floor with newspaper.

Removing plants from their pots

This can be very awkward if plants are large, an unusual shape, or have sharp spines. Water the plant thoroughly an hour before the operation; this will help it slide out of the pot more easily, avoiding root damage. It will also hold together the potting mixture around the plant's roots. Make sure all the pots are clean, and soak any new clay pots until the air bubbles stop rising; this will ensure the pot will not absorb water from the potting mixture. Repot the plant as quickly as possible to avoid drying of the roots.

REMOVING A PLANT FROM A SMALL POT

1 *Carefully place the palm of one hand on the surface of the potting mixture with the main stem of the plant lying between your fingers.*

2 *Turn the pot upside-down and gently tap the pot edge on the side of a table in order to loosen the plant enough for the whole root ball to come out easily.*

3 *The plant and its root ball should then slide out without difficulty into your hand keeping the root system intact.*

REMOVING A PLANT FROM A LARGE POT

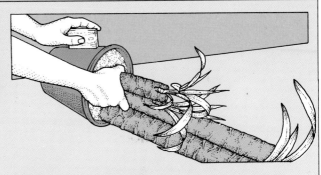

1 *Gently run the blade of a blunt knife or spatula around the edge of the potting mixture.*

2 *Lay the pot on its side and tap it with a block of wood to loosen the potting mixture. Rotate the pot slowly, tapping it on all sides. Support the plant with one hand while doing this.*

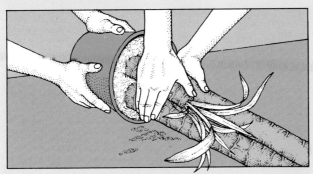

3 *Make sure the plant is completely loose before attempting to remove it. If the plant is very large, two pairs of hands may be necessary — one to hold the plant steady, the other to pull the pot away from it.*

REMOVING A CACTUS FROM A POT

1 *With a prickly plant, such as a cactus, use a rolled up piece of paper to protect your hand.*

2 *Place the paper around the cactus, making sure the paper is long enough to make a "handle".*

3 *Holding the paper "handle" in one hand, gently pull the pot away with the other.*

A potbound plant

The earliest recognizable stage of a plant becoming potbound is when new roots start to cover the root ball. The roots will eventually become densely matted and form a thick spiral in the base of the pot. Potting on at this stage is essential.

Potting on

The term "potting" refers specifically to the transfer of cuttings and seedlings to their first pot, while "potting on" is used to describe transferring a plant to a larger pot. It should be done at the beginning of the growing season. Do not pot on during, or just prior to, a rest period as no new root growth will be produced to penetrate the extra potting mixture; this will then become waterlogged and cause the existing roots to rot. Never pot on if the plant is unhealthy in any way. Do not feed potted on plants for the first four to six weeks to encourage them to send out new roots.

Mass of new roots visible on the surface of the root ball.

Roots begin to spiral at base.

Roots in a mass at the base of the pot, as they grow out of the drainage hole.

POTTING ON

1 After removing any moss from the surface, line the new pot with drainage material.

2 Prepare a mold by filling the space between the new pot and the old with potting mixture.

3 Insert the plant, fill in any gaps around the sides of the root ball and firm it in gently.

REPOTTING

1 *Remove the plant from the pot gently. Watering about an hour before will help the plant to slide out.*

2 *To allow room for the new potting mixture, you may need to prune the roots by cutting slices off the root ball.*

3 *Place the plant in a clean pot of the same size. Fill in around the edges with new potting mixture and firm down.*

Repotting

Plants do not always need potting on. If they are not potbound, or thrive better in a smaller pot, they may simply need repotting – taking them out of their pots and returning them to clean pots of the same size with some fresh potting mixture. Often, it is enough to gently tease away some of the old potting mixture and to supply the plant with a little fresh mixture which is high in nutrients. If the plant is growing too fast, or is already too big, the roots may need pruning. Use a sharp knife to slice off the outside of the root ball to allow room for the new potting mixture.

Topdressing

Eventually, with the well-established plants that have been potted on several times, it will not be practical to move them into larger pots as they will probably be an unwieldy size. You must then find a way of providing them with extra nourishment. Topdressing each spring is the best way of doing this. The method also suits house plants, such as the *Hippeastrum* hybrids (amaryllis), which resent root disturbance and flower best when thoroughly potbound. Always use new potting mixture to which a slow-release fertilizer high in nutrients has been added.

TOPDRESSING

1 *Gently scrape away the top couple of inches of the potting mixture, with an old kitchen fork or similar implement, taking care not to damage the roots.*

2 *Refill the pot to its original level using fresh potting mixture of a suitable type. Firm this down to ensure the plant is properly anchored in the pot.*

Pruning and training

House plants may need to be pruned periodically, or trained to the shape you wish them either to maintain or take on. They may become too big for the space available, or odd branches can start to grow in places where you do not want them, giving the plant an unbalanced look. Messy, tangled growth needs to be thinned out, and branches and stems should be induced to grow in a particular direction. Some plants need their growing points nipped out frequently to avoid unwanted leggy shoots and encourage a close, bushy shape. New growth on certain climbing plants will need to be supported.

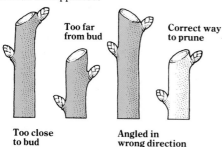

The correct way to prune
Always cut just above the bud where you want the new shoot to form. Slope the cut downward, away from the bud, and do not leave a long "snag", as this will be liable to rot.

When to prune

Spring is the best time for pruning nearly all plants, as it is the season when new, active growth begins, but overlong stems can normally be cut back in the autumn if they get in the way or overcrowd the plant.

Some plants only make flower buds on the new season's growth and you can therefore cut away a lot of old growth in the spring, confident that you are not harming the prospect of flowers in the coming season. However, when cutting back woody-stemmed plants, it is usually safest to cut back into the previous year's growth and not beyond.

Whatever tool you use for pruning, it is important that it is sharp, to avoid bruising or otherwise damaging the remaining stem. A razor blade, scalpel or scalpel-like knife is excellent for soft-stemmed plants, and a finely pointed pair of scissors will allow you to get into the leaf axils of really bushy plants. For woody stems, pruners are essential.

Deadheading and pinching out

Deadheading involves cutting away any dead or faded flowers on the plant. This encourages the plant to put more effort into producing new flowers rather than producing seeds, as would happen naturally.

Growing tips should be pinched out frequently on plants that would naturally grow long unbranched stems, but which look better when growth is more compact.

Flowers on long stalks
Deadhead plants such as Saintpaulia *hybrids (African violets), whose flower stalks arise from the plant base, by pulling and twisting out the whole stalk.*

Flowers on short stalks
Deadhead flowers that grow in clusters, or on short stalks arising from a main stem, by pinching them off between your thumb and index finger.

Pinching out
Nip out the growing tip or point with your index finger and thumb in order to maintain a bushy shape and discourage straggly shoots and spindly stems.

Cutting back

Cutting back is probably the most drastic form of pruning, but usually improves the attractiveness of a plant. It allows you to get rid of totally unwanted growth and lets you keep favorite plants that would otherwise become too big to be grown in the home. A drastic cutting back often improves growth by ridding the plant of old, weak sections and encouraging new, strong shoots with short gaps between the leaves.

Plants with long stems, such as *Hedera* sp. (ivies) or *Philodendron* sp. (philodendrons) may develop large gaps between the leaves in winter. This may be due to insufficient light or overcrowding. To correct the condition, the stems affected must be cut back to allow new, close growth (the tips can be used as cuttings). The initial cause of the problem must then be identified and improved.

Fast-growing plants which climb, or are trained around hoops and canes, can lose their shape after one, two or three seasons' growth. *Jasminum* sp. (jasmine) is a climber which needs particularly drastic cutting back. Do not be afraid to cut out all but the newest growth; if

CUTTING BACK TO CREATE CLOSE GROWTH

1 *Stems with large gaps between leaves, particularly those of trailing plants, will look better if cut back.*

2 *Using sharp scissors, cut the stem back to the point (node) where tight growth exists, taking out the elongated, leggy growth.*

3 *If the plant is then given the correct growing conditions, the new growth will have short gaps between the leaves.*

CUTTING BACK STRAGGLY GROWTH

1 *If growth around a hoop becomes very straggly, cutting back will provide attractive, bushier new growth.*

2 *Unwind the stems from the hoop and cut them off, using sharp scissors, until only two of the youngest stems remain.*

3 *Wind the remaining stems around the wire hoop and secure with wire plant ties.*

CUTTING BACK A TALL PLANT

1 *A favorite plant which has grown too tall can be cut back drastically and kept in the home for a few more years.*

2 *Use pruners to remove the head of a woody-stemmed plant. Cut down by as much as half its original height.*

3 *Staunch any flow of latex with a dusting of powdered charcoal. Give the plant the kind of growing conditions it needs to grow at its best and new leaves will be produced in four to six weeks.*

the plant is cut back in early spring, it will be covered with new growth by the summer.

Cutting back usually encourages new growth, so merely snipping away the top 4-6in of a large plant will only prove a temporary solution. When a *Ficus elastica* (rubber plant) or *Dracaena marginata* (rainbow plant) almost reaches the ceiling, it needs shortening by about 3ft if you want to keep it indoors for a few more years. The plant may look odd for several weeks but once the new leaves appear the cutting back will have been worthwhile.

Training plants

Many house plants can be trained to grow in a variety of shapes, by appropriate pruning or pinching out to obtain a bushy plant or a tall plant with a bare stem, known as a standard, or by training the plant to grow around a support. Most plants attain a rewarding shape within a few years.

TRAINING PLANTS AROUND A SUPPORT

Support can be provided by fastening the stem of the plant to thin canes, bamboo, wire hoops or trellises pushed into the potting mixture. Ties made of twine, raffia, soft wire rings or wire-and-paper twists can be used. Fasten them so that they secure the stems, but not so tight that they will bite into the stems as they thicken.

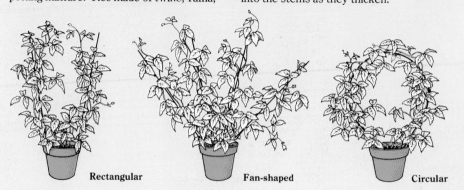

Rectangular   Fan-shaped   Circular

Propagation

All plants eventually reach the stage when they cease to be as attractive as they once were and need replacing with younger, more vigorous specimens. Propagating your own plants is a cheap and satisfying way of rejuvenating your house plant stock.

There are two main ways in which it is possible to produce new plants – they may either be grown from seed (see pp. 215-16) or propagated vegetatively.

Vegetative propagation

This method of propagation involves taking a specific part of a plant and encouraging it to make roots of its own, so that it can establish itself and become a plant in its own right. Generally, but not always, plants propagated vegetatively look just like the original plant the section was taken from. Virtually any part of a

Equipment for propagating plants

Jam jar
propagator

Plastic bag
propagator

Cold
propagator

Plant
labels

Paintbrush

Hormone
rooting powder

Peat tray

Labeling
pencil

Peat pots

plant can be used: plantlets that develop on leaf surfaces or on trailing stolons (creeping stems), offsets and stem or leaf cuttings. Alternatively, clumps may be divided (see p. 213), or stems layered or air-layered (see pp. 214-15). You can propagate some plants by more than one of the methods mentioned, others can only be propagated in one particular way. Quick rooting and establishment is, in all cases, vital. The faster the section can make roots of its own and become established as a separate plant the safer it is; unrooted sections are at risk from wilting, rot and a number of other hazards. Special rooting mixtures are available for the propagation of cuttings – these hold plenty of air and water, but have few nutrients, which would scorch the new roots.

With practically all types of vegetative propagation, the best season to choose is the spring, just as new growth is starting.

Propagating from leaf cuttings

Some plants can be propagated from leaf cuttings. A complete leaf, with its leaf stalk attached, is pulled or cut from the parent plant and then grown in barely moist rooting mixture, or, in certain cases, water. The leaves should be inserted into the mixture at a 45 degree angle, and may be rested against the pot edge to give them maximum support; the cut end should not be buried too deeply. The new roots and shoots will develop from the cut end of the leaf stalk, or along the leaf edges (veins). Leaf cuttings may be planted singly in small pots, or a number may be planted together in larger pots or shallow trays. Enclosing the container in a plastic bag creates a humid atmosphere and usually eliminates the need for further watering. *Saintpaulia* hybrids (African violets) and rhizomatous *Begonia* sp. (begonias) are examples of popular house plants which can be reproduced in this way. The leaves chosen

Equipment for propagating plants (cont.)

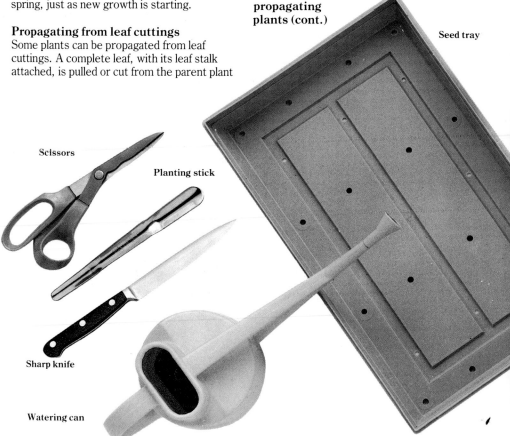

Seed tray

Scissors

Planting stick

Sharp knife

Watering can

ROOTING LEAF CUTTINGS IN POTTING MIXTURE

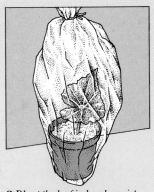

1 *Remove a complete leaf from the plant with a sharp knife or razor blade, and trim the stalk to a length of 1½-2in.*

2 *Plant the leaf in barely moist rooting mixture and fasten a plastic bag over the pot to increase the humidity.*

3 *When new plantlets appear at the base of each leaf, cut away the parent leaf. Leave to develop in the pot.*

ROOTING LEAF CUTTINGS IN WATER

1 *Trim the stalks of healthy leaves to 1½-2in. Cover a water-filled jar with plastic and insert leaves through holes in the plastic.*

2 *Roots and small plantlets will form underwater. These can then be separated and planted in potting mixture.*

Electric heat propagator

should be neither too old nor too young, so – in the case of a *Saintpaulia* hybrid, for example – the extreme inner and outer leaves of the rosette should not be used. Large-leaved *Begonia* sp. should not have their leaves cut into sections, as they are then liable to rot, but the leaves can be used whole if their outer edges are trimmed off to reduce leaf area.

Propagating from stem cuttings

Most house plants can be propagated from stem cuttings of one kind or another. Cuts should be made with a really sharp knife or razor blade, as bruised or split stems are liable to rot. If possible, water the plant about two

hours before taking the cutting, as this ensures that the stems and leaves are fully charged with moisture. If you have to use a flowering stem, gently pinch off the flowers first. Coating the cut end of the stem with hormone rooting powder will hasten the rooting process.

Rooting leaf sections in potting mixture

The leaves of certain plants, including *Sansevieria* sp. (mother-in-law's tongue), *Streptocarpus* hybrids (Cape primrose) and *Peperomia caperata* (emerald ripple peperomia), can be cut into pieces, which are rooted separately to produce many new plants. A cluster of plantlets will push up through the

ROOTING A SOFT-STEMMED CUTTING IN POTTING MIXTURE

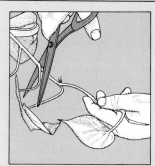

1 *Select a healthy stem, with about three nodes fairly close together, and make a clean cut, giving a 4-6in "tip" cutting.*

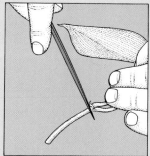

2 *Trim the cutting just below the lowest leaf node and remove the lower leaves to prevent them from rotting in the rooting mixture.*

3 *Make some holes with a stick and plant several cuttings in the same pot, gently firming the mixture with your fingers.*

ROOTING A SOFT-STEMMED CUTTING IN WATER

1 *Make a clean cut just above a leaf axil or node; the parent plant can then make new shoots from the top or upper leaf axils.*

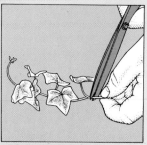

2 *Make another cut immediately below the lowest node or leaf axil of the cutting and gently remove the lower leaves.*

3 *After approximately four weeks 1-1½in of new root will have formed, and the cutting can then be transferred to potting mixture.*

TAKING A WOODY-STEMMED CUTTING

1 *To propagate a woody-stemmed plant, remove any lower leaves that remain and cut the stem into short pieces, each of which should include at least one node. The rooting process may take several weeks longer than with a soft-stemmed plant.*

2 *Place the cuttings, horizontally or vertically, in rooting mixture. Roots will develop from buried nodes and new top growth from the nodes exposed to air.*

mixture from a leaf section of a *Streptocarpus* hybrid and, most probably, just a single plantlet from the cut base of each piece of *Sansevieria* sp. leaf. The segments of leaf must be inserted base downwards in the rooting mixture – otherwise no roots will develop. The leaves of both these plants should be cut crosswise at 2-3in intervals and then planted almost vertically in a sandy rooting mixture, with

between a quarter and a half of the section buried. *Peperomia caperata* leaves should be cut into four sections (one cut down the leaf, one cut across it) and planted with a cut edge just in contact with barely moist rooting mixture. If leaves from a variegated *Sansevieria* sp. are used for rooting (as shown below), the new foliage which is produced by the section will revert to plain green.

ROOTING LEAF SECTIONS IN POTTING MIXTURE

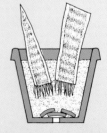

1 *Remove the parent plant from its pot and select a healthy, mature leaf which is unblemished. Cut or break off the leaf at the base of the plant.*

2 *Cut the leaf crosswise, with a sharp knife, at 2-3in intervals. Each large leaf will provide several segments from which new plants can be propagated.*

3 *Plant the leaf cuttings together at a slight angle in the rooting mixture. They may be supported by plant labels or rested against the pot side. New roots will develop from the cut edge of each leaf section. When they are well developed, pot them and treat them as mature plants.*

ROOTING PLANTLETS

1 *Cut off a leaf or stolon (shown above) which bears a well-developed plantlet. Leave about 1in of the leaf stalk or stolon attached to the plantlet. Bury this stalk in a pot of rooting mixture with the plantlet resting on the surface.*

2 *Cover with a plastic bag to provide extra humidity. Roots should develop in three weeks.*

Propagating from plantlets

A number of house plants make "plantlets" – small replicas of themselves – on their leaves or at the ends of stolons or arching stems. *Tolmeia menziesii* (piggy-back plants) produce plantlets on their leaves, while *Saxifraga stolonifera* (strawberry geraniums) produce plantlets on stolons. If plantlets are left on the parent plant until they are well developed, they can usually be detached and potted up to develop roots of their own. Alternatively, *Saxifraga stolonifera* and *Chlorophytum comosum* (spider plants) can be layered (see p. 214), although plantlets may be less inclined to make roots while they continue to be sustained by the parent through the linking stem.

ROOTING OFFSETS

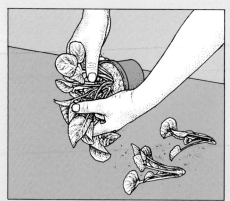

1 *Choose an offset, ideally one which already has some roots attached, and gently break it off the main stem. This may be done at the same time as you repot the parent plant.*

2 *Plant the offsets in barely moist rooting mixture in separate pots. Place the pot in a plastic bag until active growth indicates that the offset is well rooted.*

ROOTING DIVISIONS

1 You may need to use a knife to start a division so that you can get your thumbs into the cut area and successfully lever the sections apart, dividing the root ball equally.

2 Pot the divisions at the same level as previously, in a pot slightly larger than the root spread. Water sparingly until sections get established and new growth appears.

Propagating from offsets

These are small plants which appear around the base of mature plants. Most grow directly from the stem but some may be produced on long stalks or stolons. Bromeliads and succulents often produce offsets at the base, and many of the spherical cacti make clusters of them. If offsets are to survive on their own, they should not be detached until they are well established and have developed the normal shape and characteristics of the parent. Well-developed offsets often have some roots of their own already formed while still attached, and this inevitably makes subsequent establishment easier and quicker.

Propagating by division

Plants such as *Saintpaulia* hybrids (African violets), most ferns and some cacti can usually be divided by taking them out of their pots and firmly but gently pulling apart obviously separate sections, each comprising a single plant or small cluster of plants and a healthy root system. It may be necessary to tease or wash away some of the potting mixture so that you can see the separate sections. Sometimes these are joined together with tough thickened roots, and you may need a sharp knife to make the division. In addition, ferns often have densely packed fine roots that make pulling the sections apart difficult.

PROPAGATION TIMES

Soft-stemmed cutting in water: four to six weeks for adequate roots to form; then transfer cutting to potting mixture.

Soft-stemmed cutting in potting mixture: three to four weeks for adequate roots to form.

Woody-stemmed cutting in potting mixture: eight to ten weeks for adequate roots to form.

Whole leaf in potting mixture: three to four weeks for adequate roots to form; then a further two to five weeks before new topgrowth appears.

Whole leaf in water: three to four weeks for adequate roots to form; then transfer leaf to potting mixture.

Leaf section in potting mixture: four to six weeks for adequate roots to form; then a further four to eight weeks before new topgrowth appears.

Plantlet in potting mixture: three to four weeks for adequate roots to form; then a further two to five weeks before an attractive-looking new plant develops.

Offset in potting mixture: three to four weeks for adequate roots to form; then a further two to three weeks for a plant of a useful size to develop.

Division in potting mixture: two to three weeks for a plant of a useful size to develop.

Layering

This is the process by which roots are encouraged to form on a trailing stem while it is still in contact with the rest of the plant. Layering is practiced in the garden when semi-woody stemmed shrubs have their stems bent down and held in contact with the soil to encourage them to make roots. It is not often practiced indoors, except with *Philodendron scandens* (heartleaf philodendron) and *Hedera* sp. (ivies) – both of which make aerial roots at the nodes or leaf joints. As with the propagation of plantlets (see p. 212), the stems are brought into contact with a suitable rooting mixture in a nearby pot. Many creeping plants are constantly sending roots down into the potting mixture over which they grow. The new growths can be cut from the parent plants and potted separately.

Air layering

Air layering is a way of propagating a prized plant that has grown too big for convenience or one that has lost some of its lower leaves and is starting to look untidy. It is often used for woody-stemmed plants that do not root quickly from cuttings and are so stiff that their stems cannot be bent down for layering. The woody stem is "injured" to encourage it to put forth roots at the point of injury; the top section is then cut off and potted. One method involves making a single upward-slanting cut in the stem, but this puts it in danger of being broken off. A somewhat safer way of air layering is described here.

Air-layered plant, before (right) and after (far right). The plant has lost its bare, leafless stem, leaving a much more attractive bushy shape.

LAYERING TRAILING STEMS

1 *Bring the stem into contact with a pot containing suitable rooting mixture, securing it firmly in place with a hairpin or a piece of bent wire. Heap a little rooting mixture over the point of contact to further encourage rooting.*

2 *New roots form within three to four weeks at the node, and a young plant will begin to grow. When this happens, cut the new plant free, taking care not to spoil the shape of the parent. Several plants can be propagated in this way simultaneously.*

PROPAGATING BY AIR LAYERING

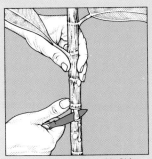

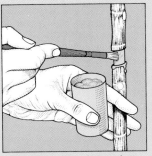

1 *Score out two rings, ½-¾in apart, just below the lowest healthy leaf on the stem. Peel off the bark between them, leaving the stem tissue undisturbed.*

2 *Brush the stripped area of stem with a thin layer of hormone rooting powder to encourage the rapid production of new roots.*

3 *Using insulating tape or strong thread, secure the end of an oblong piece of plastic around the stem, just below the point at which the stem is cut.*

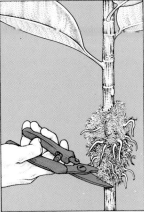

4 *Pack the cuplike plastic sheath with moistened sphagnum moss. Lash the top of the plastic around the stem to ensure that the moisture cannot escape.*

5 *After several weeks, roots will appear through the moss. Remove the plastic cover and cut the stem cleanly, just below where the roots are growing.*

6 *Plant the new root ball in a pot large enough to allow a 2in space around it. Fill with a suitable potting mixture, and water sparingly until well established.*

Growing from seeds

Very reliable strains of seeds are available for such popular house plants as *Begonia semperflorens-cultorum* (wax begonias) and *Impatiens wallerana* (impatiens), and the best hybrid forms can often be raised in this way.

Seeds are best sown in a suitable peat-based rooting mixture (see p. 208). Use half-pots, pans or seed trays depending on the quantity of seed being sown. Very small seeds, such as those of *Begonia* sp. (begonias) and *Saintpaulia* hybrids (African violets), resemble dust, and are best sprinkled over the surface of the rooting mixture. Slightly larger seeds can have a shallow layer of finely sieved mixture placed over them, and sizeable seeds should be buried at one and a half times their own depth. Once water has penetrated the outer coating of the seed, growth begins and a constant supply of moisture is then necessary. Any drying out is fatal, but too much water will result in rotting, so a balance must be struck.

Temperatures above 60°F are needed for swift germination and some of the sub-tropical and tropical plants need much higher levels. Some seeds germinate best in the dark, other types need light to grow – so always follow the instructions on the packet. It is very important to give small seedlings the quantity of bright light they need from the very earliest stages of growth. If a seedling starts to make elongated growth, due to insufficient light, it will never develop into a really satisfactory plant. Containers should be placed near to a source of bright light as soon as the first seedlings start to appear. However, it is important to avoid hot direct sunlight that could cause scorch and certainly dries up the surface of the mixture.

SOWING SEEDS

1 *Spread a thin layer of gravel in the bottom of a tray – for drainage and to prevent waterlogging. Cover the gravel with a layer of suitable rooting mixture.*

2 *Mark out shallow furrows as a guide for sowing. Sprinkle fine seed or individually space larger seeds along the furrows.*

3 *Cover the seeds, if appropriate, and moisten with a fine mist-sprayer. Then place a sheet of glass or clear plastic on top and remove to a warm place.*

THINNING OUT

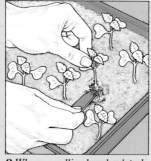

1 *Thin out seedlings growing very close together to a distance roughly equal to their height. Use your fingertips to firm the mixture around each one.*

2 *When a seedling has developed at least two true leaves, gently remove it from the mixture using a plant marker, or something similar, to ease out the young roots without damaging them.*

3 *Transfer each seedling to a pot containing mixture suitable for the adult plant. Firm the mixture around the stem. Ensure that the lower leaves are not buried and avoid handling the stem.*

Problems

Healthy, well-maintained house plants grow sturdily, look good and are less likely to develop problems or be attacked by pests or disease. Unhealthy plants are usually the result of poor cultivation, wrong treatment or simply neglect – actual pests or diseases are, in fact, rarely to blame.

The first step to ensuring that your plants remain in peak condition is to choose them carefully, bearing in mind the amount of time and effort you can devote to them and the conditions you have to offer. Buy a specimen which looks healthy and protect it on the journey home. A plant will also need a period of acclimatization to its new surroundings; try to ensure it is placed in a suitable position and not moved for a few days.

Preventive action

The successful way to care for any plant is to give it neither too much nor too little of the essential growth factors: water, food, light, warmth and humidity. Apart from meeting your plants' specific growing needs, though, it is well worth devoting a few minutes, every week or two, to cleaning them and generally looking them over. Turn over the leaves and examine the undersides carefully – this will help you to spot any problems at an early stage. Also pay close attention to the growing points; these, being soft and succulent, are more liable to attack by aphids than older, leathery leaves. In several flowering plants, such as the *Streptocarpus* hybrid (Cape primrose), the leaves are rarely attacked – it is the flower stalks and flower buds that are the susceptible parts.

Routine maintenance

The action of cleaning a plant often dislodges the odd pest and may even prevent a real infestation. Household dust spoils the look of leaves and, to some extent, clogs the pores through which they breathe – it also reduces the amount of light which can be used for photosynthesis. See that plants are not crowded together so closely that air cannot circulate freely between them, or that some fail to get enough light because others are shading them. Remove any yellowing or damaged leaves and take off all flowers as they fade. Flower stalks should be taken off at the base when all the individual blooms on the stalk are finished to prevent the plant rotting.

ROUTINE CHECKLIST FOR ENSURING HEALTHY PLANTS

In the majority of cases, ailments that affect house plants are not due to actual disease or infestation by pests but simply due to ill-treatment or neglect. It may just be that one or more of the plant's growing needs are not being met. The following checklist will help you to determine the likely reason behind any symptoms of ill health displayed by your plants. If more than one of the plant's growing needs are not being met, it will be necessary to correct them all, to ensure healthy plant growth. If any symptoms persist, examine the plant for any likely pests or diseases.

- Are you overwatering?
- Are you underwatering?
- Is the plant getting the sort of light it prefers?
- Is the temperature too high or too low for proper growth?
- Is the level of humidity conducive to the plant's particular needs?
- Have you remembered to cater for any winter rest the plant may need?

- Does the plant stand in a draft?
- Is the pot size correct?
- Are the roots of the plant completely filling all the available space in the pot?
- Is the plant growing in the most suitable sort of potting mixture?
- Would the plant benefit from being grouped with others?
- Is the plant dusty and in need of a cleaning?

KEEPING PLANTS CLEAN

Plants which are kept in the home are bound to get dusty, and regular cleaning is essential. Clean leaves look more attractive and they allow a plant to function more efficiently. Various methods of cleaning are given below, depending on the size and texture of the plant's leaves. By far the most effective method is to stand the plant outside in a gentle shower, in a sheltered position, during the milder months. Rain water leaves no nasty white deposit behind and the leaves will be freshened.

Cleaning a plant with hairy leaves
Do not clean a hairy-leaved plant with a damp cloth, as the hairs trap the water, causing rotting. You can, however, "sweep" away dust with a soft, dry ½in paintbrush.

Removing faded leaves and flowers
Remove any faded flowers or yellowing leaves that are due to old age, taking them right off to the base. Snip off brown leaf tips with sharp scissors. As these are usually due to dry air, increase the humidity.

Immersing a small plant
On warm days it is possible to wash leaves clean of dust by inverting a small plant in a bowl of lukewarm soapy water. Swirl the plant around for a few seconds, remove and allow it to drain.

Wiping with a damp cloth
Plants with large, smooth leaves can be cleaned with a damp sponge or soft cloth. Use a weak solution of soapy water and rinse with clean water afterwards.

Physiological problems

The most common problems met with in house plants are caused by overwatering, under-watering, fluctuating temperatures, drafts, strong sunlight causing leaves to scorch, cold water causing spotting on the foliage, and low levels of humidity.

Too much or too little water

Overwatering is a very common problem and can be a killer. The dangers of underwatering are less, but the signs of both faults are very similar: in each case the plant droops or wilts because it is not absorbing enough water.

Consistent overwatering, when water is frequently given to an already moist potting mixture, means that air cannot reach the roots, so they stop growing and start to break down and die. With little or no roots, a plant cannot take up enough water to sustain it. To prevent overwatering, only water when the potting mixture starts to dry out, and then wait until this happens again before giving more water. If a plant prefers a moist potting mixture, keep it slightly moist all the time, but never sodden wet (see p. 190).

If a plant is underwatered, it will be obvious that there is little or no water left in the potting mixture; there may also be a considerable gap between the root ball and the inside of the pot where the potting mixture has shrunk and, in the case of a soil-based potting mixture, the surface of the mixture may become caked hard, or even cracked.

Fluctuating temperatures

When temperatures fluctuate by more than 15°-18°F, leaf drop may occur. Aim at keeping the temperature fairly even, with only a slight fall at night. Avoid the opposite – cool days when the heating is turned off and warm evenings when the heating is turned on. It is better to keep all but the most warmth-loving plants at a lower temperature, moving them to a room that is not directly heated at night.

When temperatures soar, *Saintpaulia* hybrids (African violets) and many other gesneriads will drop most or all of their flower buds; during a heatwave try to keep temperatures down and increase the level of humidity.

Drafts

Plants abhor drafts: the thin and more delicate fern fronds will be blackened by them, the leaves of *Caladium hortulanum* hybrids (angel wings) and *Begonia rex-cultorum* (painted-leaf begonias) will droop, and *Codiaeum variegatum pictum* (crotons) will drop their leaves. Avoid sites next to drafty or open windows and, at night, do not leave plants behind drawn curtains.

Sun scorch

The leaves of plants that prefer to grow in some shade can easily develop brown dehydrated patches if exposed to really strong direct sunlight. Those plants that can tolerate direct sun, but which are not used to it, can be scalded by sudden exposure. Always acclimatize plants by gradually exposing them for longer and longer to increasingly bright light.

Insufficient light

If a plant is not receiving enough light, its growth will be generally sluggish. Flowering plants will not bloom as they should, and flower buds may drop off. The new leaves of plants with variegated foliage will revert to a uniform green. To ensure that all parts of the plant receive sufficient light, turn plants regularly, or place them where a reflective surface can throw light on to the side facing away from the light source.

Cold water spots

Saintpaulia hybrids (African violets), *Sinningia speciosa* hybrids (gloxinias) and a number of other gesneriads can have their leaves marked with lighter colored patches if they are watered with cold water, or if water is allowed to collect on the leaves at the time of watering. Always use tepid water and avoid wetting the foliage while watering..

Incorrect humidity

Low levels of humidity can cause browning of leaf tips and leaf edges; this is particularly obvious on plants with thin leaves, such as *Calathea makoyana* (peacock plants), *Chlorophytum comosum* (spider plants) and many ferns. Increase humidity by regular mist-spraying and by standing plants on trays filled with moist pebbles.

Diseases

House plants are not prone to many air-borne diseases and, of those that are found, most gain a foothold because the plant has been overwatered, or because water has lodged in leaf axils causing conditions in which fungi and bacteria can thrive. Damaged leaves and bruised stems may spark off one of several bacterial diseases, and overcrowding, resulting in a lack of adequate air circulation, can also spell trouble. Always remove diseased sections as soon as you see them, and isolate an affected plant from the rest of your collection whilst treatment is being given.

Examining for diseases and pests
It is a good idea to inspect your plants carefully at regular intervals for signs of disease or pests. Pay particular attention to the undersides of leaves.

BLACKLEG

This disease, also known as "black rot" and "black stem rot", strikes plants just where the

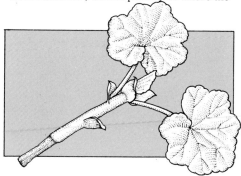

stem meets the potting mixture, but spreads both upward and downward to the roots. An attack rarely occurs unless the potting mixture is kept too wet for too long, but stem cuttings are liable to be affected during propagation.

Susceptible plants This disease is most common on *Pelargonium* sp. (geraniums).

Treatment Always use free-draining potting mixtures and be particularly sparing with water during the period that geranium cuttings are rooting. Avoid damaging stems and always remove faded leaves. There is no cure for this disease but cuttings taken from the tops of stems that are unaffected can be rooted – dip the cut ends into hormone rooting powder containing fungicide.

CROWN AND STEM ROT

If the stem of the plant starts to get soft and slimy, the reason may be stem rot. Low temperatures and soggy potting mixture may

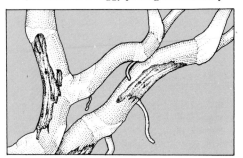

cause plants to become infected. An attack of crown rot will cause the leaves to be eaten away from the center outwards.

Susceptible plants Plants with soft stems such as *Impatiens* sp. (impatiens) and *Exacum affine* (German violets), are prone to stem rot. Other susceptible plants are cacti; when soft, dark-brown or black patches appear near to potting mixture level, it is likely to be stem rot. Rosette-shaped plants, such as *Echeveria* sp. (echeverias) and *Saintpaulia* hybrids (African violets), are liable to attack from crown rot.

Treatment An attack is usually fatal but unaffected sections may be dusted with sulphur and re-rooted.

GRAY MOLD

This fungus, which is also called "botrytis", usually starts growing on fallen leaves and flowers, but can also start when water lodges

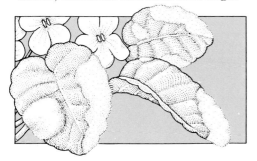

in the axils of the leaves. It strikes quickly when temperatures are low and the air is moist, and rarely in warmer weather and in dry air. Whole leaves or stems can be affected, assuming a fluffy-gray, moldy appearance.

Susceptible plants Gray mold affects plants with soft stems and leaves, such as *Saintpaulia* hybrids (African violets), *Senecio cruentus* hybrids (cinerarias), *Caladium hortulanum* hybrids (angel wings) and *Gynura aurantiaca* (purple velvet plants).

Treatment Fading leaves should be removed, and plants should be watered and mist-sprayed less frequently. A suitable fungicide may have to be used in severe cases, and to prevent further attacks.

MILDEW

Mildew appears as powdery white patches on leaves, stems and, occasionally, flowers. These patches can be distinguished from gray

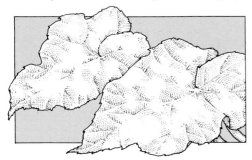

mold by the absence of fluffy growths. Stricken leaves become distorted and fall from the plant. Low temperatures combined with high humidity, poor air circulation and overwatering provide ideal conditions for mildew.

Susceptible plants Soft-leaved and succulent-stemmed plants, including some *Begonia* sp. (begonias), are particularly susceptible; other kinds of *Begonia* sp., even when growing alongside affected plants, are not attacked.

Treatment To treat plants affected by mildew, pick off all affected leaves and spray the rest of the plant with a fungicide.

SOOTY MOLD

Sooty mold grows on the sticky honeydew secreted by pests such as aphids and scale insects. As such, it is a sure sign that a plant is

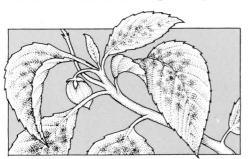

infested with some sort of sap-sucker. The mold itself looks just like a thick layer of soot and feels sticky. Although sooty mold does not directly attack the leaves, its presence spoils the appearance of the plant, clogs the breathing pores of the leaves, and reduces photosynthesis by obscuring light.

Susceptible plants Citrus plants are particularly liable to be affected.

Treatment Regular washing of the leaves with soapy water avoids the possibility of an attack, and is the only way of washing off the objectionable mold once it appears. The best means of treatment is to attack the sap-sucking pests which deposit the sticky honeydew.

Pests

House plants are sometimes attacked by insects and other pests which eat their leaves, stems and roots or suck their sap. A minor infestation is hardly noticeable and often does little damage but, if left unchecked, numbers quickly build up and then serious harm can be done. The ways in which pests arrive on plants vary, but new plants should always be very thoroughly checked and infested plants should be moved away from healthy ones. Each pest attacks a plant in a different way and can be identified by the damage which it causes, and by the season during which the plant is

affected. For instance, a drooping plant with crescent-shaped bites out of its foliage during the spring and summer might indicate an attack by adult vine weevils.

Some pests prefer to feed on particular plants – the adult vine weevil has a preference for succulents – and will leave others alone, while others are less discriminating. A few types, such as aphids and whiteflies, are very common – they thrive throughout the world, adapting to very different conditions, and are extremely difficult to get rid of – others need special conditions to do well and are therefore easily discouraged. All pests should be treated as soon as possible using the appropriate form of insecticide (see pp. 228-9).

APHIDS

Aphids, commonly called "greenflies" or "plant lice", which may be black, brown, gray or light yellow as well as green, suck sap and multiply

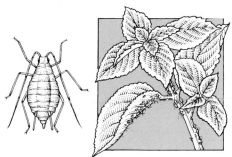

at an alarming rate. They molt their skins, and the white cases are found on infested plants.

What they do In addition to sucking sap, which debilitates the plant and causes distortion, aphids carry incurable viral diseases and exude a sticky honeydew on which a black fungus called sooty mold can grow.

Susceptible plants All plants which have soft stems and soft leaves; these include *Cyclamen persicum* hybrids (cyclamens), *Impatiens* sp. (impatiens) and *Exacum affine* (German violets).

Treatment Individual pests can be removed by hand, but a suitable insecticide is needed in most cases.

CATERPILLARS AND LEAF ROLLERS

Caterpillars, such as those found in the garden, rarely attack house plants but an infestation may occasionally be caused by moths or butterflies which fly in and lay their eggs on

 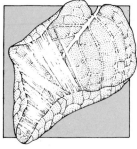

stems or leaves – usually the leaf undersides. A more common problem is the thin, bright-green caterpillar of the tortrix moth.

What they do They roll themselves up in a young leaf, inside a protective web, and eat young stems and growing points, ruining the symmetry of a plant.

Susceptible plants All soft-leaved plants, such as *Plectranthus australis* (Swedish ivies), *Fittonia verschaffeltii* (nerve plants) and *Pelargonium* sp. (geraniums).

Treatment Individual caterpillars can be picked off by hand and destroyed, but a more serious attack will need treating with a suitable insecticide.

EARTHWORMS

Although they are to be encouraged in the garden, where their feeding enriches the soil and their movements serve to aerate it,

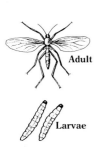

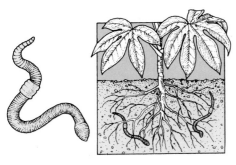

earthworms that get into the potting mixture of house plants can be a nuisance.

What they do Constant burrowing among the roots causes disturbance and loosens the potting mixture. Their presence is usually noticed when heaps of their casts appear on the surface of the mixture and plants seem loose in their pots.

Susceptible plants Worms may infest any plant which is left in the garden during a shower of rain. They enter the mixture through the drainage holes in the pot.

Treatment Water affected plants with permanganate of potash solution and pick off any worms that surface. Tapping the pot will cause them to surface.

FUNGUS GNATS OR SCIARID FLIES

Also known as "mushroom flies", these are tiny, sluggish creatures that hover above the surface of the potting mixture and do no real harm.

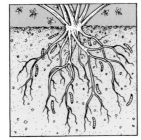

What they do The flies lay their eggs in the mixture and the hatched larvae feed on dead matter, including decaying roots. The larvae are unlikely to damage live roots on mature plants, but will sometimes attack those on very young seedlings.

Susceptible plants Fungus gnats exist in practically all peat and peat-based products. This means that plants such as *Ficus pumila* (creeping figs), *Saintpaulia* hybrids (African violets) and most types of fern are especially likely to suffer from them.

Treatment The condition can be treated by drenching the mixture with an insecticide when it is relatively dry, but the flies are really more of a nuisance than a pest.

LEAF MINERS

Leaf miners are the slim, sap-sucking maggots of a small fly. They can sometimes be seen if the leaves are examined closely.

What they do The grubs tunnel between the surfaces of the leaves of certain plants, causing a mosaic of irregular white lines. The progress of leaf miners is usually rapid and will quickly spoil the appearance of a plant.

Susceptible plants *Chrysanthemum* sp. (chrysanthemums) and *Senecio cruentus* hybrids (cinerarias) are the most popular house plants likely to be attacked by these pests. Plants that are purchased are unlikely to be affected, but *Senecio cruentus* hybrids grown by the amateur from seed can be at risk.

Treatment Damaged leaves should be picked off and a spray insecticide used on the leaves. Alternatively, a systemic insecticide can be applied to the potting mixture.

MEALY BUGS AND ROOT MEALY BUGS

Mealy bugs resemble white woodlice; they are oval in shape and around ¼in long. They can wrap themselves in a sticky white "wool" which repels water (and insecticide).

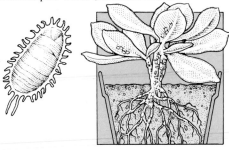

What they do Mealy bugs are sap suckers and excrete honeydew. A severe attack can result in leaf fall. Root mealy bugs congregate on the roots and will create little patches of white wool.

Susceptible plants Mealy bugs tend to attack desert cacti or succulents, but may appear on virtually any plant. Cacti, *Pelargonium* sp. (geraniums) and *Saintpaulia* hybrids (African violets) are particularly liable to attack from root mealy bugs.

Treatment Systemic insecticides can be effective against mealy bugs, if used repeatedly. For root mealy bugs, drench the potting mixture with an insecticide at least three times at two-weekly intervals.

RED SPIDER MITES

These minute reddish pests thrive in hot, dry air. The mites are barely visible to the naked eye, but their webs are the tell-tale indication of their presence.

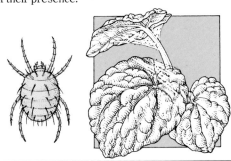

What they do Red spider mites suck sap and spin very fine, silky webs on the undersides of leaves. Infestation results in leaves becoming mottled and unattractive, new growth being stunted and, in severe cases, leaf fall occurring.

Susceptible plants *Impatiens* sp. (impatiens) and *Chlorophytum comosum* (spider plants) are two popular house plants which may be prone to attack.

Treatment As the mites dislike moisture, regular spraying with water will discourage a serious attack, but insecticides must be used in severe cases. Apply weekly, directing the spray on to both upper and lower leaf surfaces.

SCALE INSECTS

Most scale insects are brown or yellowish in color, they appear mainly on the undersides of leaves and are particularly partial to crevices.

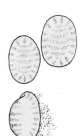

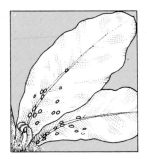

The young insects are very active and move around over the plant, but mature pests remain stationary, enclosed in their waxy cover, and appear as circular or oval raised discs.

What they do Both suck sap and excrete sticky honeydew – often the first sign that they are present is when this sticky residue is noticed on leaves or furniture. Honeydew may lead to infection by sooty mold.

Susceptible plants All plants are vulnerable to attack, but some types of scale insects prefer particular plants. The citrus family and ferns are most susceptible.

Treatment Spraying is not very effective, due to the adults' hard protective coating, and systemic pesticides should be used.

SLUGS AND SNAILS

Slugs and snails will not survive in the home for long, as their presence is soon noticed and they can be easily picked off by hand and destroyed.

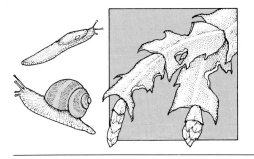

They can, however, be troublesome in greenhouses and conservatories.

What they do Both are very fond of juicy stems, and can eat away large sections of them rapidly. They are most active at night and during prolonged wet spells.

Susceptible plants Plants that are left outside in summer and autumn can be seriously damaged by these pests. Christmas and Easter cacti, such as *Schlumbergera* and *Rhipsalidopsis* sp., are especially at risk because of their succulent stems.

Treatment Protect all indoor plants while they are outdoors by sprinkling slug pellets around them. Renew pellets frequently as rain washes out the chemicals.

VINE WEEVILS

These pests are increasing in numbers and an attack can be disastrous. Adult weevils are large and almost black in color, their grubs are cream-colored.

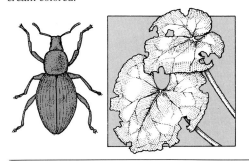

What they do Adult pests bite pieces out of the foliage, leaving a permanent scar. The grubs eat roots, tubers and corms. Often, the first sign of their presence is when a plant droops and an inspection may reveal that it has no roots left at all!

Susceptible plants The most commonly affected plants include orchids; *Cyclamen persicum hybrids* (cyclamen), *Saintpaulia* hybrids (African violets) and all types of rosette-shaped succulents.

Treatment Adult pests can be removed by hand and destroyed, and the potting mixture should be drenched with a suitable insecticide. A plant without a root system cannot usually be saved.

WHITEFLIES

These tiny, white, mothlike creatures are sometimes found in the home, but are more common in greenhouses or conservatories. When whiteflies appear indoors, they have

usually been brought in with temporary flowering pot plants.

What they do They settle mainly on the undersides of the leaves, sucking sap and depositing sticky honeydew. Their almost translucent larvae are often present in large numbers on the undersides of leaves.

Susceptible plants Whiteflies tend to attack certain flowering plants, such as *Pelargonium* sp. (geraniums), grown during the summer in the garden.

Treatment These are persistent pests which may prove difficult to eradicate. Repeated applications of a spray insecticide for the larvae and a systemic kind for the adults will eliminate them in time.

Diagnosis charts

These diagnosis charts should enable you to determine what is wrong with your plant. Most problems occur because of incorrect growing conditions but, if the symptoms continue, check the plant for any likely diseases and pests, and treat accordingly.

SIGNS OF DISEASE	
BLACKLEG	• Black shriveled sections of stem just above the potting mixture *Occurs in late autumn and winter*
CROWN OR STEM ROT	• Soft, slimy stems • Black or brown decayed areas *Occurs in autumn and winter*
GRAY MOLD (botrytis)	• Fluffy gray mold on half-rotted leaves *Occurs from autumn to spring*
POWDERY MILDEW	• Powdery white patches on leaves and stems • Twisted leaves • Leaf fall and possible total defoliation *Occurs in spring and autumn*
SOOTY MOLD	• Thin, black, sootlike deposit on leaves and stems growing on the sticky honeydew substance secreted by sap-sucking insects *Occurs in summer and autumn*

DANGER SIGNS	
• Pale elongated growth with large gaps between the leaves • Small new leaves, small or few flowers • Variegated leaves lose color contrast • New shoots that should be variegated appear plain green *Lack of sufficient light*	• Brown leaf tips and leaf edges • Some leaf curl *Air and/or potting mixture too dry* • Blackening or shriveling of small leaf sections • Serious leaf drop of large-leaved plants *Drafts or too cold a position*
• Large, irregularly shaped, light-brown patches on leaves • Drooping leaves and stems • Stunted flowers and unduly short or misshapen flower stalks *Too much sun or unaccustomed sun*	• Green slime on clay pots • Algae, moss and other plant growth on the surface of the potting mixture • Yellowing leaves and leaf drop *Overwatering*

SIGNS OF PESTS

APHIDS (plant lice or greenfly)	• Distorted stems and leaves • Damaged flowers *Occur throughout the year*	• General air of lack-luster • Honeydew on leaves and stems
FUNGUS GNATS	• Minute, sluggish, brown flies circling above potting mixture *Occur throughout the year*	• Piles of "soil" made by tiny larvae appear under the pot
LEAF ROLLING CATERPILLARS	• Nibbled leaves and stems • Rolled up leaves with fine sticky webbing holding them together *Occur throughout the year*	• Distorted growth caused by leaves or shoots being "stuck" to their neighbor
MEALY BUGS	• Yellowing leaves • Tufts of waxy, white wool in leaf axils and around areoles of cacti *Occur throughout the year*	• General air of debility • Honeydew on leaves or on cactus stems
RED SPIDER MITES	• Mottled or finely pitted leaves • Curled up leaf edges *Occur throughout the year*	• Fine silky webbing on leaf undersides and leaf axils
ROOT MEALY BUGS	• Poor growth and yellowing leaves • Clumps of white, waxy bugs on roots *Occur throughout the year*	
SCALE INSECTS	• Sticky substance on leaves which may turn black *Occur throughout the year*	• Waxy brown or yellow encrustations on leaf undersides
VINE WEEVILS (adults)	• Crescent-shaped sections eaten out of leaf edges of plants with thick, succulent leaves *Occur in spring and summer*	
VINE WEEVILS (larvae)	• Wilting of the whole plant when potting mixture is still moist *Occur in spring, summer and autumn*	• Roots or tubers eaten away
WHITEFLY	• Sticky honeydew on leaves • Pure white insects resembling moths on leaf undersides *Occur in summer and autumn*	

Pesticides

All types of pesticide are labeled as to their contents and the pests or diseases they should be used against. Always follow strictly any specific instructions, such as the dilution ratio.

Contact insecticides

Insecticides are most commonly applied in liquid form as a fine spray, so that they hit the pest directly and, with luck, kill it quickly before it has time to multiply. These "knock-out" sprays work on contact, affecting the insect's respiratory system or otherwise destroying it.

Most sprays have an unpleasant smell and should not be inhaled. Take plants to be treated out into the garden or on to a balcony, as good ventilation while spraying is essential.

Some insecticides are poisonous to animals, birds and fish, and need careful handling. Others may not be suitable for particular plants. The label should warn you of this.

Systemic insecticides

Systemic insecticides work in another way. They are taken up by the sap – either from the potting mixture or through the leaves – and the sap-sucking or leaf-chewing insect is poisoned. Some stay as a thin film on the surface of the leaves, killing the insects that eat them; these are often called "stomach insecticides". Systemics can be applied in a number of ways: they can be watered on to the mix, sprinkled over it in the form of granules or pushed into it as a "pin" or "spike". They can also be sprayed on to the foliage of plants; the active ingredients work their way into the sap and circulatory system of the plant and poison pests taking them in. All systemics are relatively long-lasting and they can kill "newcomers" (pests that arrive after the application of the chemicals), whereas contact sprays only affect insects through direct contact.

Some insecticides combine both the knock-out effect and the long-term systemic coverage. Vary your insecticide from time to time to avoid the possibility of resistance build-up.

HOW TO APPLY PESTICIDES

APHIDS
Soaking: diazinon; malathion; pyrethrum with resmethrin.
Spraying: diazinon; dimethoate; disulphon; nicotine sulfate: rotenone; safer's soap; malathion; pyrethrum with resmethrin.

BLACKLEG
No known cure.

CATERPILLARS
Soaking: dimethoate; rotenone.
Spraying: dimethoate; carbaryl; diazinone; rotenone.

CROWN AND STEM ROT
No known cure.

EARTHWORMS
Soaking: permanganate of potash.

FUNGUS GNATS
Soaking: malathion; nicotine sulfate.

GRAY MOLD (botrytis)
Spraying: benomyl.

LEAF MINERS
Spraying: dimethoate; disulfoton; malathion.

LEAF ROLLERS
Spraying: dimethoate.

MEALY BUGS and root mealy bugs
Soaking: malathion; safer's soap; dimethoate.
Spraying: dimethoate; malathion; pyrethrum with resmethrin.

POWDERY MILDEW
Dusting: gamma HCH dust.
Spraying: benomyl; dinocap and triforine.

RED SPIDER MITES
Soaking: dimethoate; malathion; pirimiphos-methyl with synergized pyrethrins; pyrethrum with resmethrin.

Spraying: dimethoate; malathion; safer's soap; disulfoton; pyrethrum with resmethrin.

SCALE INSECTS
Soaking: dimethoate; malathion.
Spraying: dimethoate; malathion.

SLUGS AND SNAILS
Pellets: metaldehyde.

SOOTY MOLD
Remove with a damp sponge.

VINE WEEVILS
Soaking: dimethoate.
Spraying: dimethoate.

WHITE FLIES
Soaking: dimethoate; malathion; pirimiphos-methyl with synergized pyrethrins; pyrethrum with resmethrin; rotenone.
Spraying: diazinone; dimethoate; disulfoton; malathion.

APPLICATION METHODS

Insecticides, fungicides and bactericides can be applied in a number of ways. In addition to the normal sprays, aerosols, dusts, granules and spikes, diluted chemicals can be used as a bath into which small plants can be dipped.

When it is necessary to treat sub-soil pests by soaking the potting mixture, a watering can may be used to apply the insecticide. Ensure adequate ventilation is provided when applying the chemicals.

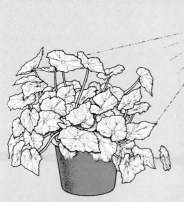

Spraying
Coat all parts of the plant evenly, paying particular attention to the undersides of leaves. If possible, use sprays and aerosols outside so that the spray is not breathed in.

Soaking
Chemical solutions can be applied to the potting mixture using an ordinary watering can – but avoid splashing the leaves. Always use at the recommended strength.

Dusting
Dusting powders are good for cut or bruised leaves. Give upper and lower surfaces, and potting mixture, a thorough coating.

Sprinkling
Sprinkle granules evenly on to the potting mixture. The chemical is gradually released with each successive watering.

Inserting a spike
Push the spike into the potting mixture using a pencil or your finger. This method is quick and convenient.

Fungicides and bactericides

The best way to prevent disease is to ensure that your plants are grown in the conditions they prefer. Because disease is less frequently met with than attack by pests, it can be controlled by a much smaller range of chemicals. These are known as fungicides, which combat fungal diseases, and bactericides which combat bacterial diseases. Most of these act systemically and are therefore capable of combating disease which occurs in any part of a plant. They are also unlikely to harm healthy plants, as can unsuitable insecticides, and are not usually harmful to people.

Fungicides and bactericides are most effective when applied in advance of attack, and it does no harm to use them purely as a precautionary device.

Glossary

Adventitious roots Roots appearing in an unusual place, such as on stems or leaves, e.g., on the stems of cuttings placed in water or on the leaves of some succulent plants.

Aerial roots Roots that appear at nodes. They are mainly used or climbing but are also capable of absorbing moisture from the air. Many only develop properly if they can grasp a suitable rooting medium such as sphagnum moss, e.g., *Philodendron* sp. and their relatives the *Monstera deliciosa, Scindapsus pictus* 'Argyraeus', *Epipremnum aureum* and *Syngonium podophyllum.*

Annual A plant grown from seed that completes its life cycle in one season. Annuals must be thrown away once this cycle is complete. A number of perennial plants are treated as annuals (a recommendation is made in *The A–Z of house plants*), because of the difficulty of overwintering them or because they seldom look attractive in subsequent years, e.g., *Exacum affine*. See also *biennial, perennial.*

Anther The male part of the flower which produces pollen.

Areole An organ which is unique to the cacti, the areole consists of a cushion or hump from which the spines and flowers arise.

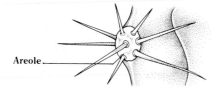

Areole

Axil The angle between the leaf or leaf stalk and stem from which new leaf or side-shoot growth and flower buds arise. Buds found here are known as axillary buds. Side-shoot growth is prevented if they are pinched out.

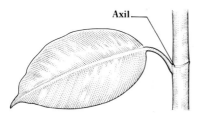

Axil

Berry A succulent fruit in which the usually small but hard seeds are embedded in the fleshy pulp. This pulp is usually brightly colored to attract animals and birds.

Biennial A plant grown from seed which takes two growing seasons to complete its life cycle. A rosette of leaves is produced in the first year, the flowers in the second. Biennials should be thrown away once this cycle is complete as it is difficult to make them flower again, e.g., *Digitalis* sp. See also *annual, perennial.*

Bleeding When sap flows freely from a damaged stem. This is particularly obvious in such plants as *Euphorbia milii* and *Ficus elastica* which bleed a milky-white latex. The flow can be staunched by applying powdered sulphur or charcoal to the damaged stem. See also *latex.*

Bract A modified leaf, often colorful, which backs relatively insignificant flowers and acts as a method of attracting pollinating insects and birds, e.g., the petal-like red bracts of *Euphorbia pulcherrima* and the bell-shaped bracts of *Bougainvillea buttiana.*

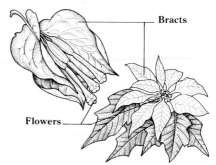

Bracts

Flowers

Bud An embryo shoot, leaf or an immature flower. A terminal growth bud is situated at the tip of a stem or side shoot, an axillary bud is one found in the axil of a leaf stalk. Growth buds are normally protected from damage and cold by closely overlapping scales or sheaths. See also *sheath, axil.*

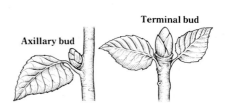

Terminal bud

Axillary bud

Bulb An underground storage organ containing a young plant. The organ stores food during the rest period and usually a complete embryo flower, e.g., *Tulipa*, *Narcissus* sp. See also *corm, tuber*.

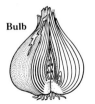

Bulb

Bulbil A small immature bulb attached to a parent bulb, it can also appear on the stems or leaves of the parent plant, e.g., some members of *Lilium* sp.

Calyx The collective name for the ring of green sepals which surrounds the petals in most flowers. The calyx protects the developing flower buds. See also *sepal*.

Capillary action Also known as capillary attraction, this is the drawing up of water by a thread or hair. The term is also used to describe the way potting mixture draws up water when the pot and mixture are placed in direct contact with a dish or bowl of water.

Cereal Plants of the grass family cultivated for their seed as food, e.g., wheat, barley. See also *grass*.

Chlorophyll The green pigment found in the stems and leaves of plants.

Compound leaf A leaf divided into two or more segments, e.g., *Cyperus alternifolius* 'Gracilis' umbrella plant. See also *pinnate, palmate*.

Corm An underground storage organ made up of a thickened stem covered with a thin papery skin. At the top of the corm a bud produces both roots and shoots, e.g., *Crocus, Gladiolus* hybrids. See also *bulb, tuber*.

Corm

Corolla The collective name for the ring of petals. It may be made up of separate petals or the petals may be fused into one unit. See also *flower, petal*.

Crown The growing point of a plant, particularly of a rosette-shaped plant, e.g., *Saintpaulia* hybrids. The crown can also be the basal part of an herbaceous plant where the root and shoots are joined. See also *root crown*.

Cultivar A type of plant or flower that has been developed in cultivation and named by the plant breeder. Cultivar names are enclosed by quotation marks to distinguish them from the scientific names. See also *variety*.

Cutting A term usually applied to a stem cutting. This is a section of stem, 3-4in long (usually the growing tip), which is used in propagation to root and develop into a new plant.

Deciduous A plant that loses its leaves at the end of the growing season. These plants do not make good house plants as they are not decorative through the resting period. New leaves appear in the spring to replace those lost in the autumn. See also *evergreen*.

Dieback The death of a section of stem. This is often caused by faulty pruning.

Double flower Flowers having at least two layers of petals. Often the stamens and pistils at the center of the flower are replaced by more petals. Double-flowered forms are usually cultivars, e.g., modern *Rosa* sp. See also *single flower, semi-double flower*.

Double flower

Epiphyte A plant that grows on another plant but is not a parasite. Epiphytes use the host plant purely as an anchor and take no direct nourishment from it. Many bromeliads and ferns are epiphytes, producing strong, wiry roots which cling to tree trunks and branches, and other plants.

Etiolation The technical name for pale, sickly growth. The gaps between the leaves become greater and the flowers fewer. Insufficient light and overcrowding cause the condition.

Evergreen A plant which retains its leaves throughout the year. See also *deciduous*.

Exotic A plant introduced from abroad. The term is often applied to plants that have their origins in tropical and sub-tropical regions. Most house plants, therefore, are exotic.

Eye The center of a flower, which is often a different color to the rest of the bloom, e.g., *Thunbergia alata*, *Primula* sp.

Family A term used to describe a large association of plants in which certain characteristics are constant. Many genera make up one family, e.g., *Compositae* is the family name for all the plants with daisylike flowers. See also *genus, species*.

Filament The stalk supporting the anther. These two parts make up the stamen. Normally, many filaments are clustered together in the middle of the flower, e.g., *Passiflora caerulea*. See also *stamen, anther*.

Floret A small flower among many others making up a flower head, e.g., most daisy flowers are made up of many florets.

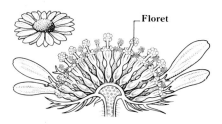

Floret

Flower Usually the most striking feature of a plant, this is an organ of very specialized parts concerned with sexual reproduction. Some plants produce flowers that carry only male parts (stamens), or female parts (pistils). These parts are usually surrounded by a ring of colored petals and green

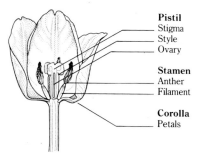

Pistil
Stigma
Style
Ovary

Stamen
Anther
Filament

Corolla
Petals

sepals, although there are many variations of this pattern. Some plants have both male and female flower heads on the same plant but, in most plants, both male and female parts are enclosed in the same flower head. *Begonia* sp. is an example of a flower which is either male, when it is a collection of bright petals with pollen-filled stamens, or female, when it has a large winged seed sac backing the petals.

Forcing The technique of bringing a flower into growth ahead of its natural season. Usually a term applied to spring bulbs when they are encouraged to flower early. *Rhododendron simsii* and *Cyclamen persicum* hybrids are also "forced".

Frond Botanically, a term used to describe the deeply dissected "leaves" of ferns which bear spores and arise from a rhizome. It is also loosely applied to palm leaves.

Fruit A widely used term that describes any mature ovary bearing ripe seeds. The outer covering may be soft and fleshy, such as the berries of *Solanum capsicastrum*, or a dry pod with hard seeds inside, such as the seed pod of *Streptocarpus* 'John Innes' hybrids. See also *nut, berry*.

Genus (pl. genera) A group of allied species. Usually a group of plants (though sometimes only one) which are similar in structure and which most probably evolved from a common ancestor. The genus name always begins with an upper case letter, e.g., all ivies belong to the genus *Hedera*. See also *species, family*.

Germination The first stage of a seed's development into a plant. The first visible stage is sprouting of the new seedling. Germination can be swift (four to six days), or take many weeks or even months. It is a dangerous period as the seed is no longer protected by the hard outer casing, and strong roots and leaves have not yet developed.

Gourd The large, fleshy fruit of climbing and trailing annual plants native to tropical America. The dried fruits can be used in decoration.

Grass Annual or perennial plants of the family *Gramineae*. In the home, their decorative seed heads and threadlike stalks can be used in flower arrangements or dried for winter decoration. See also *cereal*.

Growing tip Also commonly known as growing point, this is the tip of a shoot from which vigorous new growth emerges.

Hardy A plant capable of surviving outside throughout the year, even in areas where there is the possibility of a sustained frost. *Aucuba japonica* "Variegata" and *Fatsia japonica* are examples of hardy house plants.

Herbaceous A word usually associated with perennial plants whose growth dies down in the late autumn and is replaced with fresh growth the following spring. Plant material is stored as a bulb, corm, rhizome or tuber, e.g., *Begonia* sp. *Narcissus* sp. Herbaceous plants never have woody stems. See also *woody*.

Hip A fleshy type of fruit, especially common amongst *Rosa* sp.

Hybrid A plant derived from two genetically different parents. Cross fertilization is common between plants of different species within the same genus. Plants arising from such crossings are known as primary hybrids; they usually have some of the characteristics of both parents, but may favor one more than the other. Cross fertilization is possible, but rare, between plants of different genera, e.g., *Fatshedera* is a hybrid of *Fatsia* and *Hedera*. These crossings are known as bigeneric or intergeneric hybrids. Many naturally occurring hybrids are sterile.

Inflorescence A group of two or more flowers on one stem. An inflorescence may vary considerably in shape from the narrow and spikelike *Lavandula* sp. and *Gladiolus* hybrids to the broad round heads of *Hydrangea* sp. and *Pentas lanceolata*. See also *raceme, panicle, spike, umbel*.

Juvenile Usually applied to the leaves of a young plant that are different in shape from those of a more mature plant, e.g., *Eucalyptus gunnii* foliage, which is round when taken from young plants and thin and pointed when taken from older trees. The leaves of young *Philodendron* sp. may also be a different shape from those of older plants.

Latex A free-flowing, milky-white fluid which exudes from plants such as *Euphorbia milii* and *Ficus elastica* if stems are cut or damaged. See also *bleeding*.

Leaf The energy-producing organ of the plant. Light striking the green part of the leaf starts the process of photosynthesis. Sepals, petals, tendrils and bracts are thought to be modified leaves. In most cacti, the stems take over the function of leaves.

Leaflet A part of a compound, pinnate leaf, properly known as a pinna. See also *compound leaf, pinna, pinnate*.

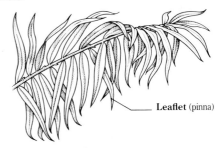

Leaflet (pinna)

Leaf mold Partially decayed leaves used in potting mixtures to provide nutrients, bacterial activity and an open, free-draining consistency. More correctly known as humus, it may be difficult to buy but can be found under deciduous trees (leaf litter) or made by composting fallen leaves.

Margin The border of a leaf or flower petal. This may be lobed or toothed, or of a different color to the main body of the leaf.

Node A stem joint at which the leaves are borne. The node may be notched or swollen and is a point from which the new roots of such plants as *Hedera* sp. and *Philodendron* sp. are commonly made.

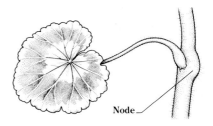

Node

Nut A type of fruit consisting of a hard or leathery shell enclosing a seed, or kernel, that is often edible. See also *fruit*.

Offset Also known as an offshoot, this is a new plant produced by the parent at its base, or on short stolons, and is normally detachable from the parent. See also *stolon*.

Ovary The basal part of the flower in which the seeds are formed. The ovary wall becomes the fruit wall. See also *flower, fruit*.

Palmate A term applied to compound leaves with several leaflets arranged fanwise from a common point, shaped like a hand, e.g., *Dizygotheca elegantissima*. See also *compound leaf*.

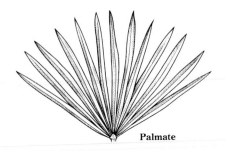

Palmate

Panicle A type of inflorescence consisting of a large branched cluster of flowers, each with a number of stalked flowers, e.g., *Syringa* sp., most grasses. See also *inflorescence*.

Perennial A plant that lives for an indefinite period, e.g., *Agapanthus orientalis*. Perennials can be herbaceous or woody. See also *annual, biennial*.

Petal Usually the showy part of the flower. Petals protect the center of the flower and, when colored, are intended to attract pollinating insects to the stamens and pistils. Sepals are often confused with petals. Petals may be few (three in many *Tradescantia* sp.) or many (as in double-flowered *Rosa* sp.). They are collectively known as the corolla. See also *sepal, stamen, pistil, flower, corolla*.

Photosynthesis The process by which carbon dioxide is converted into carbohydrates within the leaf. It is sparked off by light striking the green pigment in the leaves and stems of plants. See also *chlorophyll, leaf*.

Pinching out Also known as stopping. A form of pruning practiced by gently pulling off, with forefinger and thumb, the soft growing tips of shoots to induce bushiness.

Pinna An individual section of a much divided leaf or frond, commonly known as a leaflet. Used when describing fern fronds. See also *frond, leaflet*.

Pinnate A term used to describe a compound leaf that is divided into several or many pairs of oppositely arranged pinnae (leaflets), e.g., *Chamaedorea elegans* 'Bella'. See also *compound leaf, leaflet, pinna*.

Pistil The female part of a flower, consisting of the stigma, style and ovary. See also *stigma, style, ovary, flower*.

Plantlet A young plant. The stage beyond that of a seedling, but also used to describe "offspring" that are produced on leaves or stolons, e.g., *Tolmiea menziesii*. See also *seedling*.

Raceme A type of inflorescence. An elongated, unbranched flower head, each flower having a short stalk. The flowers normally develop and open from the bottom of the raceme, higher ones opening as the lower ones fade, e.g., *Hyacinthus orientalis* hybrids. See also *inflorescence*.

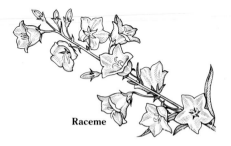

Raceme

Rest period A period within the 12-month season in which the plant should be allowed to become inactive, producing little or no leaf or root growth.

Rhizome A creeping stem, usually horizontal and often underground, from which leaves, side shoots and roots appear. It often acts as a storage organ to enable plants to survive through a short period of drought, e.g., *Begonia rex-cultorum*.

Rib A main or prominent vein of a leaf.

Root The lower part of a plant, normally in the potting mixture, which serves to hold it firm and pass nourishment and water to it from the potting mixture. There are two types of root: fine, fibrous roots and the larger, single tap roots. Most plants have one type of root or the other; few have both.

Root ball The mass of potting mixture interspersed with roots seen when a plant is taken from its pot. Examination of the root ball is a way of establishing whether a plant needs repotting or potting on.

Root crown The basal part of a plant, where the stem meets the roots.

Root hair The fine feeding hairs covering the surface of the roots.

Rosette An arrangement of leaves radiating from a distinct center, e.g., *Saintpaulia* hybrids.

Runner A creeping stem, running along the surface of the potting mixture, which takes root at its nodes and produces a new plant at that point. See also *stolon*.

Scurf Fine, scalelike particles on leaves or stems giving them a gray or silvered appearance, e.g., *Cotyledon undulata*.

Seed The fertilized and ripened part of a flowering plant (ovule), capable of germinating and producing a new plant. Seeds range in size from very tiny to around 8in in diameter; most seeds are pea-sized.

Seedling A young plant raised from seed which still possesses a single unbranched stem.

Semi-double flower A flower with more than one layer of petals but with fewer than a fully double bloom, e.g., some *Saintpaulia* hybrids. See also *single flower, double flower*.

Sepal The outer part of a flower, often green, which protects the middle of the flower and the more delicate petals. Flowers such as *Anemone coronaria* are actually made up of sepals rather than petals. See also *calyx, petal*.

Sheath A protective wrapping for a growing point, e.g., *Ficus elastica*.

Shrub A woody-stemmed bushy plant, smaller than a tree and usually with many stems which branch near the ground. It is often difficult to define the difference between a large shrub and a small tree. Most house plants are shrubs rather than trees. See also *tree, woody*.

Single flower A flower with the normal number of petals, e.g., *Chrysanthemum frutescens*. See also *double flower, semi-double flower*.

Single
flower

Spadix A small spike embedded with tiny flowers, usually surrounded by a spathe, e.g., the center part of *Anthurium andraeanum* hybrids. See also *spathe*.

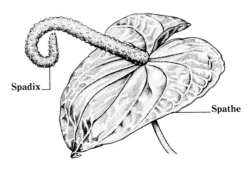

Spadix

Spathe

Spathe A prominent modified leaf or bract surrounding the spadix. Usually fleshy and white, sometimes colored, e.g., *Anthurium andraeanum* hybrids. See also *spadix*.

Species The members of a genus are called species. From its seed each persistently breeds true to type in its main characteristics. A plant's name is made up of at least two parts: the name of the genus and the name of the species, e.g., *Coleus* (genus) *blumei* (species). See also *genus, family*.

Spike A type of inflorescence, in the form of a long unbranched flower head. Very similar in appearance to a raceme except that the individual flowers of a spike have no stalks, e.g., *Gladiolus* hybrids.

Spore Minute reproductive bodies produced by ferns and mosses – the equivalent of seeds in a flowering plant. Spores are held in spore cases on the underside of some fronds (some fronds are sterile and do not bear spore cases) and may be arranged in a number of patterns – herringbone, marginal or scattered.

Stalk The organ supporting the flower (flower stalk), the leaf (leaf stalk) or the anther (filament). See also *filament*.

Stamen The pollen-bearing male organ of a flower, comprising a filament and two anther lobes containing pollen. See also *filament, anther, flower*.

Stigma The tip of the female reproductive organ (pistil) on which the pollen settles. See also *flower, pistil*.

Stolon A creeping stem that produces a new plantlet at its tip or wherever it touches the potting mixture. See also *runner*.

Stomata The pores through which gases enter and leave the plant. They are usually situated on the underside of the leaves.

Style The style supports the stigma, holding it in an effective place for pollination. See also *stigma, pistil, flower.*

Succulent A plant which has fleshy leaves or stems capable of storing water. Usually plants from arid areas, e.g., *Crassula arborescens.*

Sucker A shoot arising from below the surface of the potting mixture, usually from the roots of a plant.

Tendril A wiry projection from the stem that twines around a support and enables a plant to climb. The tendrils may be spiraled, e.g., *Passiflora caerulea,* or forked.

Topdressing The process of replacing the top couple of inches of potting mixture with fresh mixture as an alternative to repotting. Top dressing is most useful for plants which have grown too large for moving into bigger pots. It involves carefully scraping away some of the old potting mixture in spring, doing as little damage as possible to the roots, and firming in fresh mixture.

Transpiration The continual, natural water loss from leaves. This may be heavy or hardly noticeable, depending on the time of day or time of year – factors which affect the relative humidity. Heavy transpiration in warm weather causes wilting which is damaging to the plant.

Tree A woody-stemmed plant with an obvious trunk topped with branches. See also *woody, shrub.*

Tuber A thick, fleshy stem or root which acts as a storage organ. Some tuberous-rooted plants lose their leaves and stem in the autumn and the tuber stores food for renewed growth the following spring, e.g., *Begonia* sp. Occasionally tubers are produced on plant stems, e.g., *Ceropegia woodii.* See also *corm, bulb.*

Tuber

Turgid A term applied to plants that are "crisp" and healthy as their cells are full of water. Also applied to cuttings that have obviously produced roots of their own and are taking up sufficient water for their needs.

Umbel A type of inflorescence. A flower head in which the individual flower stalks arise from a common point. Commonly known as a cluster, e.g., *Pelargonium domesticum* hybrids, *Hydrangea* sp. See also *inflorescence.*

Undulate A leaf margin or petal that has a wavy edge. The term undulate does not refer to toothed or serrated edges.

Variegated A term applied to leaves streaked or spotted with another color (usually cream or yellow). Variegation is usually the result of a mutation and is sometimes due to a virus infection; rarely is it natural or built-in. Variegated-leaved plants are popularly cultivated and need good light to maintain variegation. Cuttings from certain variegated-leaved plants produce plants with plain green leaves.

Variety A word used to refer to variations of the plant that have occurred in the wild, but sometimes incorrectly used to describe a form developed in horticulture. Cultivar is a more accurate term for the latter product. Varietal names are printed in italics. See also *cultivar.*

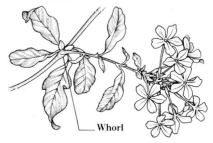

Whorl

Whorl A circle of three or more leaves or flowers produced at the nodes on a stem or stalk, e.g., *Plumbago auriculata.*

Wintering A term used to describe the simulation of winter conditions indoors to encourage winter- and spring-flowering bulbs to make good roots before top growth starts.

Woody Refers to plants which have hard stems which persist above ground all year, e.g., *Bougainvillea buttiana.* See also *herbaceous.*

INDEX

Figures in *italic* refer to illustrations

ACKNOWLEDGMENTS

Dorling Kindersley would like to thank the staff who worked on the original title *The Indoor Garden*: Elizabeth Eyres, Jane Owen, Sophie Mitchell, Tim Hammond, Cheryl Picthall and Ann Cannings.

Designer: David Allen
Editor: Catherine Tilley
Studio: Del & Co
Americanization: Candace Burch
Assistant editor: Candida Ross-Macdonald
Typesetters: Bournetype, Bournemouth and MS Filmsetting Limited, Frome
Reproduction: Colourscan, Singapore

Photographic credits
6/7 Eric Crichton Photos/The Garden Picture Library; 102/3 Ron Sutherland. The Garden Picture Library; 126/7 Camera Press; 144 Elizabeth Whiting and Associates; 155 T&B Camera Press; 158/9 Elizabeth Whiting and Associates; 177 Michael Boys; 178/9 The Garden Picture Library.